Endangered Wildlife and Plants of the World

Volume 9
RAI–SHE

Marshall Cavendish
New York • London • Toronto • Sydney

Marshall Cavendish Corporation
99 White Plains Road
Tarrytown, NY 10591-9001

Created by Brown Partworks Ltd.
Project Editor: Anne Hildyard
Associate Editors: Paul Thompson, Amy Prior
Managing Editor: Tim Cooke
Design: Whitelight
Picture Research: Helen Simm
Index Editor: Kay Ollerenshaw
Production Editor: Matt Weyland
Illustrations: Barbara Emmons, Jackie Harland, Tracy Williamson

Library of Congress Cataloging-in-Publication Data

Endangered wildlife and plants of the world
p.cm.
Includes bibliographical references (p.).
ISBN 0-7614-7194-4 (set)
ISBN 0-7614-7203-7 (vol. 9)
1. Endangered species--Encyclopedias. I. Marshall Cavendish Corporation.

QH75.E68 2001
333.95'22'03--dc21
99-086194

Printed in Malaysia
Bound in the United States of America
07 06 05 04 03 02 01 00 7 6 5 4 3 2 1

TABLE OF CONTENTS/VOLUME 9

ESA and IUCN

In this set of endangered animals and plants, each species, where appropriate, is given an ESA status and an IUCN status. The sources consulted to determine the status of each species are the Endangered Species List maintained by the U.S. Fish and Wildlife Service and the Red Lists compiled by IUCN–The World Conservation Union, which is a worldwide organization based in Switzerland.

ENDANGERED SPECIES ACT

The Endangered Species Act (ESA) was initially passed by the U.S. Congress in 1973, and reauthorized in 1988. The aim of the ESA is to rescue species that are in danger of extinction due to human action and to conserve the species and their ecosystems. Endangered plants and animals are listed by the U.S. Fish and Wildlife Service (USFWS), which is part of the Department of Interior. Once a species is listed, the USFWS is required to develop recovery plans, and ensure that the threatened species is not further harmed by any actions of the U.S. government or U.S. citizens. The act specifically forbids the buying, selling, transporting, importing, or exporting of any listed species. It also bans the taking of any listed species in the U.S. and its territories, on both private and public lands. Violators can face heavy fines or imprisonment. However, the ESA requires that the protection of the species is balanced with economic factors.

The ESA recognizes two categories of risk for species:

Endangered: A species that is in danger of extinction throughout all or a significant part of its range.

Threatened: A species that is likely to become endangered in the foreseeable future.

RECOVERY

Recovery takes place when the decline of the endangered or threatened species is halted or reversed, and the circumstances that caused the threat have been removed. The ultimate aim is the recovery of the species to the point where it no longer requires protection under the act.

Recovery can take a long time. Because the decline of the species may have occurred over centuries, the loss cannot be reversed overnight. There are many factors involved: the number of individuals of the species that remain in the wild, how long it takes the species to mature and reproduce, how much habitat is remaining, and whether the reasons for the decline are clear cut and understood. Recovery plans employ a wide range of strategies that involve the following: reintroduction of species into formerly occupied habitat, land aquisition and management, captive breeding, habitat protection, research, population counts, public education projects, and assistance for private landowners.

SUCCESS STORIES

Despite the difficulties, recovery programs do work, and the joint efforts of the USFWS, other federal and state agencies, tribal governments, and private landowners have not been in vain. Only seven species, less than 1 percent of all the species listed between 1968 and 1993, are now known to be extinct. The other 99 percent of listed species have not been lost to extinction, and this confirms the success of the act.

There are some good examples of successful recovery plans. In 1999, the peregrine falcon, the bald eagle, and the Aleutian goose were removed from the endangered species list. The falcon's numbers have risen dramatically. In 1970, there were only 39 pairs of falcons in the United States. By 1999, the number had risen to 1,650 pairs. The credit for the recovery goes to the late Rachel

Carson, who highlighted the dangers of DDT, and also to the Endangered Species Act, which enabled the federal government to breed falcons in captivity, and took steps to protect their habitat.

Young bald eagles were also successfully translocated into habitat that they formerly occupied, and the Aleutian Canada goose has improved due to restoration of its habitat and reintroduction into former habitat.

IUCN–THE WORLD CONSERVATION UNION

The IUCN (International Union for Conservation of Nature) was established in 1947. It is an alliance of governments, governmental agencies, and nongovernmental agencies. The aim of the IUCN is to help and encourage nations to conserve wildlife and natural resources. Organizations such as the Species Survival Commission is one of several IUCN commissions that assesses the conservation status of species and subspecies globally. Taxa that are threatened with extinction are noted and steps are taken for their conservation by programs designed to save, restore, and manage species and their habitats. The Survival Commission is committed to providing objective information on the status of globally threatened species, and produces two publications: the *IUCN Red List of Threatened Animals*, and the *IUCN Red List of Threatened Plants*. They are compiled from scientific data and provide the status of threatened species, depending on their existence in the wild and threats that undermine that existence. The lists for plants and animals differ slightly.

The categories from the *IUCN Red List of Threatened Animals* used in *Endangered Wildlife and Plants of the World* are as follows:

Extinct: A species is extinct when there is no reasonable doubt that the last individual has died.

Extinct in the wild: A species that is known only to survive in captivity, well outside its natural range.

Critically endangered: A species that is facing an extremely high risk of extinction in the wild in the immediate future.

Endangered: A species that is facing a very high risk of extinction in the wild in the near future.

Vulnerable: A species that is facing a high risk of extinction in the wild in the medium-term future.

Lower risk: A species that does not satisfy the criteria for designation as critically endangered, endangered, or vulnerable. Species included in the lower risk category can be separated into three subcategories:

Conservation dependent: A species that is part of a conservation program. Without the program, the species would qualify for one of the threatened categories within five years.

Near threatened: A species that does not qualify for conservation dependent, but is close to qualifying as vulnerable.

Least concern: A species that does not qualify for conservation dependent or near threatened.

Data deficient: A species on which there is inadequate information to make an asssessment of risk of extinction. Because there is a possibility that future research will show that the species is threatened, more information is required.

The categories from the *IUCN Red List of Threatened Plants*, used in *Endangered Wildlife and Plants of the World*, are as follows:

Extinct: A species that has not definitely been located in the wild during the last 50 years.

Endangered: A species whose survival is unlikely if the factors that threaten it continue. Included are species whose numbers have been reduced to a critical level, or whose habitats have been so drastically reduced that they are deemed to be in immediate danger of extinction. Also included in this category are species that may be extinct but have definitely been seen in the wild in the past 50 years.

Vulnerable: A species that is thought likely to move into the endangered category in the near future if the factors that threaten it remain.

Rare: A species with small world populations that are not at present endangered or vulnerable, but are at risk. These species are usually in restriced areas or are thinly spread over a larger range.

RAILS

Class: Aves

Order: Gruiformes

Family: Rallidae

Rails can pass through very narrow places. Many of them live in tangled forests of cattails and rushes that grow in marshes. Here the long, upright leaves and stems grow close together and offer only slits through which birds may pass. The rails that live in such places have adapted by developing bodies that are quite flat from side to side, like a fish. Viewed from the side, these birds look broad and even chunky; but viewed from straight ahead, they look "skinny as a rail."

Rails are related to sungrebes, bustards, cranes, kagus, and some of the other families that are included in the order Gruiformes.

Within the rail family itself are such birds as coots, gallinules, moorhens, and wood rails. In all, approximately 140 species make up the family. Long ago many rails settled onto remote oceanic islands. After millennia of isolation and security from predators, many of them lost their ability to fly. A bird that could not fly was no match for the aggressive predators that followed each human intrusion onto the islands. Consequently, many rail species have become extinct in the last two centuries. Several species have not been seen in decades.

Bar-winged Rail

(Nesoclopeus poecilopterus)

IUCN: Extinct

Length: 13 in. (33 cm)

Weight: Unknown

Clutch size: Unknown

Diet: Unknown

Habitat: Forests, abandoned plantations, taro fields, swamps

Range: Viti Levu of the Fiji Islands in the southern Pacific Ocean

THE BAR-WINGED RAIL ultimately suffered from many well-meaning ideas. Perhaps the tragedy of the bar-winged rail began when people discovered the wealth and riches of faraway lands.

In centuries past, such exotic items as black pepper and silk encouraged Europeans to risk great danger and hardship to acquire them. Eventually, competition for profit motivated people to sail the seas instead of marching cross-country in caravans. Those who returned nearly always brought back the wealth of new lands, but they always left behind the scourge of rats.

Dutch mariner Abel Tasman was the first European to contact the Fiji Islands, recording them in 1643. English sea captain William Bligh, infamous victim of the *Bounty* mutiny, more completely explored and described the islands in 1789. British colonists settled on the islands in 1874, after which time regular visits by ships became common.

The Fiji nation includes 840 islands, collectively covering 7,056 square miles (18,346 square kilometers). Viti Levu is the largest island and accounts for more than half the nation's land area and more than half its human population. A plain brown bird the size of a domestic chicken lived in the forests that once covered Vitu Levu. With dull brown upperparts from the forehead to the tail, a plain gray face, and underparts darkening from a gray chin to a nearly black belly, the bar-winged rail could hide very well in the dark recesses of forests and swamps. A few thin white lines on the sides did not detract from its pattern. Only its yellow beak, foot, and toe had any color. The darkly banded cinnamon wings gave the bird its name. A flightless bird, the bar-winged rail spent its life on the ground until the European ships arrived, carrying rats. Sometimes the rats would sneak ashore in cargo and sometimes they simply dropped into the water and swam ashore. They became established on the Fiji Islands and soon made a nuisance of themselves to the native people. Then Indian mongooses (*Herpestes auropunctatus*) were released on the islands for rat control, but they also became a nuisance to the rails.

Too many predators

First, terrestrial island birds such as the bar-winged rail had to contend with egg-stealing rats that also ate nestlings. Then the mongooses arrived. The nocturnal rats and diurnal mongooses seldom encountered one another. Instead, the mongooses found the ground-nesting island birds. Eggs, nestlings, fledglings, and adults were all easy prey. The bar-winged rail was not described until 1866, when only 12 specimens were collected and preserved. Within 20 years this bird was believed to be extinct. Nothing was reported of the bar-winged rail for almost 100 years.

In 1973, one was seen on the Nadrau Plateau, but the species has not been reported again.

Sugarcane fields, cement works, and copper and gold mines all promise to secure some economic growth on Fiji's islands. They all take up space and contribute to the forest destruction already begun for lumber production and agriculture. The bar-winged rail may not be able to endure this threat in addition to others it has suffered. However, it survived hidden on a well-populated island for a century. Perhaps it can accomplish the same trick twice.

Bogota Rail

(Rallus semiplumbeus)

IUCN: Endangered

Length: 10–12 in. (25.5–30.5 cm)
Weight: Unknown
Clutch size: Unknown
Incubation: Unknown
Diet: Mainly aquatic invertebrates and insect larvae
Habitat: Wetlands in savanna landscape
Range: Departments of Boyacá and Cundinamarca, Colombia

THE BOGOTA SAVANNA stretches across uneven terrain in the mountains of central Colombia. Marshes dapple the savanna, and in those marshes dwells the Bogota rail.

Medium-sized as rails go, the Bogota rail sports olive-brown upperparts, including a dark crown, that contrast with light gray underparts. A bib of white

BOGOTA RAIL
South America

streaks accents the underparts, and there are white streaks on the rail's black sides. The small feathers of the wing are reddish brown, and the outer flight feathers are dark brown. The two-tone beak is dark reddish brown toward the tip and more yellow and red at the base. Like most of its kin, the Bogota rail sports a coloring pattern that is ideal for a terrestrial life in the marsh.

Unfortunately, the Bogota rail's marshes have been drained for many years to support agriculture. Savannas are generally good grazing land for livestock and are often plowed for crops. Marshes only hinder the plow and detract from the total productive grazing area available to cattle. The bird was never abundant to begin with, and enjoyed only a relatively small distribution within Colombia.

Habitat loss has not been the rail's only problem. It was heavily hunted for many years, and even today, though its population has diminished severely, these birds are still hunted.

No study of the species has ever been done. Nothing is known of its feeding habits,

courtship and nesting, chick rearing, longevity, parasites, or predators. The Bogota rail no longer occurs where marshes have been completely destroyed. Some surviving marshes appear to be uninhabited by this bird as well, perhaps owing to pollution. Few healthy populations remain (about 400 birds at Laguna de Tota in 1991, abut 50 territories at Laguna de la Herrera, and 55 pairs at Parque La Florida), and no specific preservation work has been undertaken on its behalf.

California Clapper Rail

(Rallus longirostris obsoletus)

ESA: Endangered

Length: 13–19 in. (33–48 cm)
Weight: 8¾–12½ oz. (250–350 g)
Clutch size: 5–9 eggs
Incubation: 23–29 days
Diet: Crustaceans, spiders, mollusks
Habitat: Coastal saltwater marshes
Range: San Francisco Bay area, California

BIRDERS KNOW San Francisco Bay for the millions of seabirds, waterfowl, shorebirds, marsh birds, and wading birds it once supported. In particular, the vast coastal marshes and estuaries of San Francisco Bay once harbored a unique subspecies of clapper rail. This bird is known as the California clapper rail, and it has steadily declined as people have found other uses for the coastal wetlands in the Bay Area. The upperparts of this bird are generally striped medium brown to dark brown on a lighter gray brown. The throat and upper breast are a dark buff, with faint brown bars. The lower breast and belly turn dingy white, but the sides are boldly patterned with brown stripes, edged with slightly darker brown.

Degraded habitat

The California clapper rail's problem is that it does not have much marsh vegetation left. About 85 percent of the original habitat has been diked or destroyed, and much that remains is in a degraded condition. Estuaries were once viewed as wet wastelands where mosquitos breed. They were used as garbage dumps and sewage dumps. They were drained and then filled in with earth. Laws were enacted to protect these estuaries from further destruction, but laws are not always entirely effective. Chemical pollution from dozens of sources has degraded the San Francisco Bay estuaries. But all this abuse to the clapper rail's habitat only explains part of the California story.

During the 1800s, hunting developed in two directions. Some people shot birds to sell to markets and restaurants, while others shot them to fill leisure time. Such hunting was excessive and poorly controlled.

Then a series of treaties between the United States and Canada, and ultimately Mexico, extended international protection to migratory birds. The California clapper rail was protected by these measures, even though it does not migrate. Pockets of its estuary habitat remain, and the California clapper rail

A portrait of many brown hues, the California clapper rail is perfectly camouflaged for a bird of the marshes. The overall pattern blends well with marsh vegetation.

inhabits many of them. The rails weave through the dense vegetation and occasionally wander into more open areas, always on the lookout for mussels, small crabs, insects, and other tasty morsels. However, the population was estimated at about only 400 birds in 1991, down from 4,200–6,000 in the early 1970s. Fortunately, portions of the San Francisco Bay estuary system have been purchased by the National Audubon Society, the U.S. Fish and Wildlife Service, and other agencies.

Some tracts of estuary have been targeted for recovery and restoration work. This has been led by the California Department of Fish and Game.

Barring disasters, artificial or natural, the California clapper rail should survive, although in smaller numbers than in the past.

The light-footed clapper rail is another subspecies adapted to ever-threatened marsh ecosystems.

Light-footed Clapper Rail

(Rallus longirostris levipes)

ESA: Endangered

Length: 14–16 in. (35.5–40.5 cm)
Weight: 9–10 oz. (252–280 g)
Clutch size: 4–8 eggs
Incubation: 23 days
Diet: Crustaceans, insects, mollusks, small fish, tadpoles
Habitat: Coastal saltwater marshes
Range: California and Baja

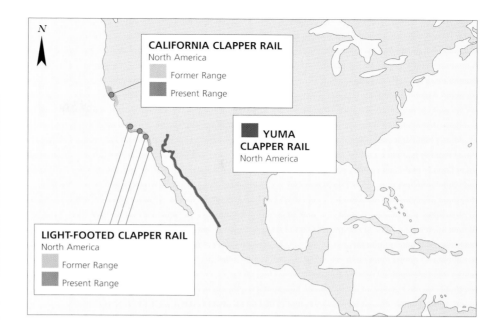

LIGHT-FOOTED clapper rails still live in southern California. That alone seems like a miracle. The light-footed clapper rail is one of seven subspecies of clapper rail found in the United States. Other subspecies live on islands of the West Indies, in Central America, and along the coasts of South America in extreme northeast and southwest Colombia, Ecuador, northwest Peru, northwest Venezuela, Guyana, Suriname, and from French Guiana to southern Brazil. Despite the species' broad distribution, the light-footed clapper rail lives only in the coastal marshes of southern California and northern Baja.

Light-footed clapper rails differ from California clapper rails in both size and color. They are slightly smaller on average, and are slightly darker. Their upperparts are olive brown, rather than gray brown. The underparts are more cinnamon and less buff. The sides are boldly striped.

Although they differ noticeably in appearance, their behaviors vary only slightly,

according to the character of the landscapes each inhabits. The California clapper rail now occupies only coastal marshes of the San Francisco Bay Area, but it once ranged as far south as Monterey Bay. The light-footed clapper rail ranged approximately from Santa Barbara in California to Ensenada in Baja.

Civilization steals habitat

The enormous human settlement of southern California has altered much of the natural landscape. Many coastal wetlands simply no longer exist. Some that remain are too small, too isolated, too polluted, or otherwise unsuitable for rails. Light-footed clapper rails need estuaries for nesting. They occasionally wander into freshwater ponds near estuaries. They catch tadpoles, small fish, crustaceans, and large insects in the freshwater pools, but concentrate on eating crabs, mussels, and other invertebrates in the estuaries.

Besides nesting and feeding areas, they also need emergency escape cover. High winds,

storms, and higher than normal tides can be hazardous to young rails. Parent rails typically construct a sheltered nest in dry, upland vegetation, well above the high tide and storm tide waterline.

Human presence in southern California has eliminated many of the estuaries and reduced the size of others. In those areas where the estuaries have been left, land development has eliminated the adjoining upland habitat so vital to the light-footed clapper rails. Where other factors have been satisfactory for the light-footed clapper rail, humans have introduced a hazard into the bird's habitat.

Dangerous mollusk

The ribbed horse mussel (*Ischadium demissum*) is an exotic mollusk that grows large enough to clamp its shell closed on rails' toes. At least one light-footed clapper rail has been found with a toe trapped in a ribbed horse mussel. Many light-footed clapper rails have been observed with partially missing toes. Presumably, all light-footed clapper rails

would be vulnerable to this particular danger, but their chicks would suffer higher mortality because of their size.

Breeding census

As of 1990, less than two dozen California estuaries still harbored light-footed clapper rails. Just six areas held about 90 percent of the total American population, and nearly half of that population lived in the estuarine marshes of Upper Newport Bay in Orange County. There were an estimated 500 to 700 breeding pairs there in 1970, but the population had declined to fewer than 150 pairs in 1990. The total U.S. population is now estimated at a mere 190 pairs, with a further 240 pairs remaining in Mexico.

Low fertility and hatching success in northern populations may result from contaminants, but could also be an indication of inbreeding depression. This trend in population decline began in

the late 1800s. At that time the greatest pressure on rails was hunting. Hunting became a commercial enterprise and also a recreational pastime, expanding without legal or moral constraints. The light-footed clapper rail entered the 20th century with a badly depleted population.

Reduced habitat

The human population of southern California continues to grow. Even human activities away from the coast influence the quality and character of the coastal wetlands. If the light-footed clapper rail is to survive, it must accept smaller parcels of habitat in less than ideal conditions. People must extend some help to the bird, and they have done so. Some coastal marshes have been improved through specific management actions. A few have been protected against further destruction, and a clever invention has been tested to help the rails.

The rare light-footed clapper rail makes its home in the highly populated region of Southern California, where humans have greatly changed the environment and thus reduced the bird's habitat.

Artificial floating platforms that rise and fall with the tides give the rails safe places to nest, and the birds have successfully made use of them.

Still more can be done. The Mexican populations of light-footed clapper rail should be monitored regularly, and the condition of rail habitat in Baja should be evaluated.

Recovery measures

The dryland habitat next to marshes must be protected, pollution must be reduced, and the estuaries must be guarded against oil spills. If the recovery work continues, substantial increase in light-footed clapper rail populations in southern California will be no surprise.

Yuma Clapper Rail

(Rallus longirostris yumanensis)

ESA: Endangered

Length: 14–16 in. (35.5–40.5 cm)
Weight: 9–10 oz. (252–280 g)
Clutch size: Probably 4–8 eggs
Incubation: Probably 23–26 days
Diet: Crustaceans, insects, mollusks, small fish
Habitat: Saltwater and freshwater marshes
Range: California and Arizona, to central Mexico

THE YUMA CLAPPER RAIL presents probably the most challenging of all questions about endangered species—is it really endangered? The question has been avoided because, regarding the Yuma clapper rail, ethics rather than science are the issue.

One interpretation of the Yuma clapper rail's natural history claims the bird only recently pioneered into its present range, the American Southwest. This subspecies naturally occurs as far south along the Mexican coast as San Blas in Nayarit.

The Yuma clapper rail now inhabits marshes as far north as Topock, Arizona. It is also known to live along the Gila River as far east as Tacna, Arizona. Its western limit is the Salton Sea of southern California. Some ornithologists argue that the

The Yuma clapper rail is one of the paler subspecies of clapper rail. Its upperparts are duller gray-brown and its underparts are more tan, with less buff than other subspecies.

Yuma clapper rail moved into the northern extremes of its present range only because of human water management.

As dams were built and reservoirs were created along the Colorado River, the flow of the Colorado's water changed enough to allow marshes to develop where none had been before. The Yuma clapper rail responded by moving into the newly available habitat. Similar circumstances occurred along Arizona's Gila River. In 1905 the Colorado River flooded into California's Imperial Valley, creating the Salton Sea. Marshes subsequently developed around the Salton Sea and the rail took up residency there, too.

Southwestern bird

The stripes on the sides of the Yuma clapper rail are faded but distinguishable. It is also one of only two subspecies that occurs inland. Its presence in marshes of southern Arizona and southern California may reflect the salinity of the rivers and lakes in that part of the country.

Population surveys conducted in the 1960s and 1970s indicated that perhaps as few as 700 pairs

of breeding Yuma clapper rails lived in the United States. No similar field studies were done at the time in Mexico to compare populations there. Surveys in the 1980s produced estimates of 1,700 to 2,000 pairs in the United States.

A rough approximation of nonbreeding birds would bring the total American population to perhaps 4,500 birds.

The Yuma clapper rail needs shallow water areas where various aquatic plants, such as cattails (*Typha* sp.), can grow thickly enough to form debris. Dead plant stalks and leaves form a base on which the rails nest. As human population growth and agricultural development of the Southwest and West continue, the demands on water resources grow. This affects the availability of habitat for rails.

Even though water management in the West and Southwest may not include more giant dams, water management and development projects may still eliminate marshes now inhabited by Yuma clapper rails. This raises the question of whether a bird should be protected if it is not legitimately endangered. Since

the Yuma clapper rail experienced a surge in population as a result of human activity within its range, the bird's population was inflated beyond what would have been its natural limits. Now that human activity threatens to reduce the newly formed habitat, the Yuma clapper rail may withdraw to more natural population levels. There is an ongoing debate as to whether such a decline qualifies as endangerment.

Usually, people only question the ethics of depriving a species of habitat or of causing that species to become extinct.

The Yuma clapper rail forces people to carefully examine the definition of endangerment and whether a naturally occurring species is truly endangered if the artificial habitat it inhabits is lost.

The circumstances surrounding the Yuma clapper rail are not clearly defined. Many useful details are now obscured by time. Still, the status of American wetlands and wildlife species argues persuasively for protecting the Yuma clapper rail. In a land where water is more useful than gold, marshes must be guarded.

Guam Rail

(Gallirallus owstoni)

ESA: Extinct

IUCN: Extinct in the wild

Length: 11 in. (27.9 cm)
Weight: Males, 6¼–10¾ oz. (174–303 g); females, 6–9¾ oz. (170–274 g)
Clutch size: 3–4 eggs
Incubation: Probably 19–20 days
Diet: Insects, snails, slugs, some carrion, fruits, and small geckos
Habitat: Woodlands, shrublands, secondary growth
Range: Guam in the Mariana Islands of the western Pacific Ocean

NOT ALL RAILS DEMAND wetlands for their life needs. On Guam a zebra-looking rail shuns the island's few remaining wetlands in favor of shrubby woodlands.

The Guam rail wears a striking plumage. Warm brown colors the upperparts from the tip of the stubby tail to the crown. A uniform brown runs up the side of the neck and cuts across the middle of the cheek to the base of the beak. A pale gray line sweeps back from the beak like an eyebrow. The chin, lower cheek, throat, and upper breast are a medium gray. From midbreast back to the tip under the tail, the Guam rail sports a loud pattern of blackish brown stripes on a white background. A long thick beak gives the Guam rail a pow-

The Guam rail has endured as the entire southern half of Guam was slowly but steadily converted to agriculture and urban development.

erful tool for opening snails, one of its favorite foods. The giant African snail (*Achatina fulica*) escaped, perhaps from a ship, onto the island and established itself. This species provides a rare example of a native species taking advantage of an exotic species. However, the Guam rail survived thousands of years without having giant African snails to eat.

A terrestrial bird with only limited ability to fly, the Guam rail spends its entire life lurking among the shrubland and woodland undergrowth.

The Guam rail evolved as a species without the pressures of reptilian or mammalian predators. Since humans arrived on Guam, an array of livestock, pets, and vermin have also found the island. Many of them directly threaten the Guam rail. A variety of rats (*Rattus* sp.), the domestic pig (*Sus scrofa*), and the brown tree snake (*Boiga irregularis*) all eat bird eggs. They also snatch nestlings, as do monitor lizards (*Varanus indicus*), feral house cats (*Felis sylvestris*), and dogs (*Canis familiaris*). The brown tree snake was unintentionally introduced to Guam after World War II. By the 1960s, its population had grown enormous. A venomous nocturnal predator that specializes in consuming birds, the brown tree snake has no difficulty finding bird nests in the trees or even on the ground.

At the end of World War II, American military personnel regularly sprayed the island with a pesticide known as DDT. Developed as a powder to kill lice on people, DDT proved effective at killing other insects. Guam was sprayed regularly, and farmers adopted the chemical for crop protection. Ornithologists now know that DDT interferes with a female bird's ability to deposit calcium in her eggshells. Thin eggs break easily and cause rapid breeding failure.

Vast tracts of shrublands and woodlands were cleared for agriculture and development on Guam, and this rail was left with less total habitat for its needs. What habitat remains harbors its predators as well, not to mention residues of DDT. Under these conditions, the Guam rail population plummeted from about 2,000 birds in the 1970s to fewer than 100 birds in 1983.

The U.S. Fish and Wildlife Service is aggressively studying ways to control brown tree snakes that prey on rail eggs. Captive-breeding efforts are also underway. The Guam rail may be lost to the wild until the snake can be effectively controlled.

per. From forehead to tail tip, the Lord Howe rail is a warm, earthy brown. The cheek and wing share the same hue. The underparts, from chin to undertail, appear a shade lighter than the upperparts. The lighter brown hue continues up the neck and over the red eye as a thin line. The stout beak is long, slightly decurved, and golden brown. The leg, foot, and toe are thick and strong, but the tail is puny and the wing short. Ground birds that inhabit remote islands have little need to fly.

Lord Howe Island offers the rail only five square miles (13 square kilometers) of land. This island lies about halfway between Sydney and Brisbane on the Australian coast, 394 miles (630 kilometers) out in the Tasman Sea. The island is mountainous and the Lord Howe rail now lives only at the top of Mount Gower and Mount Lidgbird. The moun-

tains are not especially high. Mount Gower rises only to 2,795 feet (852 meters). The summits, however, are higher than feral pigs and feral goats normally range. Rats are also less abundant higher up the mountains. Nonetheless rats have taken the eggs and nestlings of these birds. The Lord Howe rail is a terrestrial species, so its nests are particularly vulnerable to rats. Today, the Lord Howe rail stands poised for extinction.

In the early 1960s, ornithologists estimated there were 300 to 400 Lord Howe rails. The estimate dropped to 50 known birds in the early 1980s. Captive breeding has increased the total population to around 150 birds. The conditions that caused endangerment on Lord Howe Island persisted into the 1990s, despite a program to eradicate rats. If the rats are still there, releasing captive birds will only

Lord Howe Rail
(Gallirallus sylvestris)

ESA: Endangered

IUCN: Endangered

Length: 15 in. (38.1 cm)
Weight: Unknown
Clutch size: 1–4 eggs
Incubation: Unknown
Diet: Insects, bird eggs
Habitat: Forests and all other plant communities
Range: Lord Howe Island off eastern Australia

FEW BIRDS COME ANY plainer than the Lord Howe rail. Truly, it is a bird in a plain brown wrap-

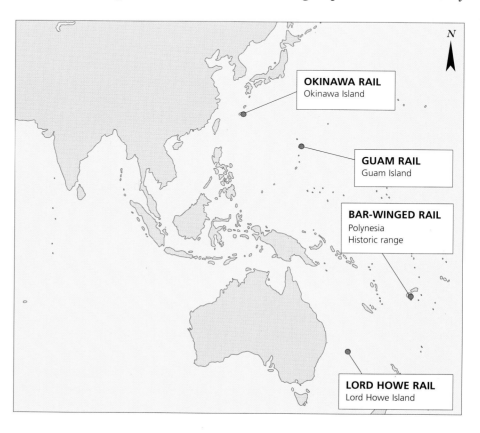

OKINAWA RAIL
Okinawa Island

GUAM RAIL
Guam Island

BAR-WINGED RAIL
Polynesia
Historic range

LORD HOWE RAIL
Lord Howe Island

replay the original problem. Additional protective measures have been recommended. These include fencing the mountain tops to protect the last suitable habitat from goats and pigs and possibly rats, and expanded programs to eradicate pigs and goats from the island. Together they have changed the character of the island's plant communities.

Saving the Lord Howe rail has nothing to do with glamor, beauty, magnificence, or power. The Lord Howe rail is just a medium-sized bird that is in trouble. Saving it will be a human expression of concern toward another species.

Okinawa Rail
(Gallirallus okinawae)

IUCN: Endangered

Length: 11–12 in. (27.9–30.5 cm)
Weight: Unknown
Clutch size: Unknown
Incubation: Unknown
Diet: Unknown
Habitat: Dense vegetation
Range: Okinawa, Ryukyu Islands of the western Pacific Ocean

NEW BIRDS MAKE NEWS. Earth's human population has grown so large and the human occupation of the planet has become so thorough that no one expects to find new species of birds anymore.

Nowadays, ornithologists can acknowledge new species by recognizing separate populations of a single species as being a distinct species. New species are therefore made by redefining them, not by discovery. However, in 1981, scientists did discover a new bird. In that year ornithologists described the Okinawa rail. The secretive bird had escaped detection for hundreds of years.

The Okinawa rail is pretty, in a plain sort of way. It has a dark gray crown that fades to olive brown on the back of the head, over the nape, back, wing, and tail. The bird has a black face including lore, entire cheek, and chin. A small, irregular white patch, or sometimes patches, below and behind each eye add the only contrasting pattern to the black face. The underparts from throat to undertail are boldly barred in fine black and white streaks. The beak is bright orange red at the base, turning yellow at the tip. The leg, foot, and toe are likewise bright orange red. Such a recognizable bird would seem quite conspicuous on a small island.

Life on an island
Okinawa lies in the middle of the Ryukyu Island chain that extends southward from Japan toward Taiwan. This island chain effectively separates the Yellow Sea from the Philippine Sea. Okinawa was once thickly covered in forest and shrubland.

A small bird like the Okinawa rail, a species adapted to a secretive life on the ground, could easily go undetected as this one did. At first ornithologists suspected that the rail had diurnal habits, but research shows that the rail calls through the night, suggesting a nocturnal lifestyle.

More details of the bird's natural history await further studies.

Exotic predators
Feral house cats and mongooses, which may be *Herpestes auropunctatus*, both exotic to Okinawa, now pose a serious threat to the Okinawa rail. This hazard increases annually as the human presence on Okinawa expands. Southern Okinawa has already been extensively developed for farming, housing, and commerce, so the Okinawa rail now inhabits only the northern third of the island. The last tracts of forest and shrubby woodland on Okinawa occur there.

Woodland birds
People often associate rails with marshes and other wetlands, but many rails are actually birds of woodlands and forests. This is true of the Okinawa rail, and such habitats once covered much of the island. Each year, however, a little more forest is converted to croplands or housing. As the rail's habitat shrinks, its population declines. Exotic predators become especially threatening to such weakened species.

Being essentially flightless, the Okinawa rail nests on the ground, where it is easy prey for cats and mongooses that take the eggs and nestlings.

There have been recommendations put forth for preserving this rail's habitat, along with ideas to control the rail's predators. The degree to which these have been tried is not known, but the Okinawa rail population was estimated at around 1,500 birds and was still declining in the mid-1980s.

The next news the Okinawa rail makes could be less cheerful than its discovery.

Kevin Cook

Lake Eacham Rainbowfish

(Melanotaenia eachamensis)

IUCN: Vulnerable

Class: Actinopterygii
Order: Atheriniformes
Family: Melanotaeniidae
Length: 4 in. (10 cm)
Reproduction: Egg layer
Habitat: Shoreline areas
Range: Lake Eacham, Queensland, Australia

BECAUSE OF THEIR wide range of body coloration, rainbowfish are aptly named. These tropical species (there are about 40) are found in the jungles of northern Queensland and on the nearby island of New Guinea. They are in demand as aquarium fish and for use in mosquito control. Their relatively small adult size and varied coloration make them particularly attractive to fish hobbyists. As with many fish species, male rainbowfish generally have brighter colors than their female counterparts.

The sole habitat of the Lake Eacham rainbowfish is in Lake Eacham on the Atherton Tableland (a plateau) of northern Queensland, Australia. Lake Eacham, a crater lake, is fairly small (123 acres or 50 hectares) and was formed when a volcano collapsed. Today it is the centerpiece of Lake Eacham National Park. Despite the lake's designation as a protected habitat within a national park, the Lake Eacham rainbowfish population suffered a "crash" sometime in the mid-1980s. During a 1987 survey, no individuals of this species could be located in the lake. Previous reports from 1984 indicated that the Lake Eacham rainbowfish was present in large numbers. What happened between 1984 and 1987 is a matter for speculation. While the evidence is not totally conclusive, biologists believe that exotic species may be responsible for the fish's decline

The back carries two dorsal fins; the first fin is short but has long and spiny fin rays that afford some protection from predators. The second dorsal fin is much longer, reaching from the fish's mid-section down to the tail; the anal fin on the belly is longest of all. Like the first dorsal fin, the pelvic fins on the belly carry defensive spines. Rainbowfish earned their name from the wide variety of colors present on each individual, and the Lake Eacham variety is no exception. Blues, yellows, reds, and other colors are blended to create what is thought to be one of the most attractive fish in the world.

The problem of exotic species introduced into a finite habitat is a common reason why native species become endangered.

LAKE EACHAM RAINBOW FISH
Australia

Four species of fish were introduced (unauthorized by public officials) to Lake Eacham during the same period when the population of the Lake Eacham rainbowfish crashed. One species in particular, the mouth almighty (*Glossamia aprion*), is an aggressive predator and is probably the primary cause of the decline. In 1989, 3,000 cultured Lake Eacham rainbowfish were put in the lake to bolster the population, but a 1990 survey located no specimens. The lake Eacham rainbowfish has been officially declared extinct in the wild by the Australian government. There are however, several captive populations held in Australia. Finding other suitable habitats for this fish has been difficult, and the future of the Lake Eacham rainbowfish is very much in doubt.

William E. Manci

Rainbowfish have a seemingly undersized head and pointed snout on a body that is deep but compressed from side to side.

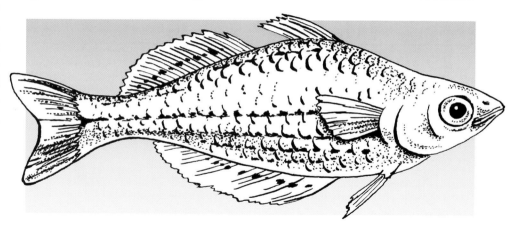

RATS

Class: Mammalia

Order: Rodentia

Family: Muridae

A typical female rat reaches sexual maturity in six weeks, and so becomes capable of giving birth to between three and as many as 14 offspring every three or four weeks for the rest of her life. In theory, this makes it possible for a single rat to have as many as 20 million descendents in a span of three years. Luckily for other forms of animal and plant life, the rat is an important food source for many of the world's most successful carnivores.

The rat has at times been responsible for human diseases. For example, black rats hosted the fleas whose bites led to outbreaks of bubonic plague that swept through Europe.

During the Middle Ages, periodic plague outbreaks claimed millions of human lives and altered the course of history. Europe has not been visited by the "black death" for more than 500 years, but rats can still spread disease, particularly in developing countries where rat-spread diseases are able to flourish because antibiotics are scarce.

Rats serve as hosts to a wealth of protozoans, flukes, tapeworms, and threadworms, and so are instrumental in spreading forms of jaundice and typhus, as well as flulike human illnesses such as leptospirosis and rat bite fever.

The rat is a prodigious eater, with an appetite for agricultural products and a knack for invading food storage facilities. Apart from its appetite, the rat regularly contaminates much of the food it doesn't eat with its urine and feces.

Rats are rodents, and the word *rodent* means "gnawing animal." Rats have been known to gnaw almost anything, from seat covers to silverware, and while they may not eat a food, they will effectively spoil it by gnawing on it.

Like all species of rodent, a rat has a pair of long incisor teeth in each jaw. These teeth continue to regenerate throughout the animal's life. Gnawing both sharpens these teeth and prevents them from growing too long. By biting into food and other things it doesn't intend to eat, the rat both sharpens its teeth and curtails their growth.

Apart from their continually regenerating incisor teeth, rats are characterized by as many as 22 nonregenerating molar teeth in the back of the mouth. These are useful for grinding food. Like people, rats have rotating bones in their forearms. These bones allow for considerable dexterity.

Rodent feet often have five fingers, or digits, in the form of claws. These are of particular use for digging, climbing, and food handling. In addition, some rats have internal or external cheek pouches for carrying food to a burrow or nest.

In all fairness to the rat, it has made some positive contributions to the well-being of people and other animals. It has, for example, always been a primary food source for the world's carnivores (including humans). Rats have provided people and other animals with an invaluable food supply during times of periodic famine.

More significantly, because it is so easily and inexpensively bred in captivity, the rat has become the ultimate laboratory animal, invaluable to all manner of medical and scientific research. As medical and genetic research continues, rats are likely to provide scientists with more answers to the many research questions of our day.

In the wild, the rat is like other animals; it struggles to find food and avoid being eaten. Like many other animals, it contends with food shortages by hoarding food as well as by reducing breeding and other activities. Natural conditions of alternating plenty and scarcity function as a population check on those species of rats that live apart from and do not depend on humans.

Rats come in all sizes, shapes, and habitat preferences. Some are arboreal, making their nests in trees. Others are semiaquatic and live along river banks. Some are burrowers. Mostly it is the burrowing rats that have reaped the benefits of living near people. These rats have taken up residence in buildings and, once inside, create nests behind panels or between floorboards. Because they are essentially omnivorous and can eat whatever people do, they flourish, especially in the older, dirtier cities of the world.

Few New York City subway riders would dispute the claim made by some biologists that half the mammals presently alive on earth are rodents. New Yorkers would probably be happy to see the ever-present urban blight, the Norwegian brown rat (*Rattus norvegicus*), become an endangered species. Urban rats can be expected to continue outnumbering the people living in cities. However, a few people-avoiding rural rat populations are dwindling and disappearing. For just as people's garbage and waste has nurtured the urban rat, human encroachment has driven other species of rat near to extinction.

It is not entirely misleading to say that rats are essentially large mice, or that mice are small rats and both belong to the order Rodentia. Rodentia consists of 29 living families, 426 genera, and more than 1,800 species, many of which have not been seriously studied.

Colorado River Cotton Rat
(Sigmodon arizonae plenus)

IUCN: Lower risk

Weight: 2½–7½ oz. (6.8–21.6 g)
Head-body length: 4¾–7¾ in. (12–20 cm)
Tail length: 3–5¼ in. (7.5–13.5 cm)
Diet: Seeds, grasses, small mammals, insects, some fish, birds' eggs
Gestation period: About 30 days
Longevity: 6 months to 5 years
Habitat: Grassy shrub areas
Range: Arizona and California (along the lower Colorado River)

THE COLORADO RIVER cotton rat is one of eight species of cotton rat. These animals prefer grassy, shrubby areas, and their presence in an area is signaled by the surface trails they make through the foliage. They dig shallow burrows under small plants, often enlarging the burrows of other animals. Sometimes they make nests of grass and sedges on the ground.

The Colorado River cotton rat is active both day and night throughout the year. It has a varied diet that includes grasses, seeds, shrub foliage, insects, fish, small mammals, and—to the dismay of farmers—sugarcane and sweet potatoes. In most cases, these animals breed year-round. The typical litter, averaging five to seven rats, is born after a gestation period of about 30 days. While captives have lived as long as five years, an average life in the wild is about six months.

Today the Colorado River cotton rat is known just from a few sites along the lower Colorado River. Although it is classified as lower risk, it faces habitat loss, mainly due to the manipulation of the river's flow by industry.

Heath Rat
(Pseudomys shortridgei)

IUCN: Lower risk

Weight: 2–3 oz. (12–90 g)
Head-body length: 3½–4¾ in. (9–12 cm)
Tail length: 3–4¼ in. (7½–11 cm)
Diet: Seeds, grass, roots, sand insects, vegetation, and fungi
Gestation period: 28–40 days
Longevity: 6 months to 5 years
Habitat: Dry heathland
Range: Southwestern Australia

THE HEATH RAT, also known as the blunt-nosed rat, is by some standards a mouse, but it belongs to the rat family Muridae. It is one of only a few native terrestrial placental mammals in Australia. Most terrestrial mammals in Australia are marsupials.

It was originally discovered in Western Australia in 1906 but had not been seen in that part of the country after 1931 until it was rediscovered in 1961 in habitats regularly subjected to burning by aborigines in the Portland region and in the Gampian Mountains of Victoria. Individuals were collected in 1983 and in 1987 a population was discovered.

The rat's pelage is soft and either gray, brown, or yellowish. Its underparts are brown, white, and grayish, invariably lighter than its upper body. The head and ears are usually paler than the back. The tail is modestly haired and bi-colored.

Rare rat
Because it is rare, its habits are not well known. It is a nocturnal animal, inclined to burrowing and napping by day and foraging for food at night. Its shallow burrows lead to cushioned, circular sleeping rooms. It feeds on seeds, roots, sand-grown vegetation, fungi, and insects.

In Victoria, breeding occurs only in the spring, with pregnant females being found from October through December. A single litter of three young is produced each year, with a second litter being very rare.

Its habitat destruction has been blamed on modern agricul-

Cotton rats prefer grassy, shrubby areas. They dig shallow burrows under small plants, often enlarging the burrows of other animals.

Poncelet's Giant Rat
(Solomys ponceleti)

IUCN: Endangered

Weight: Up to 1 lb. (0.45 kg)
Head-body length: 13 in. (33 cm)
Tail length: To 13 in. (33.5 cm)
Diet: Coconuts, nuts, fruit, seeds, foliage, small invertebrates
Gestation period: Unknown
Habitat: Deep forests
Range: Bougainville Island, Solomon Islands

tural practices. Traditionally, the heathlands favored by this rat were burned each year by the aborigines. Ironically, some experts believe that the animal's scarcity is attributable to the decline in the systematic burning of its rangeland. Fewer naturally-occurring blazes are said to have proved much more destructive to the heath rat's habitat than the annual controlled burnings once done by the aborigines.

Mice, rats, hamsters, voles, gerbils, and lemmings are part of the giant mammal family Muridae that boasts more than 1,000 species and includes countless varieties. These two rats are from Kenya in eastern Africa.

Although this species is classified as lower risk by IUCN–The World Conservation Union, it continues to suffer from the habitat degradation that has caused a grave loss of mammal species on the Australian continent.

PONCELET'S GIANT RAT is one of three rats indigenous to the Solomon Islands. This particular species is found exclusively on Bougainville Island.

By any standards, Poncelet's giant rat is truly a giant. Its color is brownish black above and below. Its pelage is longer and finer than that of most rats. The tail is prehensile (able to grip) and hairless. The feet are well-padded and have strongly clawed digits. The rat's incisor teeth are broad and stout.

The Poncelet's giant rat prefers to inhabit thick woods and is apparently arboreal. Its main diet is nuts, vegetables, and small invertebrates. It is hunted and eaten occasionally by Solomon Island natives.

This species is thought to be a casualty of increased human pressure, both in the form of land development and hunting.

Certainly because of its island isolation, its endangerment will increase, and it will remain in danger of extinction if hunting is allowed to persist.

PONCELET'S GIANT RAT
Solomon Islands

N

HEATH RAT
Australia
Former Range
Present Range

CENTRAL ROCK RAT
Australia
Former Range
Present Range

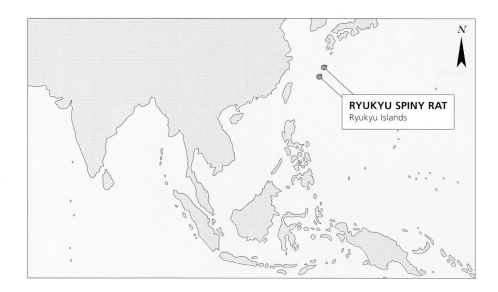

RYUKYU SPINY RAT
Ryukyu Islands

land degradation. Soil erosion is a common problem because of bad land usage and overgrazing. Much native vegetation, critical to the habitats of small mammals such as the rock rat, has been lost.

Central Rock Rat

(Zyzomys pedunculatus)

IUCN: Critically endangered

Weight: 1–4½ oz. (34–130 g)
Head-body length: 4¼–5½ in. (11–14 cm)
Tail length: 4¼–5½ in. (11–14 cm)
Diet: Fruit, vegetation, some insects
Gestation period: About 30 days
Longevity: Up to two years
Habitat: Rocky outcrops
Range: Australia

white. The tail, however, is fragile, with the skin and flesh stripping off easily.

The central rock rat eats fruits, seeds, and insects, and prefers to den in rocky crags.

Also known as the MacDonnell rat, the central rock rat was formerly found in the MacDonnell, James, Davenport, Granite, and Napperby mountain ranges in the Northwest Territories. Although apparently easy to trap, only five of these rats have been recorded since this species' discovery in 1894. Despite intensive trapping efforts in formerly inhabited areas, none have been seen since 1960. Australia has created problems for its indigenous species because of extensive

Ryukyu Spiny Rat

(Tokudaia osimensis)

IUCN: Endangered

Weight: 2½–7½ oz. (71–212.5 g)
Head-body length: 5–7 in. (12.7–18 cm)
Tail length: 4–5 in. (10–12.7 cm)
Diet: Grass, seeds, foliage, small insects
Gestation period: Unknown
Longevity: Unknown
Habitat: Subtropical grassy plains and short, shrubby forest
Range: Ryukyu Islands, Japan

THE UPPER PARTS of the Ryukyu spiny rat's body are mixed black and orange-tawny, while the ventral parts are grayish white with a faint orange wash. The tail is bicolored. The body is short and thick, and the fur is dense. The coat is made up of two kinds of

THE PELAGE OF THE endangered central rock rat is crisp and almost spiny. It is brownish gray or buff to reddish sandy. The hands and feet are white.

The feet are short and broad, the ears small and rounded. Sometimes the thick tail is all

Rock rat reproduction appears to occur year-round, with several litters of one to three young produced.

Many wood rats are nest builders and use foliage, rocks, and even bones to create comfortable homes (sometimes with more than one entrance). Other species just prefer to nestle amid rocks.

hairs. Long, coarse hair with grooved spines covers much of the body. Hair near the mouth, ears, feet, and base of the tail tends to be shorter and softer. Long black spiny hairs on its back give the Ryukyu rat an "electrified" look.

The species is listed as endangered by IUCN. This status is due to human development, human settlement, and general destruction of the natural landscape of the Ryukyu Islands. On Okinawa, specimens were collected in a thick shrub forest about 10 feet (3 meters) tall. They were found in the undergrowth of coarse grass and ferns.

Wood Rats
(Neotoma sp.*)*

IUCN: Data deficient to Critically endangered

Weight: 7–15¾ oz. (200–450 g)
Head-body length: 6–9 in. (15–23 cm)
Tail length: 3–9¼ in. (7.5–24 cm)
Diet: Roots, stems, foliage, grass, seeds, small invertebrates
Gestation period: 30–40 days
Longevity: 6 months to 7 years
Habitat: Forests, meadows, and deserts
Range: North America

UNLIKE THE NORWEGIAN brown and black rats, most species of wood rats prefer to live some distance from people. The wood rat is characteristically brown or gray, with a white or lighter-colored belly and feet. Typically, it has a more rounded snout than most other rats. About the size of the common house rat, the wood rat has a heavy, hairy tail and fine soft fur. When alarmed, the wood rat signals fellow rats in the vicinity with a curious drumming sound made by beating its hind legs on the ground.

The wood rat's diet consists of roots, stems, leaves, seeds, and some invertebrates.

Some wood rats are the consummate rodent architects, living in veritable "apartment houses" that they build over the course of many years. They use twigs, sticks, bones, leaves, branches, silverware, knife blades—whatever naturally occurring or artificial materials are to be found in their environments. These multichambered nests may reach more than 6 feet (1.8 meters) in height, have several entrances, and include individual rooms for food storage, as well as sleeping alcoves lined with bark, leaves, and grass. Within these dens, wood rats tend to be solitary. Individual den chambers are usually occupied by one adult.

Not all wood rat species build their nests on the ground. Those native to drier climates where cactus is plentiful often burrow beneath the indigenous spiky plants. As a result, an unwary predator pursuing a wood rat over its home ground is liable to experience pain from cactus spines. In more arid regions, the cactus is often doubly useful, providing a source of fresh water for these rats. Some species of wood rat are excellent climbers and prefer to nest in trees.

Wood rats can be aggressive and territorial, at least in captivity. In one captive group there were reports of individual Key Largo wood rats (*Neotoma floridana smalli*) invading rat dens and killing and wounding the other Key Largo wood rats inside. There is no confirmation that this happens in the wild, although males are known to fight over harems.

Key Largo rats are classified by the U.S. Fish & Wildlife Service as endangered.

Trade rat

When out foraging at night, they will sometimes drop whatever they are carrying if they find something else more attractive (such as a shiny trinket). This trait has led people to give them other common names such as "trade rat" or "pack rat."

Southern-dwelling wood rats breed year-round and produce three, four, or five litters of two to four young annually. Gestation is 30 to 40 days. The eyes of the newborn open between two and three weeks, and weaning occurs at about four weeks.

Reduced range

As more land is cleared for human settlement, many wood rats find themselves confined to reduced ranges. Of these, five are in danger of disappearing altogether. Anthony's wood rat (*Neotoma anthonyi*), Bunker's wood rat (*Neotoma bunkeri*), and the San Martin Island wood rat (*Neotoma martinensis*) are native to small islands off the coast of Baja California. The San Joaquin Valley wood rat (*Neotoma fuscipes riparia*) of California is confined to an area used for real estate and agricultural development, and this rat is considered threatened. The Key Largo wood rat, though, has only about 2 square miles (5 square kilometers) of suitable land remaining. Most of the wood rats are in a grave position because of their island isolation, and there is a wide range in status, from data deficient to critically endangered.

Renardo Barden

See also Kangaroo Rats and Mice.

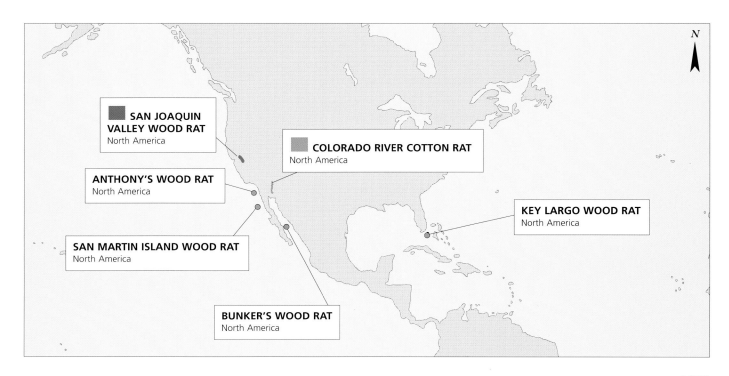

New Mexico Ridge-nosed Rattlesnake

(Crotalus willardi obscurus)

ESA: Threatened

Class: Reptilia
Order: Serpentes
Family: Crotalidae
Length: 1½–2 ft. (0.4–0.6 m)
Diet: Small mammals, birds, lizards, other snakes, arthropods
Gestation period: Approximately 390 days
Habitat: Mountainous terrain at moderate elevations
Range: Animas mountains, southwestern New Mexico; Sierra San Luis, Chihuahua, Mexico

The scientific name of the New Mexico ridge-nosed rattlesnake species comes from the man, Frank C. Willard, who collected this type of specimen.

THERE ARE FIVE subspecies of the ridge-nosed rattlesnake. All are relatively small, growing only to maximum lengths of about 2 feet (0.6 meter). Ridge-nosed rattlesnakes can be identified by the presence of a ridge along the edge of the snout. Coloration depends on the habitat of the snake. Over time they have evolved a ground color that blends with the color of the leaf

**NEW MEXICO
RIDGE-NOSED
RATTLESNAKE**
North America

debris found on the floors of the woodlands where they reside, be that light brown, reddish, or light gray.

The various subspecies also have narrow, light-colored crossbands that are bordered with slightly darker coloration.

Two additional subspecies were named before the New Mexico subspecies, *C. willardi obscurus*, was named in 1974. *C. willardi obscurus* was given subspecies status, but some herpetologists still question the validity of this distinction. Two records are also known from the adjacent Sierra San Luis of Chihuahua. This reptile has been found in four areas of canyon bottom and the adjacent slopes in a space totaling approximately 1 to 2 square miles (2.5 to 5 square kilometers). Additional areas of essential or potential habitats approximate 6½ square miles (7 kilometers), but occurrences of the rattlesnake in these areas has not been verified.

The New Mexico ridge-nosed rattlesnake prefers a habitat covered in semi-evergreen oaks, but conifers and other trees and shrubs may also be present.

Habits

The ridge-nosed rattlesnake is supposed to be a primarily diurnal reptile, and it is unlikely that it is active much after sundown except on warm summer nights. The reason for this is that these snakes may sometimes have difficulty warming themselves, especially during the rainy season. The New Mexico subspecies makes its home on canyon bottoms, and this means that clouds and vegetation often block sunlight from its habitat.

The New Mexico ridge-nosed rattlesnake has been seen climbing trees, but it is not thought to be highly arboreal. Climbing probably offers several benefits to the rattlesnake, including a better view of potential prey.

All rattlesnakes are ovoviviparous, which means that they retain fertilized eggs inside their bodies until the eggs are ready to hatch. The female then gives birth to live young. In this way the mother may regulate the incubation of the eggs through her behavior, keeping warm and thereby protecting the eggs. The estimated gestation period for the ridge-nosed rattlesnakes is approximately 390 months.

The young of most rattlesnake species are born in late summer or early fall, usually between August 1st and October 15th. While newborn rattlesnakes will share a hiding place with their mother, there is no evidence in any species that the mother actively takes care of them.

Young will generally leave the birthplace within a few days. These young snakes live a dangerous early existence and are subject to a variety of predators that could not overpower adult snakes. Difficulty in finding food and freezing temperatures are other problems that newborn snakes encounter.

Fire and excessive cattle grazing have changed the New Mexico ridge-nosed rattlesnake's habitat.

A rare snake

After the species was first documented in 1957, many collectors came to the Animas Mountains to obtain specimens of the New Mexico ridge-nosed rattlesnake. This continued until 1974, when the subspecies was named and an agreement to restrict collection and protect the habitat was signed between the U.S. Fish and Wildlife Service and the owner of the land where the subspecies was found. Unfortunately, the lands were sold in 1982, and a similar agreement was not secured with the new owners. In 1975 the snake was afforded legal protection by the New Mexico Department of Game and Fish.

The effects of collecting the New Mexico ridge-nosed rattlesnake are unknown because there are no records of population size before collection occurred. However, given the small range and the large number of individuals taken from the area, it is probable that collecting did contribute to the ever-decreasing numbers of the subspecies. Habitat disturbance occurred in conjunction with collection, adding to the problem.

Multiple threats

Future threats may include mining, land development, and harvest of wood or other resources from the area. Mining is of particular concern because mineral rights have been retained in the area for several years.

Natural threats to this snake include predation, starvation, and disease. During a 48-day search in 1976, only three New Mexico ridge-nosed rattlesnakes were found.

The way to conserve this snake is to protect its habitat. It does not appear that there are other suitable sites for transplantation. State and federal laws protecting the species must be enforced, and investigations into the status and biology of these snakes are imperative.

Elizabeth Sirimarco

REDFINS

Class: Actinopterygii

Order: Cypriniformes

Family: Cyprinidae

This group of fish is part of the large family Cyprinidae, whose members are called barbs because of the barbels or whiskers at the corners of their mouths. Some barbs are named for their bright body and fin coloration. Although most are small minnows that rarely exceed 6 inches (15 centimeters), the group includes the giant mahseer (*Barbus tor*), which may exceed 5 feet (1.5 meters) in length and can weigh over 100 pounds (45 kilograms). It is a sport fish and is found in the slow rivers of southern India, but it migrates to the mountain streams of the Himalayas to spawn.

All cyprinids have an organ called the Weberian apparatus. This internal body part is comprised of bones that connect the fish's gas bladder to its inner ear. In addition to regulating buoyancy, the gas bladder acts as an amplifier of sound, like a drum. Sounds are carried by the Weberian apparatus to the ear.

Redfins swim in schools and prefer clear water. The females scatter their eggs over vegetation and a special sticky outer layer of the eggs attaches them to aquatic plants. Males fertilize the eggs by spreading their sperm (milt) over the eggs.

Because of their small size, bright colors, courting behavior, and prolific reproduction in captivity, the redfins and barbs are favorites of aquarium enthusiasts. Many redfins and barbs are endangered due to habitat loss, introduction of non-native fish, and capture for the aquarium trade.

Berg River Redfin

(Pseudobarbus burgi)

IUCN: Critically endangered

Length: 4¼ in. (11 cm)
Reproduction: Egg layer
Habitat: Stream edges near vegetation
Range: Berg River Basin, South Africa

THE BERG RIVER BASIN in southwestern South Africa is the last remaining refuge of the Berg River redfin. This species is waging a losing battle with the forces of human activities in the basin and soon may be another victim of our mistakes. The situation for this fish is indeed grave. While there are no known extinctions of fish species in southern Africa, the principal population of the Berg River redfin in the Eerste River has been wiped out. Habitat destruction in the form of stream siltation caused by deforestation and agricultural activity is bad enough. Added to this problem is the appetite of predatory, non-native fish such as the smallmouth bass (*Micropterus dolomieu*), which takes a merciless toll on this species.

Other destructive human activities in the Berg River Basin include stream channelization for flood control and water diversion. In the process of stream channelization, habitat that is historically used by river fish for feeding and reproduction is wiped out. Water diversion dams block the movement of fishes up and down a waterway, change seasonal water flow patterns that fishes use as environmental cues (for such behavior as breeding), and reduce overall stream flow. Additionally, toxic pollution from towns and industries has been directly connected with the demise of the Berg River redfin.

Like other redfins and barbs, the Berg River redfin is in demand as an aquarium fish. While some regard this as a factor that could contribute to the eventual extinction of the species, others see aquariums as a last resort for its preservation. In the case of the Berg River redfin, the latter may be true. Under present conditions, the loss of this species is highly probable. Only after environmental policies within South Africa and the Cape of Good Hope Province change to include the needs of species like the Berg River redfin will this fish be able to survive. Until that time, aquariums and refuges outside this fish's natural range may be the only alternative for its survival.

The Berg River redfin spawns in typical barb fashion, depositing its adhesive eggs on vegetation. The small, newly hatched fry, which number between 200 and 300 from each female, are quite vulnerable to being eaten by the parents as well as other fish. To avoid predation, they remain close to some form of cover and stay together in tight groups (schools).

Favorite foods of adult Berg River redfin include small bottom-dwelling aquatic invertebrates and decaying organic material.

Fiery Redfin
(Pseudobarbus phlegethon)

ESA: Endangered

Length: 2¾ in. (7 cm)
Reproduction: Egg layer
Habitat: Stream pools and near-shore areas
Range: Olifants River Basin, South Africa

TWO TRIBUTARIES OF the Olifants River in southern South Africa are home to the fiery redfin. The Noordhoeks River and Twee River are relatively small, but they provide near-ideal conditions for this species. Historically, other tributaries located lower on the Olifants River drainage held populations of this fish as well. But years of human activity have severely depleted overall numbers of this species.

The fiery redfin shares its range with another endangered species, the Barnard's rock-catfish (*Gephyroglanis barnardi*), the rarest fish in the Olifants River Basin.

Like many threatened and endangered fish in South Africa, the fiery redfin will remain vulnerable to extinction. Because of tremendous demands on the environment by the human population, it is unlikely that the intense demands on water resources will be eased in the near future. As the need for water increases (including recreational use and the stocking of non-native fish), the prospect for an improvement in the status of the fiery redfin is gloomy.

The fiery redfin spawns like other barbs, depositing its sticky eggs on vegetation. Newly hatched young remain attached to aquatic plants for about three days while they absorb their yolk-sac. The small fry number in the hundreds, so that there will be enough to survive the hazards of the river, including being eaten by their own parents as well as by other fish. Thus, they remain close to some form of cover and stay together in tight groups or schools. The fiery redfin prefers to eat small bottom-dwelling aquatic invertebrates and decaying organic material.

Twee River Redfin
(Barbus erubescens)

IUCN: Critically endangered

Length: 4 in. (10 cm)
Reproduction: Egg layer
Habitat: Stream pools and near-shore areas
Range: Twee River and Olifants River basins, South Africa

THE TWEE RIVER REDFIN behaves like other barbs, including the way it spawns and lays its eggs so that they will stick to vegetation. Newly hatched young feed on aquatic organisms as they float past. The small fry are easy prey to other fish, which is why hundreds of eggs are laid at one time.

Adults will eat decaying organic material and small bottom-dwelling aquatic invertebrates.

Like the endangered fiery redfin (*Pseudobarbus phlegethon*), which also lives in the Olifants River Basin, the Twee River redfin is plagued by invading

BERG RIVER REDFIN
FIERY REDFIN
TWEE RIVER REDFIN
Africa

non-native fishes and habitat destruction. Years of human activity have severely depleted overall numbers.

When water is diverted for human purposes, species find their ranges permanently altered. Such action has been the primary reason for the decline of various populations of this species. Direct chemical pollution of the Twee River and Olifants River basins from agricultural, domestic, and industrial sources has also been pointed to as a chronic problem. Additionally, the introduction of non-native predatory fish such as the smallmouth bass (*Micropterus dolomieu*)—a species brought to Africa from North America as a sport fish—has contributed to the decline of this species as a whole.

The Twee River redfin will remain vulnerable to extinction, like so many other endangered fishes in South Africa, while the huge strain on the environment continues. With the ever-growing economic needs of this continent, it is unlikely that the intense demands on water resources will be eased in the near future. As demands for water increase, prospects for an improvement in the status of this fish remain poor.

William E. Manci

Copper Redhorse

(Moxostoma hubbsi)

IUCN: Vulnerable

Class: Actinopterygii
Order: Cypriniformes
Family: Catostomidae
Length: 22 in. (56 cm)
Reproduction: Egg layer
Habitat: Large lakes and rivers
Range: Quebec, Canada

Fisheries biologists have less information about redhorses than about other suckers. Shown here is the blacktail redhorse (*Moxostoma poecilurun*).

This group of specialized suckers are named "redhorses" for the red and gold body coloration that many display, their large size relative to other fish in the family Catostomidae, and the robustness of their physique. They can be found from the southern provinces of Canada to the northern states of Mexico, almost exclusively east of the Continental Divide. Only in Mexico have they been able to cross the Divide and inhabit a Pacific river system.

Sparse information

Fisheries biologists know less about redhorses than about other suckers. Information about life history, feeding habits, reproduction, and other vital details is sketchy, and disagreement about appropriate scientific names for these fish has existed for a long time. Much of this lack of certainty about redhorses is a result of the fish's preference for large bodies of water. That means access to these fish has been difficult to attain on a consistent basis. Additionally, differences between the species are few, and often a skilled eye is required to tell them apart.

Like many other threatened and endangered fish, redhorses are threatened by artificial changes in their environment, specifically of water quality. They are more sensitive to changes in water quality than other fish and usually are some of the first fish to display stress when water quality declines.

In the eastern United States and in southern Canada, acid rain caused by smokestack emissions containing sulfur dioxide and nitrogen dioxide is particularly destructive to redhorse populations. These compounds form acid rain when they mingle with atmospheric moisture and precipitate into waterways during rain and snow showers. Because of the geology of many areas of eastern North America, waterways cannot cope with this periodic assault on their chem-

istry. Such waters eventually become so acidic that fish and other organisms die.

Challenged by acid rain

The beautiful copper redhorse occupies lakes and rivers near the Canadian city of Montreal and other parts of southern Quebec. Scientists believe that, historically, this fish has never been abundant. The copper redhorse is a bottom-dwelling fish that inhabits large lakes and rivers that, by nature, are difficult to accurately survey. To illustrate just how hard it is to find these fish, consider that during the years from 1942 to 1973, only 164 individuals were recorded during numerous surveys.

The copper redhorse can reach nearly 2 feet (0.6 meters) in length and weigh 6 to 7 pounds (2.7 to 3 kilograms). True to its name, this fish displays colors that vary from bright copper to golden olive on the head and back to golden olive on the sides, with pale olive to cream on the underside. This fish has a very

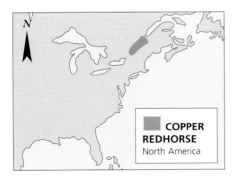

N

COPPER REDHORSE
North America

blunt snout and a sucker-like mouth on the underside of the head; the mouth is designed to pick up food from the bottom. Looking at the fish from the front, the copper redhorse appears compressed from side to side, but from back to belly the fish is quite wide, and there is a noticeable hump just behind the head. The dorsal fin on the back is square in shape, but the pectoral fins just behind the gills, the pelvic fins on the belly, and the anal fin are more triangular. The tail fin is deeply forked, with pointed lobes. The body has large scales, but the head, cheeks, and gill covers have relatively few.

This species breeds in late spring in slow-moving rivers. Little else is known about its reproductive habits. The copper redhorse is long-lived and can survive up to 15 years. The genus name *Moxostoma* means "sucking mouth," and the species *Hubbsi* was designated in honor of ichthyologist Carl L. Hubbs.

Solutions

As in other sections of southeastern Canada and northeastern United States, the environment is under heavy pressures from pollution caused by acid rain. As lakes become more and more acidic, many of the favorite foods of the copper redhorse—such as insects and snails—begin to die. Without adequate alternative sources of food, the already meager populations of copper redhorse have experienced decreases in total numbers. Compounding the problem is a seeming unwillingness of the regional or local government to significantly curtail the discharge of domestic and industrial pollutants into its waterways. These pollutants impinge on virtually all of the present-day range of the copper redhorse.

The copper redhorse inhabits important lakes and rivers within Quebec. The listing of this species as threatened is a symptom of human policies and practices that are out of control. Saving the copper redhorse from eventual extinction will require a combined effort of the federal governments of Canada and the United States, and local city government like that of Montreal. Some cooperation between the parties in acknowledging acid rain as a problem and stemming its effects has already been achieved. Hopefully these efforts will continue.

William E. Manci

Western Mountain Reedbuck

(Redunca fulvorufula adamauae)

ESA: Endangered

Class: Mammalia
Order: Artiodactyla
Family: Bovidae
Weight: 45–65 lb. (20–30 kg)
Height: 26–32 in. (66–81 cm)
Diet: Grass, leaves
Gestation period: 230–240 days
Longevity: 10–12 years
Habitat: Montane grasslands
Range: Cameroon, Nigeria

THE REEDBUCK IS an African antelope that is generally found in wet, swampy areas and habitually travels singly or in pairs. The mountain reedbuck, however, differs from all other reedbucks in that it is found in hilly terrain and not necessarily close to water. The reedbuck is also more gregarious and is seen in herds of up to 20 animals.

Reedbucks have a keen sense of hearing and excellent eyesight, which is even more efficient than that of other antelopes because reedbucks have a wider field of vision. Like most antelopes, reedbucks will flee at a sudden provocation, but will not stay spooked for long. After a short run, they will pause to look back at what set them in flight.

Most of the young are born between December and May. During the day, when the mother goes out to forage, she conceals her baby in a hiding place where the calf will instinctively stay put until the mother returns. By remaining motionless, a calf with its camouflage coloring is hard for predators to see. In addition, newborn calves have very little odor to attract predators. When the mother returns from foraging, she spends time nursing and

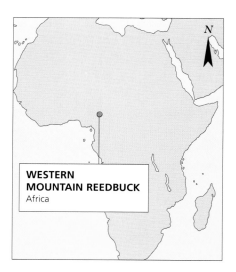

WESTERN MOUNTAIN REEDBUCK
Africa

Reedbucks are a good example of cryptic coloration (camouflage). With their olive-gray coat, they blend in with their background environment. This makes it difficult for predators to spot them except when they move.

licking her baby. After about two months, the young begin to follow the mother everywhere and remain with her until the next calf is born.

This subspecies of mountain reedbuck is found in small, declining populations, and its future is not bright. The western mountain reedbuck is not suited to compete with the larger domestic populations moving into its habitat. It is estimated that less than 600 are left in the wild, and their numbers are declining. Sadly, there are no significant captive populations.

Warren D. Thomas

Lesser Rhea

(Rhea pennata)

ESA: Endangered

IUCN: Lower risk

Class: Aves
Order: Rheiformes
Family: Rheidae
Height: 2½–3 ft. (76–91.5 cm)
Weight: 25–30 lb.(11.3–13.5 kg)
Clutch size: Up to 18 eggs
Incubation: 40–45 days
Diet: Leaves, roots, fruits, insects, small lizards, and rodents such as mice
Habitat: Floodplain and grasslands
Range: Chile, Argentina, Peru, and southwest Bolivia

FEATHERS ALWAYS look better on the bird that grows them than on a stick used for dusting. Even so, people still buy feather dusters and thus encourage their manufacture. Those who collect these feathers earn only a meager living, but the rheas that grow the feathers are the real losers.

According to traditional classification, the rheas make up their own family and order. Most ornithologists recognize only two species, but some accept three. The rheas are large, flightless birds that resemble ostriches (*Struthio camelus*).

The greater rhea (*Rhea americana*) qualifies as the largest bird in the Americas. It may stand as high as 5 feet (1.5 meters) tall and weigh 55 pounds (24.8 kilograms), although it is usually smaller than this.

The lesser rhea, also known as Darwin's rhea, is considerably smaller than its cousin, but it is still much larger than other birds.

This bird is grayish brown overall with a darker brown nape and crown. When resting, it often lies with its breast and belly on the ground and its legs and feet extending backward. Frightened birds may run swiftly away or crouch low to the ground with their necks down, Unfortunately, running and hiding are not always enough to protect them.

Feather harvest

During the eight years from 1976 to 1984, 204,322 rheas were killed so that their skins and feathers could be exported. These figures are merely for the nation of Argentina and do not include the number of rheas

killed in Peru, Bolivia, and Chile. The skins are tanned for fashionable leather and the feathers are either sold as novelties or manufactured into feather dusters. The lesser rhea faces additional threats that can only be described as wildlife vandalism.

One population of the lesser rhea lives high in the Andes Mountains on a dry plateau known as the *puna*. A little rain falls there in summer, some snow in winter, and the wind blows much of the time. Winter temperatures can get quite cold.

Feeding mostly on plant leaves and fruits, but taking occasional animal food, the lesser rhea wanders between elevations of 9,840 and 13,120 feet (3,000 to 4,000 meters) in the north of its range. Some observers have reported it at 16,000 feet (4,878 meters). To escape winter cold, the lesser rhea probably migrates down the *puna*, but this has not been verified.

Nest raiding

For many centuries people have hunted the lesser rhea and taken its eggs. Rhea nests, when found,

The lesser rhea, also known as Darwin's rhea, has suffered from excessive hunting and unnecessary harassment. The bird's skin, feathers, and even its eggs are profitable commodities in this bird's range.

are particularly vulnerable. One male courts and mates with several females. His harem may include a single female or as many as six. The male finds a natural depression and clears it of vegetation, then fashions it into a nest. Each female in his harem then lays her eggs in the same nest. The male is responsible for incubating the eggs and rearing the chicks. His brood may be a dozen or less or, in rare cases, as many as 100.

When people take rhea eggs, they immediately eliminate the total reproductive effort of many female rheas. Such heavy losses could explain swings in population, although people have been taking rhea eggs for so long that egg collecting alone seems unlikely to affect the bird's population. In the meantime, while the egg collecting continues, the lesser rhea faces other trouble.

Development within the range of the species includes road building to open up the mountains to mining. Improved road access, and the increased human populations that follow, sets the stage for disaster.

Illegal hunting

The lesser rhea seems doomed to be harassed. People now use off-road vehicles to chase the lesser rheas just for fun. Illegal hunting and idle, pointless shooting of the birds now occurs regularly.

Hunting laws cover the lesser rhea in Peru, Bolivia, and Chile, but weak enforcement offers little protection. The Convention on International Trade in Endangered Species of Wild Fauna and Flora (CITES) also lists the Darwin's rhea but does not prohibit commercial use inside the country where the animal is taken. Many of the feather dusters that are produced in Bolivia remain there.

The population in Peru was estimated at only 18 birds in 1983, but there are no overall estimates. However, the introduced population on Tierra del Fuego and the

populations in the south of its range are thought to be stable. In contrast the northern populations suffer egg collecting, hunting, and harassment, which may prove detrimental to the lesser rhea.

Kevin Cook

RHINOCEROSES

Class: Mammalia

Order: Perissodactyla

Family: Rhinocerotidae

There are five living forms of rhinoceroses. Two are from Africa, while the remaining three come from Asia: the great Indian rhino, the Javan rhino, and the Sumatran rhino—a remnant of what was once a large, thriving group of animals.

The origin of the rhinoceros goes back to the Eocene period (55 million years ago). More than 170 forms have been identified, ranging in size from about that of a small house dog to the huge Indricotherium, which stood over 18 feet (5.5 meters) at the shoulder and had a body length of over 14 feet (4.3 meters). This, and another form known as Baluchitherium, weighed between

25 and 30 tons (22,700 to 27,240 kilograms). The modern elephant weighs only from 3 to 5 tons (2,724 to 4,540 kilograms).

Rhinos are herbivores, or vegetarians, with extremely poor eyesight but an acute sense of hearing and of smell. With the exception of the white rhino, all are solitary in their habits.

Rhinos possess one or two horns that are made up of a compacted keratin material, much like fingernails. These horns have no bony connection to the skull, but are attached to the skin. During battles between rhinos, the horns may be knocked off.

The digestive system of a rhino is similar to that of the horse—they have a relatively simple stomach and a very large sack called a caecum, a junction between the large and small

intestines. The sack acts as a fermentation vat where normally indigestible, woody vegetation and grasses are changed from cellulose to digestible carbohydrates. The rhino must consume a great amount of food to receive enough nutrients for survival. Rhinos can usually be found near water.

All five forms of rhinoceros are endangered, due to loss of habitat and destruction by people. Rhinos have been slaughtered to make way for agricultural needs and for use in folk medicine. Every part of the rhino is coveted somewhere in the world as a treatment for some human malady. As the number of rhinos shrink, the value of their products grows. The rhino population has been devastated, declining from several million to less than 14,000 today.

Black Rhinoceros

(Diceros bicornis)

ESA: Endangered

IUCN: Critically endangered

Weight: 2,000–3,600 lb. (908–1,634 kg)
Shoulder height: 60–65 in. (152–165 cm)
Diet: Shrubs, scrub vegetation
Gestation period: 450 days
Longevity: 40 years
Habitat: Dry forest, scrub grasslands
Range: Africa

The black rhino is a browser, eating shrubs, young shoots, and twigs. For this purpose, its upper lip is modified with a pointed, fingerlike hook.

THE BLACK RHINOCEROS is probably the best known rhino in the world. It has received notice because of its supposedly short temper and its pugnacious personality. Only part of this reputation is deserved. Much is due to the rhino's dependence on its hearing and keen sense of smell to keep it informed of the world around it. Its eyesight is very poor indeed. That is why, when the animal is startled, it often exhibits a violent reaction.

The black rhino is also known as the hook-lipped rhinoceros because the upper lip is modified into a pointed, fingerlike hook that the rhino uses to great advantage in browsing.

The black rhino is solitary in habit, although on rare occasions a number of them will congregate around a water hole or salt lick. It is found in open savanna and forest areas south of the Sahara (excluding the central and West African rain forests), ranging

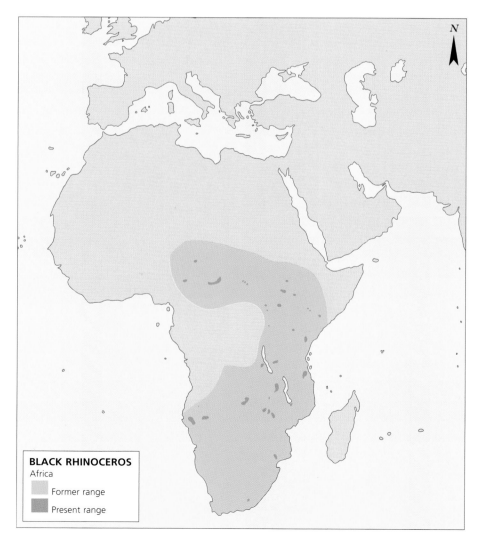

BLACK RHINOCEROS
Africa

Former range

Present range

across the countries of Sudan, Ethiopia, Somalia, Cameroon, Chad, Nigeria, the Central African Republic, Kenya, Tanzania, Uganda, Democratic Republic of Congo, Zambia, Mozambique, Malawi, Zimbabwe, Botswana, Angola, Namibia, and South Africa.

Decline

Black rhinos were once the most numerous of all living forms of rhinos. Poaching—which had risen by incredible proportions in the 1980s—has resulted in a virtual collapse of the population. For example, in 1980 Kenya recorded 1,500 black rhinos. By 1990 there were a mere 200. During that same period Tanzania recorded a drop from 3,795 to less than 200 rhinos. The Central African Republic went from 3,000 individuals to none. Only Zimbabwe, South Africa, and Namibia showed any increase in rhinos. The unprotected free-ranging days of the black rhino are probably coming to an end. Because of the incredibly high demand for its horn, it is unlikely that this rhino can be left unprotected without being under constant surveillance.

The total wild population remaining is alarmingly low, estimated at only about 3,300. The black rhino is represented in captivity by a substantial population. There are approximately 180 individuals held in some 50 zoos throughout the world. With good management this species has maintained a slow but steady increase in numbers. However, the available space in zoos is limited, and a number of health problems that occur in the animal still must be solved.

Great Indian Rhinoceros
(Rhinoceros unicornis)

ESA: Endangered

IUCN: Endangered

Weight: 4,000–5,000 lb. (1,816–2,270 kg)
Height: 65–75 in. (165–190.5 cm)
Diet: Grasses, leaves, and shoots
Gestation period: 480 days
Longevity: 45 years
Habitat: Swamp and grasslands
Range: India, southern Nepal

THE GREAT INDIAN rhinoceros is the largest of the Asian rhinos, second in size only to the African white rhino. The Indian rhino is found near water in flood plains and swampy areas. It is a browser and tends to be solitary.

Defense mechanisms

The upper lip of the great Indian rhino ends in a protuberance which it uses almost like a finger to aid it in feeding. Even though the single horn is often formidable, this rhino seldom uses it for defense, unlike its African cousin.

Instead, the great Indian rhino has a pair of lower incisor teeth that tend to curve slightly outward. By grinding them against the upper teeth, the trailing edge of these lower incisors is kept razor sharp. When fighting or defending itself, the great Indian rhino has a habit of raking backward, with these lower

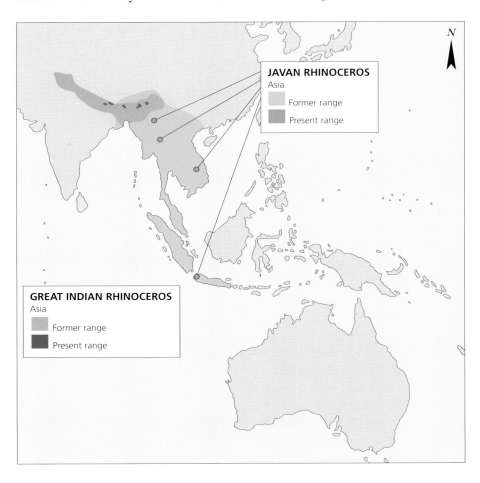

incisors. This, combined with its extremely powerful build, makes it a formidable opponent.

Reduced numbers

The great Indian rhino was once quite common over much of India, Nepal, and parts of southern China. Now, however, it is greatly reduced in numbers, and the total population is probably less than 2,000. The two biggest concentrations of the great Indian rhinoceros are found in the Kaziranga National Park in India and the Royal Chitawan National Park in Nepal. It is a constant struggle to protect these populations from poachers and from local farmers who use the national parks to graze their own livestock. The captive population is growing, with some 120 making up the well-managed group.

Javan Rhinoceros
(Rhinoceros sondaicus)

ESA: Endangered
IUCN: Critically endangered

Weight: 2,500–3,000 lb. (1,135–1,362 kg)
Shoulder height: 50–65 in. (127–165 cm)
Diet: Leaves and shoots
Gestation period: 480 days
Longevity: 40 years
Habitat: Lowland rain forest
Range: Java, Laos, Kampuchea

In appearance, the Javan rhino strongly resembles the great Indian rhino, but differs in two

The Indian rhino is easy to identify by its skin, which is divided into great overlapping plates covered by large tubercles.

ways. First, it is a much smaller animal than the great Indian rhino. Second, although its skin lies in folds like the Indian rhino, it lacks the protuberances seen in the Indian rhino. Instead, the surface of the skin has a more mosaic-like appearance.

The Javan rhino was once found over much of Southeast Asia, as well as on the Indonesian islands of Sumatra and Java. It now exists only on a small peninsula off the west coast of Java. This area is called Ujung Kulon, and it is a protected national park.

The Javan rhino may have been sighted in Myanmar (formerly Burma) and northern Thailand, and was seen in Cambodia. How-

Although the Javan rhino was once found over much of Southeast Asia, as well as on Sumatra and Java, it now exists only on Ujung Kulon, a small peninsula off the west coast of Java.

ever, none of these sightings have been confirmed. This rhino is quite solitary and secretive in its habits. Even in Ujung Kulon it is rarely seen. The Javan rhino is a browser, and its habitat is deep tropical rain forest—another reason it may be so hard to find.

The last population?

The Ujung Kulon population—the only confirmed population in existence—is a small one, reaching only about 100 individuals. This number is about the maximum that could be sustained by the resources of the park.

Since this rhino has no place to which it can migrate, a stagnant population has resulted. Because of the limited number of new genes available with which to breed, there is a tendency to inbreeding that can only create an unhealthy population. This makes the species very difficult to maintain indefinitely.

There are currently a number of studies underway to translocate some of these rhinoceroses, in stages, to more suitable habitats. This could establish new populations and perhaps revitalize the existing population. At present there are no Javan rhinoceroses held in captivity.

The Sumatran rhinoceros generally does not gather in groups, although it is not unheard of to see more than one near a water source. Still, individuals prefer to wallow in streams and pools by themselves. For days they will remain in one location, eat available vegetation, and stay in the water to keep cool and avoid insects.

Sumatran Rhinoceros

(Dicerorhinus sumatraensis)

ESA: Endangered

IUCN: Critically endangered

Weight: 1,400–1,800 lb. (636–817 kg)
Shoulder height: 50–60 in. (127–152 cm)
Diet: Leaves and shoots
Gestation period: Probably 450–480 days
Longevity: 35–40 years
Habitat: Tropical rain forest
Range: Indonesia, possibly a few left in Southeast Asia

THE SUMATRAN RHINO is perhaps the most unusual of the Asiatic rhinos. Unlike the great Indian and Javan rhinos, the Sumatran rhino has two horns.

This is the smallest of all rhinos, and it is the only rhino species covered by a considerable amount of long hair, which varies from black to reddish brown. Like the Javan rhino, the Suma-

tran rhino dwells in deep tropical rain forests. It is solitary in nature and extremely shy. It is rarely seen in the wild. This species is a leaf eater and browser. With regard to physical characteristics, it is the most primitive rhino, remaining virtually unchanged since the mid-Pleistocene Age (three million years ago).

This rhino has few natural enemies other than people. Once it was found over much of Southeast Asia, and some may remain in Thailand, Laos, Vietnam, and Cambodia. Today it survives on the islands of Sumatra, Borneo, and Sarawak, and on the peninsula of Malaysia.

Even though some population estimates list as many as 800 individuals, most of these are in small, genetically isolated pockets of habitat. The only significant concentrations that remain can be found on peninsular Malaysia. There are a small number in the northern part of Borneo, and the bulk are on the island of Sumatra.

The remaining population is seriously endangered because of poaching and, more important, destruction of the rain forest.

Northern White Rhinoceros
(Ceratotherium simum cottoni)

ESA: Endangered

IUCN: Critically endangered

Weight: 4,200–6,000 lb. (1,907–2,724 kg)
Shoulder height: 65–75 in. (165–190.5 cm)
Diet: Grasses and some leaves
Gestation period: 480 days
Longevity: 45 years
Habitat: Dry savannah, grasslands, some open forest and scrubland
Range: Democratic Republic of Congo

Captivity

Up until recently there were very few Sumatran rhinos in captivity. However, due to major efforts by the wildlife departments in Indonesia, private interests in Great Britain, and a group of North American zoos, the captive population has grown considerably, and is now estimated at between 20 and 25.

It is hoped that this population will reproduce sufficiently to establish the species in captivity. This could act as a reservoir to

It is not uncommon to find northern white rhinos in small groups. They are grazers; with their huge square lips they can go through a grassy plain like a mechanical harvesting machine.

repopulate safe areas of the wild. If it proves possible to reintroduce the Sumatran rhinoceros into the wild, there is some hope that this remarkable little rhino—which has already survived for hundreds of thousands of years—can continue to survive into the 21st century.

THE RHINOCEROS IS the third largest land mammal, and the largest of these is the white, or square-lipped, rhinoceros.

They have the largest skull in proportion to their body size. It is attached to the shoulders by huge neck muscles that give these rhinos a humplike appearance. The largest rhino horns on record are from white rhinos. The females have the longer horns, but the males' horns are bigger at the base.

The northern and southern subspecies of white rhino are separated by 1,000 miles (1,609 kilometers), and have been isolated from each other for 1,000 years. The southern subspecies was nearly driven to extinction toward the end of the 19th century. However, with protection and good management, they have made a comeback. There are around 500 in captivity and 5,000 in the wild, in protected

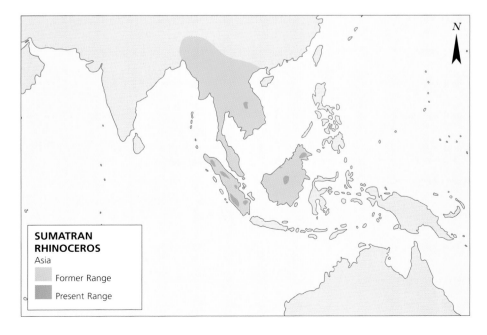

SUMATRAN RHINOCEROS
Asia

Former Range

Present Range

areas. They sustain a healthy population. The same is not true for the northern subspecies. The northern white rhino was once found in large numbers in the Democratic Republic of Congo, Uganda, and the Sudan, but due to heavy hunting, its numbers are probably less than 30 in the wild, most of which are in the Democratic Republic of Congo. The Ugandan population is gone, and Sudan may have one or two left. The northern white rhino is the most endangered rhino today.

There are only a total of 10 in captivity in two zoos, in San Diego, California and in the former Czechoslovakia. Some of the European animals were moved to America to increase their breeding capabilities, but the future for this species looks bleak.

Warren D. Thomas

NORTHERN WHITE RHINOCEROS
Africa
Former Range
Present Range

ROBINS

Class: Aves

Order: Passeriformes

Family: Muscicapidae

All the birds with the name "robin" belong to the Old World flycatcher family (Muscicapidae). Possibly the largest of all bird families, the Old World flycatchers are separated into several subfamilies. At least two of these subfamilies have species commonly called "robins." One is the thrush subfamily, which includes the American robin (*Turdus migratorius*) and the North American bluebird (*Sialia* sp.). The other subfamily is Muscicapinae. The diversity of various classifications of robins reflects their very different forms and behaviors.

Chatham Island Robin

(Petroica traversi)

ESA: Endangered

IUCN: Endangered

Length: 5½–6 in. (14–15.2 cm)
Weight: Unknown
Clutch size: 2 eggs
Incubation: Unknown
Diet: Insects
Habitat: Forests
Range: Chatham Islands of New Zealand, southern Pacific Ocean

ONLY FIVE Chatham Island robins survived in 1980. They lived on an island so small, with such little habitat, that every one could be counted. Yet by 1988 the population of Chatham Island robins had grown to 38.

Ornithologists have assigned the Chatham Island robin to the subfamily Muscicapinae. Other subfamilies include babblers, Old World warblers, and thrushes. Deep, sooty brown from beak tip to tail tip and toenail to topknot, the Chatham Island robin was not heroically saved for its great beauty. People saved the robin from extinction because people had originally imperiled it.

During the 19th century, human enterprise changed the character of the Chatham Islands. Whalers, sealers, and colonists all played a part in the change. Ships carried stowaway rats, and colonists brought livestock and pets. Soon after

The Chatham Island robin once inhabited several, if not all nine, of the Chatham Islands.

humans arrived on the Chathams, black rats (*Rattus rattus*), pigs (*Sus scrofa*), goats (*Capra hircus*), cattle (*Bos taurus*), sheep (*Ovis aries*), house cats (*Felis sylvestris*), and dogs (*Canis familiaris*) added to the islands' population. The goats, pigs, sheep, and cattle ate island vegetation; the rats and cats went to work eating the eggs and nestlings of island birds. The collective result was a degraded native plant community, with native birds either eliminated or disappearing.

The Chatham Island robin quickly perished from several islands. By the early 20th century, the robin occupied only Mangere and Little Mangere

Islands. Both islands rise steeply from the sea and are surrounded by cliffs. Nevertheless, people settled Mangere and cleared much of the forest to open the island for grazing.

Rats eventually got to Mangere, and the robins died out there, too. Little Mangere ranks as smallest of the Chatham islands. Together, the Chathams cover only 372 square miles (967 square kilometers), and Little Mangere accounts for only 37½ acres (15 hectares) of that space. By 1976, only 12½ acres (5 hectares) of forest habitat remained on Little Mangere. The robin population fell from 17 birds to just 7 in three years. Officials with the New Zealand Wildlife Service then decided to rescue the Chatham Island robin. The rescue was no small task.

Amazing rescue

Beginning in September 1976, the robins were netted and placed in special backpacks. Field workers then carried the birds to the cliffs, climbed down using ropes, placed the birds on boats, then took them to Mangere Island to more stable tracts of habitat. All seven robins were moved. They began nesting, but some deaths occurred, leaving only five Chatham Island robins in 1980. Using knowledge of robin natural history, ornithologists turned the robin's behavior to their advantage.

Chatham Island robins nearly always lay two eggs but only raise one chick. Ornithologists took the eggs of the robins soon after they were laid. The missing eggs prompted the robins to lay a second clutch. The first eggs were

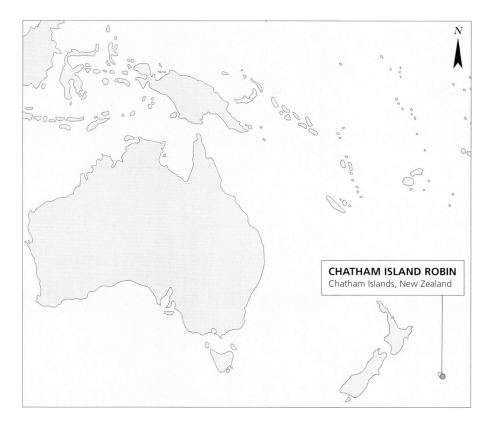

N

CHATHAM ISLAND ROBIN
Chatham Islands, New Zealand

Seychelles Magpie Robin

(Copsychus sechellarum)

ESA: Endangered

IUCN: Critically endangered

Length: 8½–9 in. (21.6–22.9 cm)
Weight: Unknown
Clutch size: 1 egg
Incubation: Unknown
Diet: Insects, giant millipedes, small lizards, human "handouts"
Habitat: Forests, woodlands, yards
Range: Frigate, Cousin, Cousine, and Aride Islands in the Seychelles

placed in a different species' nest, where they were raised by foster parents. This technique is called cross-fostering. Chatham Island warblers (*Gerygone albofrontata*) were the first species chosen to cross-foster the young robins, but Chatham Island tits (*Petroica macrocephala*) have proved a better choice as foster parents.

The cross-fostering program successfully raised the population from five in 1980, to ten in 1983, and 38 in 1988.

Nature reserve

Mangere Island only offers 10½ acres (4.2 hectares) of suitable robin habitat, and robins have completely filled it. Plans called for a second population to be established on South East Island. The New Zealand government bought South East Island in 1954 and immediately protected it as a nature reserve. All livestock were removed by 1961, and the island has no rats or cats. Landings on the island are prohibited because of the very real threat of a fishing or pleasure boat unintentionally transporting rats to the island.

Exotic predators

Fishers ignore the ban on landings, however, so the potential exists for accidental introduction of an exotic mammal. Other islands either offer no habitat or else they have rats, cats, or both.

Some restoration work, including tree planting, has been done to increase the habitat on Mangere. Meanwhile, the forest on Little Mangere has continued to deteriorate. New Zealand plans to continue monitoring the islands for rats and cats, and to continue cross-fostering the robin eggs into tit nests.

Much maintenance will be necessary to ensure that the robin survives.

SAILORS LONG KNEW of the islands clustered between northern Madagascar and the equator. France colonized the Seychelles Islands in 1768, but Great Britain took possession in 1794. The islands and their human inhabitants became an independent nation in 1976. The group includes 86 islands and islets that collectively cover only 171 square miles (445 square kilometers). Many of the Seychelles are low expanses of ancient coral, grown thick with tropical vegetation. A few of the islands are blocks of granite thrust up from the sea.

The Seychelles magpie robin originally inhabited many of the granitic islands. With human settlement, however, came rats and cats and agriculture. People cleared many of the island forests to develop pastures for grazing livestock. Plantations of cinnamon and coconut were also developed. Some land was cultivated into vegetable crops just for local consumption. Converting native plant communities into agricultural lands doubtlessly affected many native birds. What pockets of native vegetation were left intact became degraded by predators, with which island birds had no experience.

Easy prey

Black rats (*Rattus rattus*) and Norway rats (*Rattus norvegicus*) established themselves on islands all over the world. Without predators to suppress their populations, rats quickly became nuisances to struggling colonists. Soon house cats (*Felis sylvestris*) were taken along on ships as rat catchers. But both rodents and felines soon learned that island birds were easy prey. Rats easily climb trees, where they find eggs and nestlings. Cats spend more time prowling the ground than in the trees. They catch fledglings and adults. The total pressure of rats, cats, and habitat loss caused several extinctions on the Seychelles and pushed the magpie robin to the brink of extinction. The extinction of the species on some of the islands has been attributed to the capture of birds to keep in cages.

The Seychelles magpie robin vanished from all the Seychelles except Frigate Island (often spelled Fregate). The history of bird extinctions and declines prompted bird enthusiasts to support a move to eliminate cats from Frigate. The last of the cats were exterminated in 1981, although another threat came from Norway rats, which colonized in 1995 and are now

probably a threat to the population. The Seychelles magpie robin responded. Ornithologists had hoped the bird would recover and the population begin to increase. Instead, the magpie robin's population simply stopped declining and leveled off at roughly two dozen birds. Seychelles magpie robins live in fragments of woodland habitat squeezed between coconut plantations and farmland. The bird is black, with a bluish sheen in adults. The small feathers of the wing form a broad white patch for the bird's only contrasting pattern. An inquisitive little bird, the magpie robin routinely visits yards and gardens. People encourage them by putting out rice and other food scraps, which the birds have learned to enjoy.

The population declined until the bird was only found on Frigate Island, reaching a low of 12–15 birds in 1965. Numbers increased

slightly to a steady two dozen birds in the 1980s, and by early 1994 this had increased to 46 individuals, while an additional two birds (a male and a female) had been translocated to the island of Aride. Although this was largely unsuccessful, later translocations to the small islands of Cousin and Cousine have produced very encouraging results. In 1999 the total population in the Seychelles was around 80 fledged birds, 45 on Frigate, 20 on Cousin, 14 on Cousine, and one on Aride.

Frigate Island covers only 1,750 acres (700 hectares). Portions of the island provide unsuitable habitat for the robin. The species probably now fills all suitable nesting habitat, so the population on Frigate will not grow. It is essential for the long-term survival of the species to establish self-sustaining populations on islands other then Frigate.

Kevin Cook

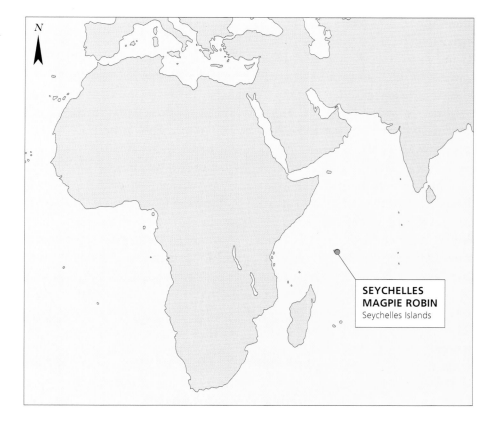

SEYCHELLES MAGPIE ROBIN
Seychelles Islands

Barnard's Rock-catfish

(Austroglanis barnardi)

IUCN: Critically endangered

Class: Actinopterygii
Order: Siluriformes
Family: Bagridae
Length: 4¾ in. (12 cm)
Reproduction: Egg layer
Habitat: Riffles and shallows over gravel and sand
Range: Noordhoeks and Twee Rivers, South Africa

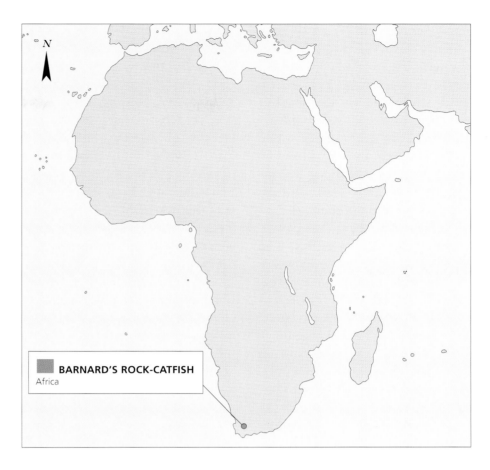

BARNARD'S ROCK-CATFISH
Africa

TWO TRIBUTARIES of the Olifants River in southern South Africa are home to the Barnard's rock-catfish. The Noordhoeks River and Twee River are relatively small, but they provide near-ideal conditions for this species. Historically, other tributaries located lower on the Olifants River drainage held populations of this fish as well. Years of human activity in and around the Olifants, however, have severely depleted overall numbers. Agricultural activity and the associated deforestation, deposition of smothering silt within the rivers, and diversion of water have been primarily responsible for the decline. Also, the introduction of non-native predatory fish such as the smallmouth bass (*Micropterus dolomieu*) have contributed to the decline of the Barnard's rock-catfish as a whole.

The name *catfish* conjures up an image in the minds of most people. The most distinguishing features of this ancient group of fishes are the barbels, or "whiskers," that all catfish exhibit. Barbels are not hairs, they are sensitive organs containing taste buds and other sensors that collect chemical cues from their surroundings. Their whiskers do not qualify catfish as cute and cuddly, however—most people consider them downright slimy and not worthy of attention. But catfish have not needed human help—they have been hugely successful in adapting to a wide range of environments, colonizing all of the earth's continents except Antarctica.

A large family of fish

All catfish, including the Barnard's rock-catfish, are not only diverse in their distribution but also in their various forms, and they are categorized under several scientific genera and families. There are many species called catfish that occupy differ-ent continents and belong to different genera. Other types of catfishes are known as blindcats and cavefish.

Catfish are remarkably hardy. They are able to occupy warm water environments and even withstand high temperatures, low levels of oxygen, and other insults —both natural and artificial. They occur in streams and lakes, caves and springs, and at both deep and shallow depths. When introduced to areas in which they do not naturally occur, they can thrive to the point where they become pests. The exotic walking catfish (*Clarias batrachus*) of Florida is a perfect example of a species that adapted well to a totally new environment. Native to Asia, the walking catfish was introduced to Florida and dis-placed some of the less aggressive native fishes. This species is appropriately named; when state officials tried to poison some of the walking catfish, the catfish swam to the surface, crawled on land while breathing air, and moved to untreated waters—leaving the native fish to die. Despite their success and adaptability, however, some catfish are in danger of extinction from human destruction of their habitat.

As well as barbels, catfish share other characteristics. The skin is scaleless, they have an adipose (fatty) fin on their back, some fins have spines for protection, and the anal fin is unusually long and deep. This feature helps keep the thin, wide mouth in contact with the bottom as the fish swims in search of food. Catfish are in demand around the world as food fish. In the United States, the channel catfish is cul-

tured on southern farms just like other livestock. The process, termed aquaculture, involves stocking large ponds with small catfish and feeding them until they reach market size. Several species of *Clarias* are raised to provide food in India and the Philippines. Presently, because of its small size and status as an endangered fish, the Barnard's rock-catfish is not generally considered a food fish or a candidate for aquaculture.

Appearance

This fish is small in size but displays an interesting and distinctive pattern of skin coloration. The light brown background is covered with randomly spaced dark brown spots and blotches. The Barnard's rock-catfish has a low sloping forehead, four pairs of barbels, a

mouth placed low on the head for easy capture of bottom-dwelling food, rounded fins, defensive spines on the dorsal fin on the back and on the pectoral fins just behind the gills, and a prominent and fleshy adipose fin between the dorsal fin and tail fin.

This species spawns in the spring within protected areas of the river. Eggs are laid in an adhesive mass and are fertilized immediately by the male; some parental protection is provided. The Barnard's rock-catfish shares its range with another endangered species, the fiery redfin (*Pseudobarbus phlegethon*), but records indicate that the Barnard's rock-catfish is the rarest fish in the Olifants River Basin.

William E. Manci

See also Blindcats, Catfish, and Cavefish.

ROCK CRESS

Class: Magnoliopsida

Order: Capparales

Family: Cruciferae

Arabis is a cosmopolitan north temperate genus of about 180 species. They are either perennials or biennials. The plants have a rosette growth form, with rosettes forming tall, terminal flowering axes.

Arabis is in the family Cruciferae (Brassicaceae) and shares the family characteristics of four-petaled flowers with six stamens, two of which are longer than the other four. The Cruciferae are also characterized by the separation of the ovary into two chambers. Some species of *Arabis* are mat-forming alpine plants that are often grown in gardens.

Braun's Rock Cress

(Arabis perstellata)

ESA: Endangered

IUCN: Endangered

Height: 8–24 in. (20–61 cm)
Leaves: 1½ in. (4 cm) long and ½ in. (1.3 cm) wide
Flowering season: Late March to early May
Habitat: Wooded hillsides and ledges
Range: Kentucky and Tennessee

BRAUN'S ROCK CRESS is a perennial, with stems that typically reach a height of 12 inches (30 centimeters) when in flower and

extend to 16 inches (41 centimeters) in fruit. The basal leaves are narrow and irregularly toothed (pinnately lobed). The leaves are covered with stellate (star-shaped) formations of hairs. These appear on both the upper and lower surfaces, which gives the leaves a grayish appearance. The rosette of leaves from the last growing season is present at flowering time, but later dies back. New rosettes are formed between the fruiting stems.

Braun's rock cress blooms in April and has white or pink flowers, sometimes with dark pinkish purple veins. The flowers have four petals, each 2 to 4 millimeters long and 1.2 millimeters wide. The seedpods are ½ to 1½ inches (1.3 to 4 centimeters) long and are straight or slightly curved. They are held in a posi-

This rocky limestone shore is a typical preferred habitat for Braun's rock cress (*Arabis perstellata*).

tion inclining slightly upward along the stem. The wingless seeds sit in one row, and are ½ to 1½ inches (1.3 to 4 centimeters) long.

Taxonomy

The taxonomy of Braun's rock cress is confusing. In some books it has been considered a form of *Arabis laevigata*. In addition, a hybrid between Braun's rock cress and *A. laevigata* has also been discovered where Braun's rock cress was first found and described: Elkhorn Creek in Franklin County, Kentucky. The

existence of these hybrids has not helped to simplify the question of taxonomy. Braun's rock cress also resembles *A. dentata*, which is now called *A. shortii*. *A. shortii* is smaller than Braun's rock cress and is an annual with yellowish flowers. Two varieties of Braun's rock cress are recognized: *A. perstellata* var. *ampla* and *A. perstellata* var. *perstellata*. *A. perstellata* var. *ampla* can be distinguished from *A. perstellata* var. *perstellata* by its larger size and by its thinner, less hairy leaves, which have a more entire margin.

Distribution

A. perstellata var. *perstellata* occurs in 27 populations in Kentucky. Of the 27 populations, 24 occur

in Franklin County, two are in Owen County and one is in Henry county. All of these populations are from the Eden Shale Belt Subsection of the Blue Grass Physiographic Region. Population sizes tend to be small. Ten of these populations have fewer than 100 plants, and 12 populations have fewer than 20 plants.

A. perstellata var. *ampla* occurs in only 2 populations in Rutherford County, Tennessee. These populations are both from the Cumberland River Subsection of the Central Basin Physiographic Region. One population is small, containing only 25 plants in an area covering 2,600 square feet (240 square meters) The other population contains several hundred plants and is scattered over 2¼ acres (0.9 hectares). Historically, three sites also existed in Davidson County, although today all populations in that county have disappeared.

Habitat

Braun's rock cress usually grows on rocky limestone outcrops that are moist but not wet. It can also occur on steep wooded slopes and in areas with little competition from other plants, such as around the bases of large trees or inclines scoured by erosion. These plants prefer full shade or filtered sunlight and do not occur in full sun. Both varieties show

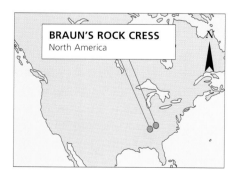

BRAUN'S ROCK CRESS
North America

distributions that correlate with the river systems of the Kentucky River and its tributaries, particularly Elkhorn Creek, and Stones River in Tennessee.

Threats

Braun's rock cress is threatened at many of the sites where it occurs. Weedy competition is a significant problem for this species, with 14 of the 27 populations affected. Six populations are threatened by trampling, and one population by logging. One of the sites with the largest numbers of individuals was damaged by roadwork while the species was being proposed for listing. Another population is also immediately threatened by roadwork. The remaining populations are not currently threatened, but are vulnerable to the same problems in the future.

There is an increasing danger of potential inbreeding, with subsequent failure to reproduce successfully as population sizes decrease and neighboring populations become more distant. *A. perstellata* var. *ampla* already seems to be suffering from inbreeding depression, since many plants are older individuals, and there is little evidence of reproduction occurring.

All populations of Braun's rock cress in Kentucky occur on privately owned land, though three receive limited protection as state-designated natural areas. Active management is required for this species at all sites.

The Kentucky Nature Preserves Commission is contacting the owners of the land on which this species occurs and they are developing a management plan for the plant.

Hoffmann's Rock Cress
(Arabis hoffmanni)

ESA: Endangered

IUCN: Endangered

Height: 6–27½ in. (15–70 cm)
Flowering season: February–April
Habitat: Cliffs and rocky hillsides, 200–430 ft. (60–130 m)
Range: Santa Cruz Island, California

HOFFMANN'S ROCK CRESS is a perennial herb with a course habit and a woody base, or caudex, covered in the scaly remainder of old leaf bases. This plant grows in rosettes of basal leaves with leafy inflorescence stalks that reach a height of 6 to 27½ inches (15 to 70 centimeters). The basal leaves are from 2 to 4 inches (5 to 10 centimeters) long and are linear to lanceolate (long and thin to spear-shaped). The upper surfaces of these leaves are hairless, while the lower surfaces are covered with many-branched hairs. The leaves on the upper parts of stems are crowded and are 1 to 2 inches (3 to 6 centimeters) long. The flowers of Hoffmann's rock cress have four white to lavender oblong petals from 6 to 10 millimeters long. The flattish seedpods, called sliques, are narrowly oblong, from 2½ to 3½ inches (6 to 9 centimeters) long and 2 to 4 millimeters wide. When mature, the seedpods are held in an upright position along the stem. Seeds form two rows per chamber in the capsule; they are round

Non-native species and feral pigs have caused much of the decline of Hoffmann's rock cress.

with a narrow wing. This plant is closely related to the mainland species *Arabis maxima*, and could have evolved from this plant. However Hoffmann's rock cress is distinguishable in form and structure and has been isolated in its island habitat for long enough to have evolved into a distinct species.

Distribution and habitat

Hoffmann's rock cress is of particular environmental concern because it is found only on Santa Cruz Island off the coast of Southern California. It occurs on the north side of the island on sea cliffs, at Plats Harbor, and in a canyon nearby. It also occurs in the central valley north of Centinela. It was recorded near El Sobrante on Santa Rosa Island, but was last seen at this site in December 1936. This plant is restricted to igneous and metamorphic substrates, and it is nearly always found on north-facing slopes. Although it favors these volcanic rock faces and rocky hillsides, it can also occur on coastal bluffs, in chaparral, and in coastal scrub grasslands at elevations of 200 to 430 feet (60 to 130 meters).

Santa Cruz Island

Santa Cruz Island is one of the eight Channel Islands off the coast of California. These islands are a westward extension of the Santa Monica Mountains and are found between 12½ and 27 miles (20 and 44 kilometers) from the mainland of California. Santa Cruz Island is 18½ miles (30 kilometers) long and 7½ miles (12 kilometers) wide at its widest point, with a total area of 96 square miles (249 square kilometers). It is located 18½ miles (30 kilometers) off the coast.

Parts of Santa Cruz Island have been continuously above sea level for the last 500,000 years, and it was probably never connected to the mainland by a land bridge. The terrain of the island is very rugged, with two mountain ridges running along its length and a central valley between them. The maximum elevation of the island is 2,470 feet (753 meters), and there are many peaks and canyons.

Santa Cruz Island has a Mediterranean climate, with mild wet winters and dry, warm summers. There is a prevailing northwest wind, which brings a marine influence and frequent summer fogs to the north-facing coastal slopes. The central valley, which is more isolated from the marine influence, freezes in the

winter, but the rest of the island is frost-free. Average monthly temperatures range from 53 degrees Fahrenheit (12 degrees Centigrade) in December to 70 degrees Fahrenheit (21 degrees Centigrade) in August. There is an average of 19¾ inches (50 centimeters) of rain annually.

Wildfires were probably very important in this ecosystem. This island has suffered from much human disturbance throughout its history, and most natural habitats have been damaged. In the 1800s livestock, including sheep, cattle, horses, and pigs, were transported to the island. For many years parts of the island were used as ranches and fig trees, olive trees, and vineyards were planted. Sheep were overstocked on the island for most of the time that the ranches existed, and this took a heavy toll on the vegetation.

Many species of native plants became rare, and others such as *opuntia* species increased and became weedy. Introduced species such as fennel, eucalyptus, and annual grasses became weedy and further threatened the native flora by competition.

The Channel Islands support 37 endemic plant species, 8 of which are endemic to Santa Cruz Island, and nearly all of which are threatened by habitat destruction. There are 16 plants, including Hoffmann's rock cress, which have extremely limited distributions.

Recently the importance of these islands has been recognized, and now 90 percent of Santa Cruz Island is owned by the Nature Conservancy. The eastern 10 percent has recently been purchased by the National

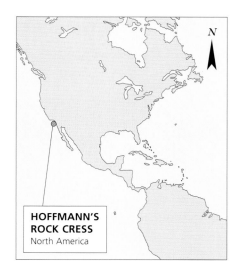

HOFFMANN'S ROCK CRESS
North America

Park Service from a private owner. The Nature Conservancy removed feral sheep from its land. The last sheep were removed in 1989, and totaled 37,171 animals. The last cattle were removed in 1988, though feral pigs are still active and have proved to be quite a bit more difficult to eliminate.

There is also concern about the presence of European honeybees on the island. These compete with local insects and contribute to the expansion of alien plants such as fennel, which would not otherwise be efficiently pollinated.

Threats

Since the removal of the feral sheep, some of the native flora has started to recover, and plants that were once limited to inaccessible cliff faces are becoming more widespread. It will, however, be many decades before the island rock cress habitats recover completely.

In the meantime, Hoffmann's rock cress and other species endemic to this island still face threats from feral pigs, competition from alien vegetation, and chance disasters.

McDonald's Rock Cress

(Arabis mcdonaldiana)

ESA: Endangered

IUCN: Vulnerable

Height: 3–30 in. (7.5–75 cm)
Leaves: Spatula-shaped, ¼–¾ in. (1–2 cm) in length
Flowers: March to June. 2 to 20 purple or pink flowers
Habitat: Serpentine soils in yellow pine forests
Range: Mendacino County, California

MCDONALD'S ROCK CRESS, also known as Red Mountain rock cress, is one of a group of six perennial species of *Arabis* with pink or purple flowers from the coastal ranges in northwestern California and southwestern Oregon. McDonald's rock cress has a rosette growth habit and a branching stem. The evergreen leaves have wavy margins or a few teeth that may be tipped with bristles. Otherwise, the leaves are glabrous (smooth). The flattened seedpods are held erect. Seeds are oblong and do not have a wing. Information is not available on the breeding system or pollinators of this species, though the colorful flowers are probably visited by insects relatively frequently.

Habitat

McDonald's rock cress is found only in a 2-square mile (5.2-square kilometer) area between 3,000 and 4,000 feet (915 and 1,220 meters) high in the Red Mountains in Mendacino County, California. This species shares its location with yellow pine forests. The climate in this region is moist, particularly in the winter, and the temperature is mild. McDonald's rock cress is most abundant in rock crevices, but it also can be found on steep slopes and dry ridges. This species appears to benefit from some burning of its habitat, since the most numerous and robust populations present now exist on land that was burned in a fire in 1985. This plant prefers filtered sunlight.

Distribution

Populations are known at 21 sites that contain 10 to 1,000 individuals. A survey conducted in 1998 estimated that 10,000 plants existed. Most of these plants are

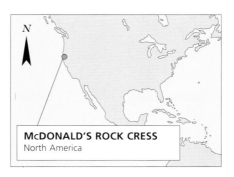

McDonald's rock cress (*Arabis mcdonaldiana*) lives on land that may soon be designated as a wilderness area to prevent development there.

McDONALD'S ROCK CRESS
North America

on land administered by the Bureau of Land Management, though several populations are located on private property. There are heavy mining activities in this area, since the soil is rich in nickel and chromium, and some populations of this species occur on land owned by a mining company. However, when this rock cress was listed as an endangered species in 1978, the mining company suspended activity and sold the land to a forestry firm, the current owner.

Threats

Although it is unlikely that trees will ever be planted on the sites where McDonald's rock cress grows, the plants could still be affected by wind-blown herbicides and by other disturbances. This species is also threatened by commercial collecting.

A project is underway to study the biology of this species, and the Bureau of Land Management is considering designating this species' range as a wilderness area. The plant is also in cultivation, both in gardens and in research collections. Attempts have been made to reintroduce greenhouse-grown plants back into the wild. However, the greenhouse plants were eaten by rodents that would normally avoid eating this species. This observation suggests that in the wild, McDonald's rock cress takes up minerals from the nickel- and chromium-rich soils where it grows, and that these minerals discourage herbivores from eating the plant's leaves.

Populations of a similar species occur in Del Norte County, California, and Curry County, Oregon. These plants are a near relative but have not yet been fully described. Some sources of information include these populations with McDonald's rock cress. However, at present these plants do not have federal protection.

Research needs to be done to resolve the taxonomy of these populations on the California-Oregon border so that appropriate conservation measures can be taken in the near future.

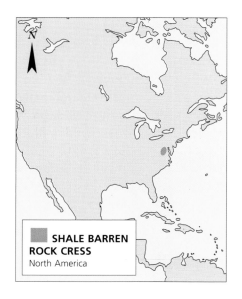

SHALE BARREN ROCK CRESS
North America

Shale Barren Rock Cress

(Arabis serotina)

| **ESA:** Endangered |
| **IUCN:** Vulnerable |

Height: 12–24 in. (30–60 cm)
Flowering season: Late June to September
Habitat: Shale barrens
Range: Appalachian Mountains of Virginia and West Virginia

SHALE BARREN rock cress is a biennial herb that forms a rosette close to the ground during the first year of growth, and in the second year forms a spreading compound inflorescence.

The basal leaves of this species die back completely by the time of flowering. The inflorescence is made up of many whitish flowers, each 2 to 3 millimeters across. The yellowish brown seeds are narrowly elliptical and 1½ to 2 times as long as they are broad.

Close relative

This plant is closely related to *Arabis laevigata* var. *burkii*, and they are easily confused. Many floras do not include shale barren rock cress on the basis that it is not distinct from *A. laevigata* var. *burkii*, though the shale barren rock cress continues to be written about in conjunction with the endemic shale barren flora. There are differences in form and structure that can distinguish the two species, such as the larger size and smaller calyxes of shale barren rock cress. Both species have elongated clusters of flowers

Shale barren rock cress lives on exposed slopes known as shale barrens.

(racemes), but shale barren rock cress commonly has secondary branching on the raceme, in contrast to the unbranched raceme of *A. laevigata*. However, the easiest way to distinguish these two species is by their different flowering times, with *A. laevigata* flowering in April and May, and shale barren rock cress flowering from late June to September.

Habitat

Shale barren rock cress is endemic to exposed south- or southwest-facing shale slopes at 1,300 to 2,500 feet (400 to 760 meters) elevation in the lower Appalachian Mountains.

These isolated habitats, called shale barrens, are distinct from the surrounding forest habitats. Appalachian shale barrens are characterized by southern exposures, slopes of greater than 20 degrees, a surface pavement of hard, weather-resistant rock fragments, and they have a sparse vegetation cover.

This region has a rainy temperate climate with 28 to 43 inches (72 to 110 centimeters) of annual precipitation, and no month receives less than 1 inch (2.5 centimeters).

Average monthly temperatures range between 32 and 72 degrees Fahrenheit (0 and 22 degrees Centigrade). Shale barren soil has a pH (a measure of acidity or alkalinity) range of 4.8 to 5.8 and contains half the organic matter of vegetated slopes. Except for this, the soil is similar to wooded areas, and it is believed that the sparse vegetation of shale barrens is due only to the high surface temperatures of the soil, which can reach 145 degrees Fahrenheit (63 degrees Centigrade), but which also drop quickly just below the soil surface. This temperature is enough to prevent establishment of the seedlings of all but the most sun- and heat-tolerant plants.

There are 18 species that are endemic to the Appalachian shale barrens, and they form biological islands in the surrounding forest vegetation.

Distribution

Shale barren rock cress can be found only on shale barrens in Alleghany, Augusta, Bath, Highland, and Rockbridge Counties in Virginia; as well as Greenbrier, Hardy, and Pendleton counties in West Virginia.

The patchy distribution of this plant is thought to be a natural distribution that results from specific habitat requirements and not as a result of recent land use changes. This plant is known from only 26 populations, comprising fewer than 1,000 reproducing individuals. Of the 26 populations, 15 contain fewer than 20 individuals. At least 16 of the 26 known populations are in the Monongahela National Forest in West Virginia and the George Washington National Forest in Virginia.

Threats

Numbers of shale barren rock cress are declining. A population in Virginia of 100 plants in 1995 contained only 9 in 1997, and a West Virginia population that contained 136 reproducing individuals in 1995 had only 12 plants that set fruit in 1997.

The National Forest populations are safe from human disturbance but are threatened by browsing deer. Deer populations are increasing, and 8 of 11 West Virginia rock cress populations showed a 30 percent loss of seed to deer browsing.

This plant is also threatened by habitat destruction caused by road construction. In Virginia and West Virginia a total of eight shale barrens that are known to support shale barren rock cress have been partially destroyed by road construction.

Conservation

One population in West Virginia is situated on a shale barren that is leased by the Nature Conservancy, who are seeking voluntary protection for two other sites.

Christina Oliver

Eastern Province Rocky

(Sandelia bainsii)

ESA: Endangered

Class: Actinopterygii
Order: Perciformes
Family: Anabantidae
Length: 10 in. (26 cm)
Reproduction: Egg layer
Habitat: Coastal rivers
Range: Eastern South Africa

LONG VALUED AS an aquarium fish, the eastern province rocky is listed as threatened in the wild and is close to being listed as endangered. This species belongs to the family Anabantidae, a group well known to aquarium hobbyists and professionals as gouramies. These warm-water jewels can be found from Africa to Southeast Asia and, interestingly, some of the larger species even are grown as food in African and Asian aquaculture systems (outdoor ponds).

Pristine habitat

The genus *Sandelia*, of which the eastern province rocky is a member, is important to the native ecosystem and to fish fanciers. This species occupies small coastal river systems along the Cape of Good Hope in eastern South Africa and thrives in undisturbed, relatively pristine environments. The principal threats to its continued survival include habitat destruction caused by dams (which also prevent migration) and pollution from nearby cities. Predation and competition from non-native fish such as the brown trout (*Salmo trutta*), sharptooth catfish (*Clarias gariepinus*), smallmouth bass (*Micropterus dolomieu*), and rainbow trout (*Oncorhynchus mykiss*), are also a problem. Trout and bass are popular sport fish in South Africa, and many escape from fish production facilities to waters in which their release is not intended.

Altered river systems

Unfortunately, human activities such as water transfer projects to link river systems compound the problem of unintended introduction of non-native fish species. These transfers are used to balance water supplies to major cities. While they may be beneficial to humans, alteration of historic stream patterns and the resulting unrestricted transfer of fish from one river basin to another only serve to disrupt aquatic communities.

Deforestation is another problem, because the increase in erosion ultimately leads to more siltation in streams, and the increased clouding of habitat is often stressful to native fish. When breeding is disturbed, a population is bound to decline. Curiously, the construction of dams on the rivers this fish occupies (particularly on the Tyume River) has provided some benefit to the eastern province rocky in the face of soil erosion and siltation. By creating reservoirs that act as settling basins for solids, the dams improve water quality by preventing the movement of those solids downstream. However, dams overall have a more negative than positive influence on river systems.

William E. Manci

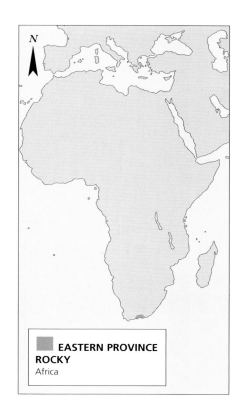

EASTERN PROVINCE ROCKY
Africa

ROSEMARY

Class: Magnoliopsida

Order: Capparales

Family: Cruciferae

Conradina, more commonly known as rosemary, is a genus of six species in the Labiatae, or the mint, family. The genus is restricted to the southeast of the United States, with one widespread species and five species that have very narrow distributions.

Conradina are all aromatic perennial shrubs that can be recognized by the densely matted hairs on the undersurfaces of their leaves.

Conradina have characteristically bilabiate flowers with a hood-shaped upper lip and a three-lobed lower lip. The middle of the corolla tube is bent sharply in a way that is unique to the genus, instead of being straight or curving gradually.

Apalachicola Rosemary

(Conradina glabra)

ESA: Endangered

IUCN: Endangered

Height: Up to 6½ ft. (2 m)
Flowers: March to June. White with purple dots
Leaves: Opposite, evergreen, and needlelike
Habitat: Rims of steepheads (bluffs)
Range: Liberty County, Florida

Apalachicola rosemary (*Conradina glabra*) is a much branched perennial shrub. The spreading upright branches root where they touch the ground. The leaves are evergreen, and needlelike. They are nearly linear, 10 to 15 millimeters long, with the margins rolled under. The top surface of the leaves are bright green and dotted with conspicuous glands. The leaves are also hairless on their upper surfaces, unlike all other species of *Conradina*. The lower surface is grayish and hairy. Additional leaves are formed by short shoots in the axils, giving the plant a fascicled appearance.

Flowers

Flowers are produced in the leaf axils in groups of two or three. The peduncles holding the flowers are 2 to 3 millimeters long. The calyx is hairless and about 8 millimeters long. The corolla is ½ to ¾ inch (1.5 to 2 centimeters) long, with a tube bending in the manner characteristic of the genus. The corolla is white and has two lips; the lobes are blue at their tips, and a row of purple dots runs down the throat of the lower lip. This plant has four stamens in two pairs.

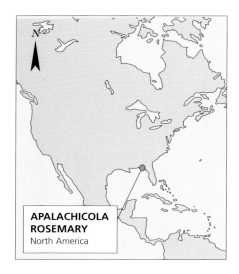

**APALACHICOLA
ROSEMARY**
North America

Distribution

Conradina glabra is restricted to Liberty County, Florida, west of Tallahassee and northeast of Bristol. It occurs in an area of several square miles near State Road 12 and County Road 271, to the east of the Apalachicola River.

Currently the population of *Conradina glabra* is estimated to be over 1,000 individuals. It occurs in four natural colonies on land owned by a forest products company and on public road rights-of-way. A fifth artificial population is being created in the Apalachicola Bluffs and Ravines Preserve, owned by the Nature Conservancy.

Habitat

Apalachicola rosemary grows on upland areas originally covered by longleaf pine and wiregrass vegetation, but now largely been covered by slash pine plantations. These uplands are dissected by ravines of the Sweetwater Creek system, which drain into the Apalachicola River. The heads of the ravines, called steepheads, often slump gradually as a result of groundwater in the bottom, causing the sides to become undermined. Apalachicola rosemary predominantly occurs on the rims of steepheads but can spread down the sides of bare ravines or colonize edges and openings in the pine stands. This plant seems to compete most successfully in open, newly disturbed areas in full sun or light shade. It is less successful in closed hardwood or pine forests. It seems to be an early succession species, and in the past may have been dependent on fire to create disturbance necessary to release it from competition and allow for a wider distribution.

Threats

Apalachicola rosemary is potentially threatened by the forestry practices of the forest product company that owns the land on which it occurs. The pine trees that are currently being planted

Apalachicola rosemary (*Conradina glabra*) thrives in areas such as this longleaf pine forest in Florida.

at the site are young, and as they mature they are likely to become denser than native longleaf pine, creating a degree of shading that would kill Apalachicola rosemary. Furthermore, the planted sand pines do not tolerate prescribed fire, which may be important in keeping the habitat open enough for this species of rosemary to survive.

Threats

Some of the land in the range of Apalachicola rosemary was cut and prepared for replanting in 1987; and today no plants survive on areas that were cut. The herbicide hexazinone is sometimes used on this property, and this could also affect the plant.

Threats are magnified because the entire range is under the jurisdiction of the same landowner, and any potentially damaging changes in forestry practice will most probably be carried out over the entire property and at the same time.

Often many of the flowers of *Conradina glabra* are male sterile and therefore produce no viable pollen grains. In extreme cases flowers occur with malformed stamens that resemble petals in their form and color. This sterility could be a result of inbreeding and homozygosity due to small population sizes, and could impact the long-term survival of the species.

Conservation

Measures being taken for the management and protection of this species include establishing three artificial sites on the Apalachicola Bluffs and Ravines Preserve. These populations were established from cuttings taken from plants growing within 1¾ miles (3 kilometers) of the preserve.

Interested bodies

The Nature Conservancy is also conducting studies on the effects of shading and fire on the growth of Apalachicola rosemary.

There is also some interest from the Florida Department of Transportation. They are exploring the maintenance of existing populations that are situated along roadsides.

The banks of this fork stream in Tennessee are typical habitat for Cumberland rosemary (*Conradina verticillata*). The movement of water may play a part in distributing the plant along rivers.

Cumberland Rosemary

(Conradina verticillata)

ESA: Endangered

IUCN: Vulnerable

Height: Up to 1½ ft. (0.5 m)
Stems: Reddish, quadrangular when young, 14–33 mm long
Leaves: 1 in. (2.54 cm) long, dotted with glands
Flowering season: Mid May to early June
Habitat: Sandy and rocky places, stream banks
Range: Kentucky and Tennessee

CUMBERLAND ROSEMARY is an aromatic shrub that branches at the base. Branches tend to spread along the ground and root. Young stems are quadrangular and often reddish. The leaves are stalkless and linear to club-shaped. They are 1 inch (2.5 centimeters) long, with a revolute margin. The leaves are conspicuously dotted with glands. One to three, or sometimes as many as seven, flowers are borne in the leaf axils. The calyx is persistent and 7.5 to 9 millimeters long. The corolla is lavender to purple, with darker dots, and is ½ to ¾ inch (13 to 20 millimeters) long. The corolla tube is bent upward in the manner characteristic of the genus. The fruits are dark brown nutlets. This species outcrosses, and studies have indicated that the insects that pollinate it can efficiently travel relatively long distances. It is believed that plants all along a river system can interbreed and should be considered a single population.

Evolution

This is the only species of *Conradina* found inland on the Cumberland Plateau, while the other four species are restricted to the coastal plain in Florida. *Conradina verticillata* lacks variability within populations and shows little variability between populations. This has led to a hypothesis that it could be a relict from a more widespread ancestral type. *Conradina verticillata* is closest morphologically to *Conradina grandiflora*, and this plant is probably its closest relative.

Morphological and geographic evidence suggests that it is possible that the other coastal plain species could be a more recent evolutionary radiation, diverging after the Cumberland Plateau had been uplifted, and the geologicaly younger coastal plain was formed.

Habitat

Conradina verticillata is restricted to sandy soil and grows on riverbanks, sandbars and islands. It often inhabits gravelly places, and branches root where they touch the ground. It is always closely associated with the floodplains of watercourses. This species requires open space and freedom from competition and shading. Because of this it benefits from the natural disturbances that occur in the sandy riverside habitat where it grows. Vegetative growth can root, and the movement of water may play a role in its distribution along rivers.

Distribution

With the exception of one disjunct population, *Conradina verticillata* occurs only along two river systems in Tennessee and Kentucky. In Tennessee, there are 44 sites where *Conradina verticillata* occurs. It can be found in Morgan County, along Clear Creek and Daddys Creek, two tributaries of the Obed River. It also occurs in Scott County, along South Fork Cumberland River, and in Morgan and Fentress counties along the Clear Fork tributary of South Fork Cumberland River. The disjunct population is located in White and Cumberland counties, along the Caney Fork River. There are four sites in Kentucky.

Conservation

Conradina verticillata can be propagated easily by cuttings and is in cultivation at several botanical gardens and arboreta. This plant in Morgan County, including those in the Clear Creek and Daddys Creek populations, are protected because part of the Obed River system has been designated as part of the Wild and Scenic River System. Also, the South Fork Cumberland, as well as its tributary, Clear Fork River, are in the proposed Big South Fork National River and Recreational Area. It will be necessary to take the distribution of this plant into consideration when trails, canoe access points, and camping areas are designated. Much of the area where this plant occurs is accessible only by canoe, and because of this exact numbers are difficult to estimate.

Surveys need to be done to assess the number of individuals of *Conradina verticillata* that still remain.

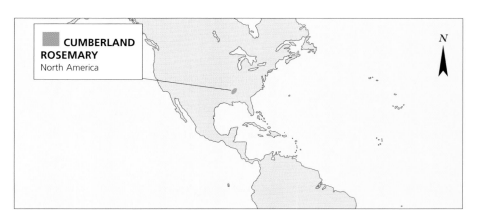

Etonia Rosemary

(Conradina etonia)

ESA:	Endangered
IUCN:	Endangered

Height: Up to 5 ft. (1.5 m)
Flowers: Early spring to late fall. Lavender and cream with purple spots and streaks
Habitat: Sand scrub
Range: Putnam County, Florida

ETONIA ROSEMARY
North America

CONRADINA ETONIA is a perennial shrub with many arching branches. The stems of new growth are reddish brown and four-sided. With age, stems develop grayish bark that exfoliates in long strips. The oblanceolate or spatulate leaves are 15 to 30 millimeters long, 3 to 9 millimeters wide and deciduous after two or three years. The leaf margins are narrow and tightly revolute (rolled backward or downward). The upper surface of the leaves is downy, dull green, and densely dotted with glands. The lower surface has prominent lateral veins, is slightly paler, and very densely covered in fine hairs. Short leafy shoots generally develop from buds in the axis of the leaves, giving the foliage a fascicled appearance (like a slender bundle). Most nodes produce three to seven flowers. The calyxes are bilabiate, 7.5 to 8 millimeters long, and downy. The corolla is ¾ to 1 inch (20 to 25 millimeters) long and strongly bilabiate. It is lavender with a zone in the throat that is cream, mottled with purple spots and streaks. The anthers are dark purple, and the flowers usually produce four brown obovoid nutlets, 1 to 1.2 millimeters long.

Taxonomy

This plant is most closely related to *Conradina grandiflora*, the species that occurs in the closest geographic area. The flowers of *Conradina etonia* and *Conradina grandiflora* are difficult to distin-

This critical wildlife area on Marco Island, Florida, is suitable habitat for Etonia rosemary (*Conradina etonia*).

guish. These species, however, can be identified by several other traits. The hairs covering the young shoots of *Conradina grandiflora* are mostly upcurved, while they are spreading in *Conradina etonia*. The leaves are also different, with *Conradina etonia* possessing broader leaves, with lateral veins evident on the undersurface. No other species of *Conradina* shows these prominent lateral veins. Also, the anthers of *Conradina etonia* have a distinctive fringe of long white hairs, while the hairs on the anther of *Conradina grandiflora* are fewer and shorter and are concentrated at the tips and bases of the anther sacks. Although the characteristics that separate the two species require a close look at the plants, *Conradina etonia* is one of the most distinct species in this genus.

Habitat

The habitat of *Conradina etonia* is natural or artificial clearings in a deep white-sand scrub. Because of its preference for clearings, this plant seems to respond positively to disturbance, which in the past was probably fire. Associated vegetation is primarily *Pinus clausa*, *Quercus chapmanii*, *Quercus geminata*, and *Quercus myrtifolia*. The threatened Florida scrub jay also occurs here.

Distribution

Conradina etonia is a relatively new species; it was discovered and described in 1990. It is a narrow endemic, known from only two sites near Etonia Creek northeast of Florahome in Putnam County, Florida. This is at the northern limit of the sand scrub ecosystems in Florida. The

scrub in this region is the northeastern range limit for several Florida scrub species, including *Persea humilis* and *Ilex cumulicola*. Since *Conradina etonia* was discovered in 1990, it is hoped that more populations will be found; however, the area has been fairly well explored botanically.

Threats

This species is threatened by habitat destruction due to development. The two sites where this plant is known are privately owned, and the first is within a subdivided housing tract where building has already begun. The second is in an area where the landowner has already obtained the necessary permits to create a residential development.

The extent of the sand pine scrub that is a suitable habitat for *Conradina etonia* is limited, which makes the establishment of artificial populations on less threatened land more complicated. There is no information on the breeding system or pollination of this species, although studies indicate that other species of *Conradina* are outcrossers, and that their insect pollinators can transfer pollen over relatively long distances. This could be a problem for *Conradina etonia*, either through inbreeding depression due to reduced population size or through hybridization that could occur with more frequent species such as *Conradina grandiflora*.

Conservation

Living plants of *Conradina etonia* have been propagated from cuttings and are now in cultivation at Woodlanders, Inc., in South Carolina.

Short-leaved Rosemary
(Conradina brevifolia)

ESA: Endangered

IUCN: Vulnerable

Height: Up to 6½ ft. (2 m)
Flowers: May to June. White, with a bluish or lavender tinge
Habitat: Sand scrub
Range: Interior peninsular Florida

SHORT-LEAVED ROSEMARY is a shrubby aromatic perennial. The branches are spreading and can root where they touch the ground. The opposite leaves are nearly linear and are shorter than the internodes, with the longest reaching 6 to 8 millimeters in length. Both the upper and lower surfaces of the leaves are covered in hairs, and the upper surface is dotted with glands. The flowers are produced in groups of from one to six in the axils of the leaves and are almost stemless. The calyx is hairy, and the corolla is white with a bluish or lavender tinge and purple markings on the lower lip.

This plant is very similar morphologically to the more widely distributed and variable *Conradina canescens*, and some researchers do not separate the two species. The doubts about the status of *Conradina brevifolia* as a species delayed its federal listing, though it is more narrowly distributed than most of the other listed species.

Conradina brevifolia is probably pollinated by the introduced honeybee, *Apis mellifera*, and a hybrid has been reported with a species of *Calamintha*, which produced pyloric (small and circular) flowers.

Habitat

Conradina brevifolia inhabits sand pine scrub vegetation of Lake Wales Ridge in Polk and Highlands Counties in Florida. It occurs in only about 30 fragments of scrub with a combined area of less than 6,000 acres (2,400 hectares). Scrub ecosystems are characterized by fine textured, often eolean, white sand, which supports the shrubby evergreen oaks *Quercus geminata* and *Quercus myrtifolia*, the sand pine, *Pinus clausa*; they also contain open areas where herbs and small shrubs grow. Sand scrub historically burns infrequently but catastrophically.

It is rich in endemic plants, which often have very limited ranges. Lake Wales Ridge contains 13 plant species that are federally listed as endangered or threatened, as well as the threatened Florida scrub jay and two species of threatened lizards.

Fire suppression, along with agricultural and other development, has left only fragments of this ecosystem remaining, and these fragments are very often degraded.

Conservation

Conradina brevifolia is protected where it grows in the Lake Arbuckle State Forest and also on land owned by the Nature Conservancy and Saddle Blanket Lakes. The Saddle Blanket Lakes property is 568 acres (227 hectares), and the state plans to acquire the surrounding 878

acres (361 hectares) of land. The proposed Lake Wales Ridge National Wildlife Refuge would also benefit *Conradina brevifolia*. Outside of these sites, *Conradina brevifolia* is threatened by the destruction of its scrub habitats for agricultural purposes such as the creation of citrus groves and pastures for livestock.

Small population sizes and fragmentation of its habitat could create further problems for this plant by causing inbreeding and a loss of genetic variation.

Christina Oliver

Brazilian Rosewood

(Dalbergia nigra)

IUCN: Vulnerable

Family: Fabaceae (Leguminosae)
Height: Up to 82 ft. (25 m)
Trunk: 1–1⅓ ft. (0.3–0.4 m) wide
Branches: Dark, roundish branches grow in a zigzag way
Leaves: Compound leaves with 12 to 18 alternate leaflets
Flowers: October to November. Pale, violet-scented pealike flowers
Habitat: Tropical lowland and submontane rain forest
Range: Brazil, including Bahia and Rio de Janeiro

BRAZILIAN ROSEWOOD is a precious timber species found only in the Atlantic coastal forests of Brazil, the home also of many unique birds and mammals. Populations of Brazilian rosewood are scattered from southern Bahia to Minas Gerais, growing under a range of climatic conditions. Usually the tree is found in hilly or mountainous areas with relatively fertile soil.

Forest loss

The Atlantic coastal forests occur in the areas of Brazil that were first settled by Europeans 500 years ago. The forests have declined dramatically, particularly over the past hundred years, and are now reduced to less than 5 percent of their former range. Timber exploitation, clearance

for plantation agriculture, and the impact of mining have been the main causes of forest loss. Only a tiny proportion of the remaining forests are protected in national parks and reserves.

Brazilian rosewood trees with thicker trunks are rare because most have been logged. The bark is thin, gray, and rough with irregular parallel fissures and is

Brazilian rosewood (*Dalbergia nigra*) displays a profuse lilac flower mass.

one of the most highly prized woods in Brazil. The species also yields useful resin and oil and is attractive as an ornamental tree. The timber has been harvested since the time of the first European settlers for use in decorative veneers, high-quality furniture, and musical instruments. Although there is some small-scale cultivation of *Dalbergia nigra*, no plantations have been developed to meet the international demand for this valuable timber. In recent years, with most rosewood trees already logged, timber cruisers, known as *madereiros*, have searched large areas to find any remaining stands of the trees that can be cut and sold for high prices. The scattered remaining trees do not produce many offspring. This may be because the seeds of the rosewood are eaten by rodents.

Protected species

Dalbergia nigra is included in the official list of threatened Brazilian plants. The export of logs of Brazilian rosewood has been banned for over thirty years.

This species was added to Appendix I of the Convention on International Trade in Endangered Species of Wild Fauna and Flora (CITES) in 1992, which means that no international trade in timber taken from the wild is allowed. The tree can be found in a number of protected areas, but, because of its high value, illegal cutting and smuggling out of Brazil continue to threaten the survival of this precious species of rosewood.

Sara Oldfield

Santa Catarina Saberfin

(Campbellolebias brucei)

IUCN: Vulnerable

Class: Actinopterygii
Order: Atheriniformes
Family: Aplocheilidae
Length: 2¾ in. (7 cm)
Reproduction: Egg layer
Habitat: Shallow ponds, fresh or salt water, cool or hot conditions
Range: Ponds near Tubarao, Santa Catarina, Brazil

IN TERMS OF THEIR distribution around the world, killifishes (of which saberfins and pearlfishes are loosely considered a part) have been very successful and can be found across the tropical and temperate latitudes of the world. As a group, the killifishes are capable of tolerating a wide range of environmental conditions, especially high salinity. They can be found in fresh water as well as in water that is more saline than sea water, and can survive cool conditions or thermal (hot) springs. Most killifishes prefer shallow water that is rich in aquatic vegetation; they use vegetation for cover and as a likely source of their favorite food, aquatic insects.

Killifishes are well known to aquarium hobbyists because they are enjoyed for their diverse color patterning, relative tolerance to the close quarters of aquarium life, and ease of spawning in captivity. Pearlfishes are small and unassuming creatures that have won the hearts of aquarium hobbyists all over the world. Their bright coloration, feathery-finned appearance, and ease of reproduction make them ideal for the aquarium environment and as display fish. In some cases, this demand has been at least partially responsible for the status of some killifishes as threatened or endangered.

Because of their small size, many killifish species are captured and used as bait fish. This type of exploitation is difficult to combat when profit is involved. However, by educating the general public to the plight of sensitive species, the demand may begin to be curbed.

Waterless fish?

Many species of the family Aplocheilidae, including the saberfin, are called annual fishes because they have developed the ability to survive for long periods without water. This amazing adaptation—a seemingly impossible feat—is achieved by laying drought-resistant eggs in the bottom of ponds and other small basins that dry up during rainless periods. While the adults of the species fail to survive these waterless intervals, their offspring wait for the rainy season and then they emerge. The young saberfins then grow, reproduce, and perpetuate the species.

Appearance

All saberfins are extraordinarily spectacular in both color and form. Brilliant colors across the body and fins are accented by a blizzard of white dots or broken stripes. The dorsal fin on the back, the anal fin on the belly, the pectoral fins just behind the gills, and the tail fin are long and wide relative to the body and are almost feathery in texture. In contrast, the pelvic fins on the belly are exceedingly short and are nearly nonexistent.

The Santa Catarina saberfin breeds at least once during the rainy season, producing about 100 fish per cycle; two or three groups of offspring produced during a year are not uncommon.

The Santa Catarina saberfin feeds primarily on mosquitoes and other aquatic insects.

Safer environment

This beautiful South American fish is in a predicament. Because it inhabits a relatively small zone along the southern Brazilian coast, urban growth threatens to overrun the current range of this highly endangered fish.

Unless the Santa Catarina saberfin can be moved to a secure environment (possibly to aquariums and suitable, remotely located ponds), this species will decline and become lost in the wild forever.

William E. Manci

SANTA CATARINA SABERFIN
South America

BEARDED SAKIS

Class: Mammalia

Order: Primates

Family: Cebidae

Sakis are among the least known and studied of the South American or New World primates. They belong to the family Cebidae, along with howler monkeys, squirrel monkeys, and many other species that share such traits as a well-furred, prehensile tail, with a rough pad underneath for grasping. The digits are usually long and thin. Most interesting are the eyes of New World primates, which are set forward in the skull and are quite human in appearance, with well-defined eyelids. The eye is not unlike a human eye in its internal structure as well. Most New World monkeys, or cebids, are great at running, leaping, and swinging through the trees.

Bearded sakis are fairly social, living in groups of up to 30 or more monkeys, both male and female. These large groups may break up into smaller family groups for foraging.

There are two distinct species of bearded saki, and both are endangered. Experts believe these bearded sakis may be the most endangered of all the New World monkeys.

Southern Bearded Saki
(Chiropotes satanas)

White-nosed Bearded Saki
(Chiropotes albinasus)

ESA: Endangered

Weight: 5½–6½ lb. (2.5–3 kg);
Length: 15–19½ in. (38–49.3 cm)
Diet: Leaves, nuts, seeds, fruit, and flowers
Gestation period: About 150 days
Longevity: 18 years
Habitat: High tropical rain forest
Range: Brazil

PERHAPS THE MOST remarkable feature of the southern bearded saki is its appearance. It has long black fur over its back and sides, with a long, heavily furred tail. The saki has a thick head of hair that grows in a way that resembles a bouffant hairdo, and the long hair around its lower chin has the appearance of a beard. All in all, the southern bearded saki is unique in appearance.

There are two subspecies of this saki: *Chiropotes satanas satanas*, which ranges in northeastern Brazil in a small area around the Rio Tocating and near the mouth of the Amazon; and *C. satanas chiropotes*, which ranges north of the Amazon. It was also spotted recently in eastern Venezuela, southern Surinam, and French Guiana (a research project has studied *C. satanus satanus* on an island in Guri Lake, Venezuela). The other member of this genus, the white-

The long hair growing around its lower chin gives the saki the appearance of having a luxurious beard.

nosed bearded saki, is equally bizarre in appearance. It is black with close-cropped hair. A white triangle is formed between the eyes and the base of the lower lip. This triangle is covered with thin, white hair and, depending on the distribution of the hair, pink skin shows from underneath. Seen from a distance, it either appears to have a white nose or, if the hair is thin enough, a pink or red nose.

Agile eaters

Sakis are very agile, hanging upside down with their hind feet while feeding. They have large canine teeth adapted for eating unripe fruit, nuts, and seeds with hard outer coverings.

Little is known about either of these saki's habits in the wild. The saki apparently prefers undisturbed primary forest for habitat, where it stays mainly in mid- to upper canopy. Over most of its range, it is hunted for meat and for its luxurious tail. The tails are used for decoration or as fly switches.

Unfortunately, rain forests are disappearing at the rate of millions of acres per year in the Amazon region alone. To make matters worse, both the southern bearded and the white-nosed sakis' habitat is being cleared and bisected by the Transamazonian Highway, resulting in an even wider destruction of bearded saki habitat. With the influx of more people, the hunting inevitably increases. No population numbers are available.

There have only been a few sakis from either species held in captivity, with never a sufficient number to establish a captive

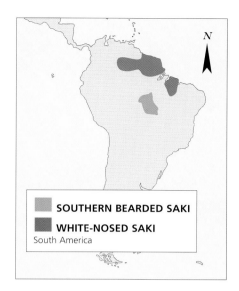

SOUTHERN BEARDED SAKI
WHITE-NOSED SAKI
South America

reservoir. However, those that have been kept have demonstrated substantial longevity—over 15 years for some. The potential for captive breeding success, and perhaps later reintroduction in the wild, is there.

Warren D. Thomas

SALAMANDERS

Class: Amphibia

Order: Caudata

There may be as many as 500 living species of salamanders in the world. Salamanders are tailed amphibians that resemble lizards in appearance, but salamanders lack scales and have a smooth, moist skin.

Salamanders range in size from less than 2 inches (5 centimeters) to one species that may be more than 5 feet (1.5 meters) long. These amphibians have four limbs with clawless feet, and their skin can be dull, brightly colored, or almost transparent. Some salamanders live on land, while others make their homes in water. They are generally nocturnal, but sometimes they can be seen searching for food on rainy days.

Their food can include a mixture of insects, snails, and worms.

Most salamanders lay eggs; few salamanders are live bearers. Generally those that give birth to live young belong to the genus *Salamandra*. Usually, the male will deposit sperm that the female picks up. The eggs are fertilized internally in the female before they are laid. Most species will lay eggs in moist areas on land. However, some species breed in water and, in this situation, the eggs are fertilized externally.

Three additional species are considered to be threatened: the California tiger salamander (*Ambystoma tigrinum californiense*), Jemez Mountains salamander (*Plethodon neomexicanus*), and Sardinian or brown salamander (*Speleomantes genei*).

Barton Springs Salamander

Eurycea sosorum

ESA: Endangered

Class: Amphibia
Order: Caudata (Urodela)
Family: Plethodontidae
Length: 2½ in. (6.3 cm)
Clutch size: Unknown
Incubation: Unknown
Diet: Small aquatic invertebrates
Habitat: Springs in limestone rock formations
Range: Springs in Zilker Park, Austin, Texas

The Barton Springs salamander was only described to science in 1993, even though its existence

The flatwoods salamander (*Ambystoma cingulatum*) is classified by the U.S. Fish and Wildlife Service as threatened. This salamander lives in Florida, Georgia, and South Carolina.

was known in 1946. It is very slender, with long, spindly legs and small eyes. Its color is pale purple brown, yellow, or cream, and these colors are often mixed to create a mottled effect.

This is a salamander that never grows up; it lives its entire life as an aquatic larva and never metamorphoses into a terrestrial form. A small number of other salamanders, the best known of which is the Mexican Axolotl (*Ambystoma mexicanum*), also display this phenomenon, known as neotony. There are other related neotonic species in the genus *Eurycea* from Texas and neighboring states. It has a highly specialized lifestyle and a narrow ecological niche. In Barton Springs Pool it occurs only within a layer of gravel and small rocks overlying a coarse sandy or bare limestone substrate near the place where the spring

BARTON SPRINGS SALAMANDER
City of Austin, Texas

enters the pool through fissures in the limestone bedrock. The water is crystal clear, pure, and contains no mud or silt. Although little is known of the salamander's breeding habits, it is probable that, like related species, it attaches small numbers of eggs to the stones and gravel on the stream or pool bed. These hatch into tiny replicas of the adult after a period of development that is relatively long due to the low temperature of the water.

Threats

This salamander is extremely rare. Its known range is among the smallest of any vertebrate species and, because it lies entirely within the city of Austin, there are grave concerns over its continued existence. A recent survey by the University of Texas, using scuba equipment, found only one individual. Its survival depends on the pristine water quality of the springs and the pools into which they empty. The main threat is the degradation of the water quality that feeds the springs. The springs are fed by an underground lake that extends to the south and west of the center of Austin and the rapid growth of the city threatens to contaminate these springs. The

amounts of heavy metals, petroleum by-products, pesticides, and other toxins entering the system have increased in recent years. The amount of silt has also increased, resulting in poorer water quality. The small invertebrates on which the salamander feeds, and the salamander itself, are very sensitive to any changes in water quality.

Freeport-McMoRan, a multinational corporation, attempted to develop an enormous 4,000-acre (1,620-hectare) site within the Barton Springs watershed despite overwhelming opposition by Austin's incensed citizens. The Save Our Springs (SOS) movement was formed in order to fight any future development. The Barton Springs salamander become a symbol of their efforts because it acts as an indicator for the water quality, and so its scientific name, *sosorum*, was created in recognition of the organization's efforts.

To protect both the salamander and Barton Springs, the U.S. federal government was requested, in 1992, to list the salamander as an endangered and threatened species. But the government failed to act in 1993 and the battle between the citizens of Austin, the U.S. Fish and Wildlife Service, and the developers, continued until April 14, 1994, when the relevant city authorities agreed on guidelines for the management of the Springs.

On April 30, 1997, the Barton Springs salamander was given total legal protection.

Cheat Mountain Salamander

(Plethedon nettingi)

ESA: Threatened

IUCN: Vulnerable

Length: Up to 4 in. (10 cm)
Clutch size: 4–17 eggs
Diet: Insects, including mites, beetles, flies, and ants
Habitat: Moist highland woods at elevations above 3,000 ft. (915 m)
Range: West Virginia

THE CHEAT MOUNTAIN salamander belongs to the family Plethodontidae, the largest family of salamanders, containing about two-thirds of the world's species. It is the most widely distributed family of the suborder Salamandroidea. All members of the family are lungless and respire directly through their skin. They also possess a groove extending from the nostril to the edge of the snout that appears to aid the sense of smell. These amphibians are also called woodland salamanders. First described in 1935, the Cheat Mountain salamander was once considered a subspecies of the ravine salamander (*Plethodon richmondi*) but was reclassified as a distinct species in 1971. It has been considered a threatened species by the U.S. Fish and Wildlife Service since 1989.

The Cheat Mountain salamander has a dark back, marked with brassy or white flecks, and a dark gray to black belly. It has 17 to 19 vertical grooves down the sides of its body that show the position of the ribs. This salamander tends to be nocturnal, spending the day under different kinds of cover, from rocks and logs to small crevices.

At night, particularly in wet weather, it forages for food on the forest floor. Mating habits have not been observed, but they are assumed to be similar to other woodland salamanders; that is, the eggs are fertilized internally. Eggs are then deposited on logs or moss from May to June.

The life span of the Cheat Mountain salamander is not known, but experts believe that most small *Plethodon* live for approximately 20 years.

The Jemez Mountains salamander (*Plethodon neomexicanus*) is another North American salamander that is considered threatened.

The Cheat Mountain salamander lives in the forests of West Virginia, often in areas where red spruce (*Picea rubens*) is the predominant tree species. It is also known to occur in areas of mixed deciduous forest where few red spruce occur, but red spruce may indeed have occurred in these areas before deforestation began.

The current known range of the Cheat Mountain salamander is an approximately 700-square mile (1,800-square kilometer) area within West Virginia.

The precise former range is unknown, because much of its preferred habitat was deforested in the late nineteenth and early twentieth centuries, before the discovery of the species.

Decline

Since people have moved into the range of the Cheat Mountain salamander, a number of habitat modifications have occurred. These include changes such as removing the forest canopy, which has adversely affected this salamander. Other activities involve timber harvesting, recreational skiing, road development, and mining, which have all played a part in the deforestation of West Virginia. As trees are cut down, the salamander is exposed to hot, dry conditions in which it cannot survive.

Loss of forest

During the last 100 years, most of the forest within the Cheat Mountain salamander's range has been completely cut at one time or another. When European settlers arrived in the area that is now West Virginia, there were nearly 1.5 million acres (600,000 hectares) of red spruce; this was reduced to just 225,000 acres (91,000 hectares) by 1899 and was estimated at just 110,685 acres (45,000 hectares) in 1986. Wildfires in the early twentieth century have also affected the species. Pollution problems, such as acid rain, may also affect this salamander. The Cheat Mountain salamander has managed to survive in some of the less damaged areas. One of the strongest populations occurs in the only tract of untouched red spruce that remains.

It is believed that there are currently around 68 populations of the Cheat Mountain salamander, but other populations probably exist. All known groups are restricted to elevations above 2,980 feet (900 meters). Detailed census-taking is underway, but during initial surveys, fewer than ten specimens occurred in 51 of the 68 populations.

Recovery

The first step in recovering the Cheat Mountain salamander is to intensify surveys that determine its total range, and to search for additional populations. Currently known populations must be monitored closely.

Protection of habitat known to support populations of the salamander is vital. As more is learned about this amphibian, specific plans for protection and management of the individual populations can be made.

Goals of the U.S. Fish and Wildlife recovery plan include securing ten stable or expanding populations over a period of ten years and having at least 100 populations situated in areas of permanent protection.

Ongoing surveys will continue to be conducted until sufficient information about the life history of the salamander is learned, and regular monitoring and management of populations will be scheduled for at least five years after the species is considered recovered from endangerment.

Desert Slender Salamander

(Batrachoseps aridus)

ESA: Endangered

IUCN: Critically endangered

Length: 4 in. (10 cm)
Clutch size: Unknown
Diet: Arthropods, including insects such as flies and ants
Habitat: Canyon lands
Range: Hidden Palms Canyon, Riverside County, California

THE DESERT SLENDER salamander was first discovered in 1969 in the lower desert slopes of the Santa Rosa Mountains in southern California. It is a member of the family Plethodontidae, the largest family of salamanders, containing about two-thirds of the world's species. This salamander is the most widely distributed family of the suborder Salamandroidea.

All members of the family are lungless and respire directly through their skin. They also possess a groove extending from the nostril to the edge of the snout that appears to help their sense of smell. These amphibians are also called woodland salamanders.

The desert slender salamander is considered to be a primitive species of its genus, and some scientists suspect that it has been isolated from other salamanders for hundreds of thousands to several million years.

The coloration of the desert slender salamander is a blackish maroon to deep chocolate on the back, with many tiny bluish silver and large gold markings. The belly is dark blackish maroon, and the tail is a light flesh tone.

Little is known about the reproductive habits of any species of *Batrachoseps*, but like most salamanders, this species are egg layers, although the eggs of the desert slender salamander have never been observed.

The habitat of the desert slender salamander has low and sporadic rainfall, high summer temperatures, and strong winds, which are all difficult climatic conditions for the salamander.

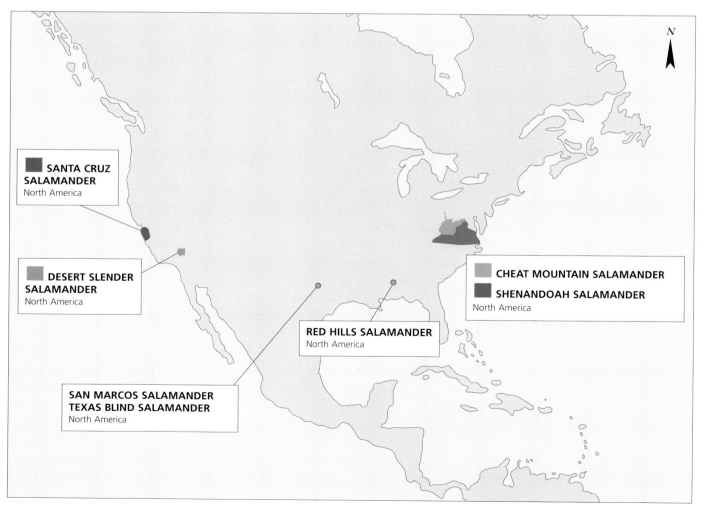

N

SANTA CRUZ SALAMANDER
North America

DESERT SLENDER SALAMANDER
North America

SAN MARCOS SALAMANDER
TEXAS BLIND SALAMANDER
North America

RED HILLS SALAMANDER
North America

CHEAT MOUNTAIN SALAMANDER
SHENANDOAH SALAMANDER
North America

Plant life in its habitat is typical of desert areas, including agave, cacti, and yucca.

Because salamanders must have a constantly moist environment, the desert presents a challenging environment. Lungless salamanders breathe only through their damp skin, and exposure to warm, dry air results in rapid water loss that can eventually lead to death. The desert slender salamander is, therefore, restricted to a small area within its habitat where water drainage provides the moisture it needs to survive. It finds such a water supply in a small area of less than ½ acre (0.2 hectare), although it depends on an approximately 440-acre (182-hectare) watershed for subterranean water. Water reaches the habitat not as a stream flow, but as seepage from groundwater.

The desert salamander also depends on the limestone sheeting that covers portions of the canyon walls where it lives. This area is shaded, providing a moist interior environment, so that when surrounding areas dry out, the desert slender salamander can retreat to the damp limestone crevices.

Threats

A variety of factors threaten the existence of the desert slender salamander. Its extremely small range puts it in a perilous position, should any natural or artificial occurrence severely alter the habitat. Prolonged drought or groundwater pumping of the watershed, for example, could be disastrous. The watershed is currently undeveloped except for a highway, scattered home sites, and dirt roads; but because it is

The Red Hills salamander has an elongated body and stubby limbs. It also has a prehensile tail, meaning that the tail is able to grasp objects.

almost entirely privately owned, additional development can be expected. The maximum number of desert slender salamanders seen in a single night was 21, and it is estimated that probably fewer than 600 individuals exist. However, there is no precise population estimate available.

Although this species is not in any danger of commercial exploitation, unrestrained scientific collection could cause its decline because of the limited number of individuals.

Surveys needed

Additional surveys must be conducted to determine if there are additional populations of the desert slender salamander in existence. Maintenance of the species would be unlikely without the presence of at least two healthy, self-sustaining populations whose habitats rely on different watersheds.

Red Hills Salamander

(Phaeognathus hubrichti)

ESA: Threatened

ESA: Endangered

Length: 9 in. (22.5 cm)
Clutch size: Probably 4–9 eggs
Diet: Insects
Habitat: Ravine slopes in mature hardwood forests
Range: Alabama

LIKE THE CHEAT MOUNTAIN and desert slender salamanders, the Red Hills salamander belongs to the family Plethodontidae. This is the largest family of salamanders, and the most widely distributed family of the suborder Salamandroidea. All members of the family are lungless and respire directly through their moist skin. These salamanders rely on a damp environment in order to survive. They possess the characteristic groove extending from the nostril to the edge of the snout. These amphibians are also called woodland salamanders.

The Red Hills salamander is a relatively large member of its family, reaching up to 9 inches (22.5 centimeters) when it is full grown. Its color is a uniform dark gray to brown.

This salamander burrows into hillsides, where it finds loamy, easily crumbled topsoil for habitation. Its preferred habitat is on forested ravines and bluffs with a northern exposure.

Often, a layer of siltstone will rest beneath a populations site, and the salamanders will frequently extend their burrows into this soft, easily manipulated rock. Siltstone retains moisture, providing the moist environment that is necessary for the lungless salamander's survival.

Cavities are formed within the burrows where the female will deposit her eggs, usually in a clutch size of from four to nine. It appears that the species has a low reproductive rate.

This amphibian is endemic to the Red Hills region of the gulf coastal plain of southern Alabama. Today it is in found only in a narrow band of the Red Hills, a distance of about 69 miles (115 kilometers). The amount of suitable habitat within the range is estimated at about 55,000 acres (22,200 hectares).

Precarious existence

Two biological factors place the Red Hills salamander in a precarious position: its low rate of reproduction and its very specific habitat requirements. Deforestation has also hurt the species. Much of its range was clear cut, then replanted with pine, creating conditions that do not support this salamander. Paper companies own approximately 44 percent of the remaining habitat and are using it for a variety of purposes. However, many of the companies are adjusting their practices to help ensure the survival of the salamander.

Santa Cruz Salamander

(Ambystoma macrodactylum croceum)

ESA: Endangered

Length: Minimum 2 in. (5 cm)
Clutch size: 200 eggs
Diet: Insects
Habitat: Chaparral and woods
Range: Central California

THE SANTA CRUZ salamander was first discovered in 1954 at Valencia Lagoon in Santa Cruz County, California. Ten to twelve thousand years ago, the species was probably common throughout much of what is now California. As conditions became drier, populations were restricted to the area that is now Santa Cruz. Because of their isolated

The distinctive markings of the Santa Cruz salamander are clearly seen as it basks on a wet log in its habitat along the coastal area of California.

habitat, these populations evolved into a distinct subspecies from similar California species.

This salamander spends most of its life underground in burrows along the root systems of plants, where it seeks shelter from heat and the drying rays of the sun. Adults migrate to a breeding pond in late September or early October during times of rain, mist, or heavy fog. When salamanders enter the pond, they pair up to breed. Eggs are usually laid on underwater stalks of spike rush (*Eleocharis*) or other vegetation, although eggs have been spotted floating in the water. A single female will lay about 200 eggs. After the eggs are laid, the adults retreat to their former habitats, leaving the larvae to fend for themselves.

Drought threat

Today four populations of the Santa Cruz salamander are known. The major threats to this salamander include drought, available habitat, natural enemies, disease, and the activities of humans. As long as there is a threat of drought in California—and the ongoing development of once rural lands—this amphibian will be in jeopardy.

Predators of the Santa Cruz salamander are not known, primarily because this amphibian is particularly secretive in its habits. However, it is likely that other amphibian species account for some predation. The non-native bullfrog, along with various bird species, may also be potential enemies, and some Sant Cruz salamanders may be lost each season to these threats.

Habitat destruction has been the primary cause of this species'

decline. By 1955, just one year after this salamander was discovered, Valencia Lagoon had been reduced by at least one-third due to the construction of a major highway. By 1969 the remaining lagoon was drained. To survive, the Santa Cruz salamander must have a relatively shallow pond with submerged vegetation. Although an artificial pond was constructed in 1970, it is not expected to add much to the salamander population.

However, additional ponds and the restoration of former habitat could ensure that the Santa Cruz salamander will not join the growing list of endangered amphibians.

San Marcos Salamander

(Eurycea nana)

ESA: Threatened

IUCN: Vulnerable

Length: 2½ in. (6 cm)
Clutch size: Egg masses
Diet: Amphipods
Habitat: Lakes and rivers
Range: Texas, between San Antonio and Austin

THE SAN MARCOS salamander belongs to the family Plethodontidae. This is the largest family of salamanders, containing about two-thirds of the world's species. All members of the family are lungless and need moisture to respire directly through their skin. They need a damp environment in order to survive. The groove extending from the nostril

to the edge of the snout appears to help with the sense of smell. These amphibians are also called woodland salamanders.

The San Marcos salamander is relatively small, at just under 2½ inches (6 centimeters) in length. It has a slender body and can be recognized by a prominent gill fringe, which is situated behind the head. It is light brown above, with a row of pale flecks on either side of the middle. Its belly is a yellowish white color. It has rather large eyes, with dark rings around the lenses. The limbs are short, with four toes on the forefeet and five on the hind feet.

This salamander is among the species that prefer to breed in water. It lays its eggs in standing pools in thick aquatic vegetation. Eggs hatch in about 24 days.

Carnivore

This carnivorous amphibian will feed on amphipods ranging from fly larvae to aquatic snails. When hunting, it will remain motionless until the victim is near. Then it will abruptly snap its head, catching the prey.

This species appears to be endemic to the sources and upper portions of the San Marcos River. Today it can be found in a very limited area that is located primarily in Hays County, Texas. The largest number of these salamanders occurs in the San Marcos Springs, in Spring Lake, and in a few hundred feet of the San Marcos River. A second, smaller population was discovered in Comal River, located to the west of the San Marcos population, in Comal County. In 1984, the total population of San Marcos salamanders was estimated to be from 17,000 to 21,000 individuals.

The threat to this salamander comes from the potential of degradation or modification of its very small habitat.

The San Marcos salamander is found only in one area, and this is located between two highly populated cities, San Antonio and Austin. This area has seen a rise in residential and agricultural development.

Together with an increased demand for water by humans, the habitat of the San Marcos salamander is at risk.

Hope for the future

The owner of Spring Lake has cooperated with biologists and safeguarded the spring sources to ensure that wildlife populations are protected.

If the amount of water taken from the ground is controlled and critical habitat is designated for this species, it has a good chance of survival.

Shenandoah Salamander

(Plethedon shenandoah)

ESA: Endangered

IUCN: Endangered

Length: 4½ in. (12 cm)
Clutch size: 4–17 eggs
Diet: Insects
Habitat: North-facing rocky slopes
Range: Virginia

THE SHENANDOAH salamander belongs to the family known as Plethodontidae. This is the largest family of salamanders, comprising about two-thirds of the world's species. It is the most widely distributed family of the suborder Salamandroidea. These amphibians are also called woodland salamanders.

The Shenandoah salamander spends its days under cover from the sun. At night it comes out to forage for food.

The Shenandoah salamander has a dark back that may or may not feature a red stripe down the middle. The back is also marked with a few gold or silver flecks, and the belly is dark gray to black. This salamander was once thought to be a subspecies of *Plethondon richmondi* and later of the Cheat Mountain salamander (*Plethondon nettingi*), but in 1979 it was recognized as a distinct species. At night, in wet weather, the Shenandoah salamander will forage for food.

Although its reproduction has not been observed, it is presumed to be similar to others of its genus, and like them, its eggs are fertilized internally.

The historic range of the Shenandoah salamander is not known because the species was so recently discovered, but it is suspected that this salamander was never particularly prevalent. Today it is found on north-facing slopes at elevations of at least 3,000 feet (915 meters). This species can withstand drier conditions than other Plethondon species, but it must still live in areas where conditions are moist. The primary threat to the Shenandoah salamander has been competition from other salamander species, particularly the red-backed salamander (*Plethondon cinereus*).

Sonoran Tiger Salamander
Ambystoma tigrinum stebbinsi

ESA: Endangered

Class: Amphibia
Order: Caudata (Urodela)
Family: Ambystomatidae
Length: 2½–5 in. (6.5–12.5 cm) snout to vent; tail slightly shorter than body
Clutch size: Unknown
Diet: Aquatic invertebrates (larvae); earthworms and insects (adults)
Habitat: Hillsides and grasslands in mountain valleys; breeds in small pools
Range: Huachuca and Patagonia mountain ranges, southeastern Arizona

THE SONORAN Tiger Salamander was discovered in 1949 at a site in Parker Canyon, Arizona, and named in 1954.

Subsequently it was considered to belong to a wider-ranging population of tiger salamanders, which are found throughout most of the United States but was confirmed as a distinct and valid subspecies in 1988.

It is stocky with a rounded snout, small eyes, and a "rubbery" body. A series of grooves, known as costal grooves, are prominent along its flanks and the sides of its tail. Adults are gray in color, with irregular bars, blotches, and reticulations of lighter gray or cream. It has a distinct breeding season, in spring, when the adults leave their retreats under rocks and in burrows, and make their way to small pools of freshwater.

During mating, the males deposit small packages of sperm on the bed of the pool and the females draw these into their cloacae to fertilize their eggs. A few days later, the eggs, surrounded by a capsule of jelly, are attached in small clusters to aquatic plants, twigs, and other debris. They hatch into larvae with external gills, and feed on small aquatic invertebrates during this stage of their life. Only about 17 to 40 percent metamorphose into adults normally, from late July to early September, and leave their pools to disperse over the surrounding countryside. The remainder stay in the water and either change into sexually mature larvae that remain in the breeding pond, or, metamorphose the following year. Salamanders that metamorphose live secretive lives but probably begin migrating back to pools to breed after two or three years.

Threats

The main area of concern over this subspecies is its restricted range and the impact of human activities within the region. The Huachuca and Patagonia Mountains are surrounded by the Sonoran Desert, a habitat that is completely hostile to amphibians, which must keep their skins moist at all times. The Sonoran Salamander, then, is isolated in its montane "island" and leads a precarious existence. Within its range, it is found in grasslands and adjacent montane slopes. It breeds only in a limited number of cattle tanks and modified water holes. Historically, it would have bred in naturally occurring water holes, or *cienegas*, and springs. It has been estimated

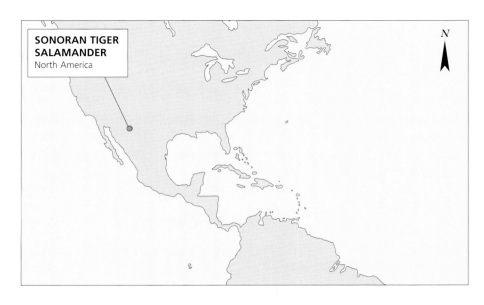

SONORAN TIGER SALAMANDER
North America

N

that 90 percent of the potentially suitable habitat in the area has been lost, degraded, or altered in some way.

Of the water holes where it was known to breed in the 1960s, several have dried up in times of drought, killing any larvae remaining in them, although metamorphosed individuals living nearby may be able to recolonize them when they fill up again. Disease killed all the salamanders at three sites in 1985, and diseased individuals were also found at another seven sites. An associated problem is the introduction of non-native species, especially the bullfrog, *Rana catesbeiana*, and fishes, which may prey upon the tiger salamanders or their larvae. These also spread diseases, notably a virus that causes periodic outbreaks of disease and which is implicated in the decline or loss of several populations. The larvae of tiger salamanders are also widely used as fishing bait in Arizona, and where sub-species from other parts of the state have been introduced to the area for bait propagation, there is a danger of interbreeding with the tiger salamanders. In summary, then, these tiger salamanders are under threat from a variety of sources: loss of breeding sites through drought or disturbance; predation and diseases caused by introduced amphibians and fish; and possible interbreeding with other salamanders.

Multiple problems

As well as the problems that apply to this population of tiger salamanders are other threats that have been affecting amphibian populations on a global scale in the last decade. Many species have disappeared, in countries as widespread as Australia and Costa Rica, and many species that were formerly common are now becoming rare. Possible causes, in addition to those listed above, include the effects of acid rain, increased ultraviolet radia-

Many salamanders have specific habitat requirements, so human developments can cause them to decline.

tion due to alterations in the atmosphere, and hormone-mimicking chemicals that reduce the fertility of populations.

The Sonoran tiger salamander was officially declared endangered in February 1997. This status affords it some protection, especially from human activities such as collection or the destruction of its habitat.

In parallel with this, populations are being monitored by teams of scientists, while other experts are investigating the occurrence of the viruses and other diseases that have already eliminated some colonies, in the hope that they can be controlled. Much of the research is funded by the Declining Amphibian Protection Task Force (DAPTF), which actively co-ordinates the conservation of all amphibians throughout the world.

Chris Mattison

Texas Blind Salamander

(Typhlomolge rathbuni)

ESA: Endangered

IUCN: Vulnerable

Length: 5 in. (13 cm)
Clutch size: Unknown
Diet: Insects and small invertebrate
Habitat: Underground water systems
Range: Central Texas

THE TEXAS BLIND salamander is aptly named, as it is a sightless animal—an adaptation to the dark, underground water systems of its habitat. It is almost transparent in appearance, showing white or pinkish color, with a fringe of red behind its head. The head and the snout are flattened, and there are two black eye spots that mark the location of its undeveloped eyes.

Biologists know of only a single population of this salamander, occurring in the San Marcos Pool in central Texas between Austin and San Antonio. The population appears to be stable, although it is rather small. Nonetheless, a single catastrophic event could render this amphibian extinct. For many years, water has been pumped from the region to supply water for agriculture and residential needs. As San Antonio and Austin have been developed, the demand for water has grown and, consequently, the Texas blind salamander's habitat has been reduced. Water levels have dropped and will probably continue to drop as the region continues to be developed.

Survival of this salamander and other cave-dwelling creatures depends on the stability and purity of the San Marcos Pool. Fortunately, local, state, and federal agencies are working to realize an agreement between the needs of the region's people and its wildlife.

However, such an agreement is bound to be controversial, as access to water is directly tied to any development or economic growth in this region.

Elizabeth Sirimarco

See also Olm.

The Texas blind salamander is a slender and frail cave dweller that spends its life in complete darkness.

SALMON

Class: Actinopterygii

Order: Salmoniformes

Family: Salmonidae

The name "salmon," when applied to a number of species can be a bit confusing. The term is applied to species in several genera and not always in a consistent manner. For example, various members of the genera *Oncorhynchus*, *Salmo*, *Hucho*, and *Salmothymus* are called salmon. Some are found in the Pacific basin, some in the Atlantic basin, and some in the Mediterranean, Caspian, Aral, and Black Sea basins. Most, but not all live in both freshwater and salt water during different periods in their lives. Most, but not all, migrate to freshwater to spawn.

The only consistent characteristic of salmon is that the majority belong to the family Salmonidae, the family that includes salmon, trout, char, grayling, and whitefish. Salmon that migrate from rivers to the ocean after hatching and then back to rivers to spawn, are called anadromous fishes. The internal body transformation required to withstand such drastic changes in environment is profound.

After hatching, the physiology of these fishes changes through a process called smoltification. This allows them to migrate downstream and enter the saltwater environment of the sea. For several years these smolts roam the ocean, feeding and growing to sexual maturity. At an appropriate time, they migrate back to the precise location from which they hatched to spawn.

In the case of salmon from the Pacific Ocean, such as the chinook (*Oncorhynchus tshawytscha*) and coho (*Oncorhynchus kisutch*), these fish die after they spawn. Atlantic Ocean salmon survive their spawning ordeal and may return to spawn for several years. Because of their need to migrate and roam freely between rivers and oceans, salmon are extremely vulnerable to the activities of people. Even those salmon that do not move from rivers into an open saltwater environment migrate up and down their natal streams in search of food and to spawn in the upper reaches as they reach sexual maturity.

Dams and other barriers to migration are a principal cause of declines in salmon populations because they impede or block these migrations.

As most people can attest, their high nutritional value and good taste makes salmon a favorite and popular food. In some arid and semi-arid regions, such as the western United States, diversion of water from salmon streams for use in agriculture adds to their demise.

The seemingly endless bounty of salmon does have its limits, and that limit is quickly being reached. If salmon are to continue to survive in their native ranges, they must be afforded the protection they deserve.

Adriatic Salmon

(Salmothymus obtusirostris)

IUCN: Endangered

Length: 16 in (40 cm)

Reproduction: Egg layer

Habitat: Stream pools and riffles

Range: Krka River and other coastal streams of southeastern Europe

THE ADRIATIC SALMON, locally known in the former country of Yugoslavia as the *mekousna* or softmouth, is a true freshwater, stream-dwelling fish. Contrary to its common name—and unlike Atlantic salmon (*Salmo* spp.) and Pacific varieties (*Oncorhynchus* spp.) that spend significant periods of time in their respective oceans—this salmon does not migrate into the relatively warm waters of the Adriatic Sea. This endangered fish, however, does migrate up and down the rivers it inhabits along the eastern Adriatic coast, and herein lies part of the Adriatic salmon's problem.

As the newly-emerging nations of this region move to bolster their economies and raise their standard of living—in part by building hydroelectric power dams—the Adriatic salmon will rapidly lose its remaining suitable habitat. Dams create reservoirs that inundate suitable areas, they block the movement of the salmon up and down the rivers as they search for food or spawn, and they significantly alter water flow and quality in streams. Without a doubt, dams are the most destructive form of stream-fish habitat alteration.

Lack of knowledge

Unfortunately, many dam construction projects are approved without regard to their impact on endangered fish like the Adriatic salmon.

Often, decision-making officials know little or nothing about the plight of this or other species, their low population numbers and, additionally, any alternatives or design changes that could minimize the impacts of construction on these fish.

The chinook salmon grows to a relatively large size after living for several years at sea.

Appearance

The Adriatic salmon closely resembles the brown trout (*Salmo trutta*) in shape, coloration, and patterning. The body is long and slender, with a pointed snout to minimize drag. Unlike the brown trout, the Adriatic salmon has a thicker upper jaw, and the mouth is positioned lower on the face. Overall, this fish has green-brown coloration on the back and sides and a yellow-brown belly. The sides, back, top of the head, gill covers, and dorsal fin carry numerous black and red spots. The body fins are square or triangular, and the large tail fin is unforked or only mildly forked. This species consumes small fish, insects, and other small aquatic invertebrates.

Another threat to this fish is competition with other salmonid fish, primarily trout, that have been raised in close proximity to the last remaining strongholds of the Adriatic salmon.

Trout that have been raised at production facilities often escape to the wild and establish themselves in the same habitat areas as the resident fishes. They can be aggressive predators, and competitors for habitat.

Chinook Salmon
(Oncorhynchus tshawytscha)

ESA: Endangered

Length: 35 in. (90 cm)
Reproduction: Egg layer
Habitat: Coastal streams and open ocean
Range: North Pacific basin, Bering and Chukchi Seas

WITHOUT A DOUBT, the chinook or king salmon (along with other Pacific salmon), is one of the most prized fish in all of North America and Asia. The chinook salmon is woven into the cultures of human populations from California and Alaska to eastern Siberia and northern Japan.

For thousands of years, Native American and Asian populations of this salmon have endured because species such as the chinook salmon have provided a major part of their food supply.

Today, for most people who occupy the northern Pacific coastal areas, the chinook salmon is not a necessity for life but is more the focus of contention than ever before. This species consists of many distinct populations, which are also called races or runs. The life history of these populations varies. After they hatch in rivers and move to the ocean to feed and grow, some populations return to spawn after one year, while others do not return for five to eight years. Some migrate upstream only 10 or 20 miles (16 to 32 kilometers) and others, like populations in Alaska's Yukon River, migrate over 1,000 miles (1,600 kilometers).

Overall, this species maintains large and healthy populations. Indeed, 50 million pounds (22,700,000 kilograms) or more were marketed annually as food. However, over parts of its range (particularly those populations that utilize rivers along the western coast of the United States), the chinook salmon is threatened by overfishing, barriers to migration, and a struggle between various special-interest groups. These groups include native peoples that claim historical fishing rights, commercial fishers who rely on the salmon for their livelihood, sport fishers who demand

CHINOOK SALMON
Asia

CHINOOK
SALMON
North America

access to the fish, and environmentalists who want to preserve the species for the future.

The debate over habitat

For many years, aquaculture, or the production of aquatic organisms in controlled environments, has been used to enhance wild stocks and provide more fish. Now aquaculture is under attack by those who claim that hatchery-reared and stocked fish undermine genetic integrity.

In the late 1800s the production of salmon in the Snake River was about 1.5 million. By the 1990s only several thousand were passing through. In California, there is always the problem of overfishing, plus the farmer's demand for unlimited use of water in the Sacramento and San Joaquin Rivers for agriculture. The salmon requires this water during its reproductive and juvenile stages. Throughout this salmon's range, dams that impede or prevent upstream migration and stream water diversion have helped to either reduce reproductive success or wipe out populations. An example is the extinct runs of the San Joaquin River. Human activities mean an uncertain future for the chinook salmon, and tighter reg-

ulation of fishing by all parties is probable. This species may become extinct, but given the large range of the chinook salmon and its importance as a renewable resource, this species may survive in the remoter regions of its range. A National Marine Fisheries review in 1997 concluded that populations in Washington and Oregon were not in danger, but the Ozette lake population in Washington was likely to become so in future, due to degradation of spawning areas and genetic mixing with hatchery fish.

Color shifts

The chinook salmon is a strong swimmer. Its streamlined body, pointed snout, and triangular body fins minimize drag; the tail fin is mildly forked. During its ocean phase, its body coloration overall is steel blue and gray, with a hint of green on the back and upper sides, and silvery blue-white on the lower sides and belly. The upper half of the body as well as the dorsal fin on the back and the tail fin carry numerous dark spots; all fins are greenish blue in color.

As the summer spawning season approaches, the body color changes to a more pronounced green tone across the head, back, and sides. The snout of the male becomes hooked, and the jaw teeth are exposed in anticipation of territorial disputes with other males. Unlike other members of the genus *Salmo*, the chinook salmon does not survive the reproductive phase of its life.

During the ocean phase, herring, amphipods, and marine crustaceans are eaten, while plankton and aquatic invertebrates are consumed in the juvenile freshwater phase.

Coho Salmon
(Oncorhynchus kisutch)

ESA: Threatened

Length: 24–30 in. (61–76 cm)
Reproduction: Egg layer
Habitat: Coastal streams and open ocean
Range: North Pacific Basin from western United States to Russia and Japan

ALTHOUGH THERE ARE some artificially introduced coho populations in the Great Lakes, the wild salmon is a migrant, spending some time in salt water between hatching and eventual breeding in fresh water.

Older and larger males may return from the sea after two years or more, while smaller individuals, jacks, may spend as little as six months in the marine environment.

The potential disadvantages of smaller size when competing for mates seems to be balanced by spending less time at sea, where predators and parasites are more likely to pose a threat to survival. Smaller fish might also survive in waters reduced in depth by human activity, where more mature fish flounder in the shallows, thereby introducing an artificial selection pressure on coho populations.

Compared to other salmon, the cohos are late breeders and may be seen excavating their nests, or redds, at the turn of the year. At this time the males take on a darker greenish coloring above and a vivid red below. This coloring resembles that of the sockeye salmon, but the spots on

After living in a marine environment, the coho salmon makes a hazardous journey back to a freshwater environment in order to spawn.

the back, the dorsal fin, and the tail of the coho salmon serve to distinguish it from other species.

The behavior of the emerging fry also sets them apart from those of other species, which immediately swim downstream on hatching. The young coho remain near the nursery grounds, where they establish a small feeding territory and begin to devour prey the moment they are released from the gravel. Resisting the safety of life in a school, they spread themselves out, with the largest and strongest fish in the best feeding areas, often with a descending hierarchy of lesser individuals strung out behind. Aquatic and terrestrial insects

that fall into the water and small crustacea provide the main food.

With the onset of winter, coho move out of the threat of raging floodwaters into quieter pools, ponds, and backwaters. Before they are two years old, most coho will leave their freshwater environment and move out to sea. Some have only a short journey to make from coastal streams,

while fish of the Yukon may have to travel hundreds of miles.

Life at sea can be hazardous, but it is the return journey that has led to the serious decline in wild populations. Traditionally coho would return from the sea each year in their millions to the western United States and Canada. This provided a food source for animals, supported a

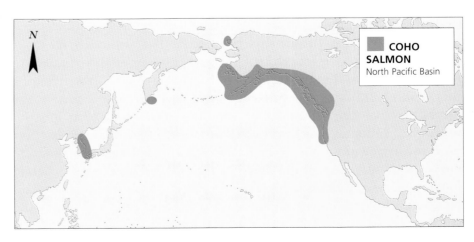

COHO SALMON
North Pacific Basin

thriving fishing industry, and provided huge quantities of nutrients for plantlife. However, over the last century numbers have declined by 99 percent over much of this species' range, and it has become extinct in about 50 percent of its native rivers.

River damage

For a fish that remains in fresh water for so long, the condition of the rivers is critical. Logging causes siltation and damage to gravel beds, as well as reduces the amount of shade over streams and rivers, which results in an increase in water temperature. The effects of logging combined with mining activities, pollution, overgrazing, and channel diversion produce a combination of destructive impacts. The decline of this species has been extreme: The coho population of California has been reduced from 500,000 to only a few thousand. In Oregon the population has been reduced from 1.4 million to 20,000, and virtually none of Washington's 1.2 million coho salmon survive.

In some areas it is already too late to save the coho, but where populations still exist, conservation strategies include wise management of logging, restrictions in oceanic fisheries to protect stocks, and restoration of spawning areas. Local action has been the favored approach so far, but many scientists, naturalists, and anglers believe that if stocks continue to dwindle, a more coordinated effort that includes local, state, and federal governments will be necessary for the continued survival of the coho salmon.

Kelvin Boot

Danube Salmon (Huchen)

(Hucho hucho)

IUCN: Endangered

Length: 60 in. (150 cm)
Weight: About 100 lbs. (45 kg)
Reproduction: Egg layer
Habitat: Small- and medium-sized tributaries, large rivers
Range: Danube River Basin, eastern Europe

EXCEEDED IN SIZE ONLY by its close relative in Asia (*Hucho taimen*), the southeastern European Danube salmon and its counterpart are two of the largest fish in the family Salmonidae, and that makes them two of the largest freshwater fish in the

world. While the populations of the Asian subspecies are somewhat large and cover a vast range, the Danube salmon is in worse shape and is considered to be endangered.

As its common name implies, this fish occupies the Danube River Basin in small- and medium-sized tributaries and in the main stem of the river. Its historic range within the Danube used to be much larger, but today the Danube salmon is common in only one-third of its former range. Only the upper reaches of these rivers in the sub-mountain regions carry fish in substantial numbers; far fewer inhabit the Danube River proper.

Given the Danube salmon's large size, one might at first suspect that overfishing is the primary reason for the decline of

ADRIATIC SALMON
DANUBE SALMON
Europe

this species. Actually, fishing pressure is only a secondary concern to biologists interested in this salmon's preservation. Other factors, in fact, do more damage: stream channelization to prevent flooding, construction of dams that prevent fish migration, municipal sewage and industrial chemical pollution, industrial thermal pollution, and deforestation, which leads to stream siltation. All these have contributed more to the Danube salmon's plight than overfishing or poaching. However, fishing does appear to take its toll on the species, given the current low numbers of reproductive adults.

The Asian subspecies is considered a pest in some areas, and is fished without legal restriction. The Danube salmon is particularly sensitive to elevated water temperatures, and the use of river water for cooling in industrial processes has produced an increase in average water temperatures, with temperatures above 68 degrees Fahrenheit (20 degrees Centigrade) causing the most damage.

What is being done?

Efforts to save the Danube salmon have been weak and relatively unsuccessful.

Much emphasis has been placed on the education of anglers, and on restrictions such as bag limits. However, as mentioned, fishing pressure takes a back seat to the more serious environmental problems.

Some production and stocking of this fish was attempted but, again, the impact was minor because of the inability of the environment to support fish. Given the reluctance or inability

on the part of the government to mandate restoration of the environment, the future of the Danube salmon within its range, as well as other fish that make their homes in this region, appears to be bleak.

Handsome specimen

An adult Danube salmon is an impressive fish, possibly reaching lengths in excess of 70 inches (178 centimeters) and a weight of over 100 pounds (45 kilograms). This fish is well designed for life in a river, with a streamlined body, pointed snout, triangular body fins, and a tail fin that is broad and mildly forked. These characteristics makes it a strong swimmer. Its overall coloration is silvery, with darker shading on the back and sides and lighter areas on the throat, lower jaw, and belly. Small black spots pepper the sides and back.

An annual cycle

After three-to-five years of life, Danube salmon begin a yearly breeding cycle; sexually mature fish, especially males, become red in color. Spawning occurs early in the year, when water temperatures reach 40 to 50 degrees Fahrenheit (5 to 10 degrees Centigrade). The female builds a nest in river gravel and deposits large yellow eggs into the depression. After they are fertilized and covered, the eggs incubate for about 20 days. The offspring hatch and move downstream to feed on bottom-dwelling aquatic invertebrates until they are large enough to eat small fish.

The enormous adults are able to consume fish, reptiles, amphibians, and even waterfowl and small mammals.

Sockeye Salmon
(Oncorhynchus nerka)

ESA: Endangered

Length: 30 in. (75 cm)
Reproduction: Egg layer
Habitat: Coastal streams and open ocean
Range: North Pacific basin, Bering and Chukchi Seas, Sea of Okhotsk

THIS PHOTOGENIC salmon has appeared on numerous television programs documenting the lives of salmon of the Pacific basin. The brilliant red body and hooked snout of the sockeye salmon, as it returns to its birth river to spawn, are its trademarks. Its range covers a broad area from Oregon and Alaska to eastern Siberia and northern Japan. Most sockeye populations are anadromous (spawning in freshwater streams and living to adulthood in the Pacific Ocean), but some live their entire lives in land-locked, freshwater environments. These are called kokanee salmon. While the species as a whole certainly is not in danger,

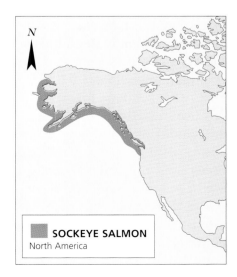

SOCKEYE SALMON
North America

distinct populations are in serious trouble or are in decline.

Like chinook salmon, this species has many distinct populations (also called races or runs), and the natural life processes of these populations are not alike. The sockeye hatch in rivers and migrate to the ocean to feed and grow, but they do not always return to their spawning grounds at the same time. Some populations return after a few years, while others take as long as five years. The migration could be from 20 miles (32 kilometers) to 1,000 miles (1,600 kilometers).

Over 100 million pounds (45,400,000 kilograms) are marketed annually as food. This big catch implies that salmon are not in danger. However, in the United States, the Snake River sockeye salmon (from the Redfish Lake population) is on the verge of extinction. The Columbia River and its tributary, the Snake River, have for decades been dammed for hydroelectric power. There are eight dams between Redfish Lake and the Pacific Ocean. Before the installation of fish ladders (devices designed to allow salmon safe passage past high dams), it was nearly impossible for salmon to migrate upstream to their historic spawning grounds. Reproductive success was, therefore, reduced.

Today, even with fish ladders, many fish still fail to move upstream to spawn. The offspring of fish that do spawn are preyed upon by non-native fish like the walleye pike (*Stizostedion vitreum*) and the northern squawfish (*Ptychocheilus oregonensis*); and some fish are ground up by turbines at power dams. In 1990, no salmon nests were found near Redfish

Lake. The status of the sockeye salmon in this lake is uncertain. Other populations of salmon throughout their range are at risk from declining river levels, hydroelectric development, and pollution. As an adult, the sockeye salmon displays two distinct body conformations. During the ocean phase, which lasts one to four years, the sockeye salmon has a streamlined body, with a straight, pointed snout, triangular fins, and forked tail. The dominant color is silvery white

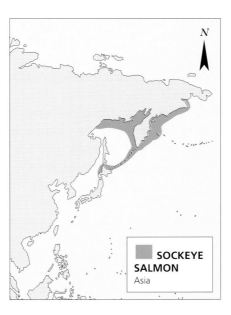

SOCKEYE SALMON
Asia

The only consistent characteristic of salmon is that the overwhelming majority belong to the family Salmonidae, a family that includes salmon, trout, char, grayling, and whitefish—all popular with fishers.

on the lower half of the body. The back, upper sides, and top of the head are dark green and gray as are all of the fins; a hint of orange or pink may be present at the base of the fins on the belly. The body is scaled but the head is nude.

Fish ready for spawning change dramatically. In both sexes, body coloration changes to brilliant red with patches of brown. Most of the head turns dark brown, except for the lower jaw, which remains white. The tail fin becomes light or cream-colored, and other fins change color to match the body.

Ocean-phase sockeye salmon feed on krill, squid, small fish, and amphipods. Juvenile fresh-water-phase sockeye consume plankton, insects, and other aquatic invertebrates. Sockeye salmon die after spawning.

William E. Manci

SARDINILLA CUATRO CIÉNEGAS
North America

to dry out, and the resident fish and other animals will be forced to concentrate in smaller and smaller tracts. Competition for space and food has increased, and changes in the population are already evident in the sardinilla Cuatro Ciénegas and other organisms.

Nearby towns also demand water from the Cuatro Ciénegas region for domestic and commercial purposes. The relatively small amount of water that is returned from these towns contains sewage and other pollutants. Overall, reduced water flows and levels in Cuatro Ciénegas streams and marshes increase average temperatures, destroy fast-flowing stream riffles and other critical habitat and, if allowed to continue, may cause the extinction of unique fish species such as the sardinilla Cuatro Ciénegas.

The sardinilla Cuatro Ciénegas is a member of the family Cyprinodontidae, the killifishes. In their distribution around the world, killifishes have been a very successful group, and can be found across the tropical and temperate latitudes of the world. Killifishes are capable of tolerating a wide range of environmental conditions, particularly extremes in temperature and salinity. They are just as readily found in freshwater as salt water, in water temperatures that are both hot and cold.

Most killifishes prefer shallow water rich in aquatic vegetation; they use vegetation for cover and as a likely source of aquatic insects—their favorite food.

Killifishes are popular with people who keep aquariums because these fish come in many varied color patterns. They can tolerate imperfect aquarium conditions, and they spawn easily in captivity. These features make them easy specimens to keep. With such popularity, it is no wonder that the market demand for these fish could be partly responsible for their status as threatened or endangered. Additionally, because of their small size, many species are captured and used as bait fish, but this has not been a major factor in their decline. Such over-exploitation is difficult to combat because of the profit motive. However, educating the public and those directly engaged in exploiting sensitive or declining species may begin to curb the demand.

Almost without exception, killifishes are less than 4 inches (10 centimeters) in length, with an elongated, robust body and a plump belly. The rounded and fan-shaped fins are never large, and they lack spines for protection against predators. An upturned mouth, jutting lower jaw, and eyes set high on the head aid them in capturing insects at the surface of the water.

The tiny sardinilla Cuatro Ciénegas is difficult to find, but the male, at least, is easy to identify because of its spectacular colors. The bronze-gold male body carries several horizontal rows of blue spots, with the rows separated by olive and orange lines. The head is olive on top and orange-brown underneath. The eyes have a black bar across the lower portion and a shiny blue patch just behind them. The dorsal fin on the back and the anal fin are blue, contrasting with the orange pectoral and pelvic fins just behind the gills and on the belly. The female is not nearly as garish in appearance, and is yellow-brown from head to tail.

Efforts are under way to declare the Cuatro Ciénegas Basin a national park, a move that would curtail water use for outside purposes. Additionally, proponents of a conservation plan hope to acquire funds for continued biological research of the unique plants and animals that occupy the region.

William E. Manci

SARDINITAS

Class: Actinopterygii

Order: Cypriniformes

Family: Cyprinidae

The sardinitas, also known as Mexican shiners, are included in one of the largest North American fish groups. They are often referred to as minnows. Although most minnows are small, some such as the grass carp (*Ctenopharyngodon idella*) or the Colorado squawfish (*Ptychocheilus lucius*), are able to attain great sizes. For the most part, sardinitas, or shiners, belong to two genera (*Notropis* and *Cyprinella*), although other smaller cyprinids are sometimes referred to as "shiners."

Shiners are found throughout much of North America, from Mexico to northern Canada and Alaska. They can be found in a wide variety of aquatic habitats: ponds, lakes, creeks, and both large and small rivers.

Various species of shiners are restricted to clear, cold-water environments, while others require muddy, warm water in order to survive.

All shiners are spring spawners, but some reproduce more than once a year, spawning in early spring and again sometime before fall. The male shiners are more colorful than the females, particularly when reproductively active. The dynamic colors of these spawning males give the group its name.

In addition to spectacular coloration, the males also develop nuptial tubercles—tiny bumps on the top of the head extending toward the dorsal fin on the back. These are more prominent during the mating season, hence the term "nuptial."

Some shiners are nest builders and deposit their eggs in prepared sites. Some require clear, clean, flowing water over gravel bottoms, while others spread their eggs on vegetation. Others scatter their eggs randomly. This group has a wide variety of reproductive strategies, although all are egg layers.

Shiners have relatively large scales on the body but none on the head. Although the scales are round, they often take on a diamond-shaped appearance, due to a cross-hatched pattern in the skin color. Shiners have pharyngeal teeth in the back of the throat but none in the mouth. Their stomachs are usually an enlargement of the intestine, although there is some variability according to the food they prefer.

Shiners have only one dorsal fin and no fleshy adipose fin behind the dorsal fin, as do salmon and trout. They also lack hardened spines in any of their fins. Many shiners have small barbels in the corners of their mouths. Another anatomical feature of shiners and all cyprinids is the Weberian apparatus—a series of bones that connects the swim-bladder to the inner ear. This gives shiners a sharp perception of sounds and movement in surrounding water.

Shiners are small, but they are of critical ecological importance. A wide range of animals including larger fish, turtles, snakes, birds, and various mammals prey on shiners. Shiners are essential to the functioning of aquatic ecosystems from Mexico to Alaska.

Sardinita Bocagrande
(Cyprinella bocagrande)

IUCN: Critically endangered

Length: 2¾ in. (7 cm)
Reproduction: Egg Layer
Habitat: Impounded spring
Range: Ojo Solo Spring in Guzman Basin, Mexico

THE TINY SARDINITA bocagrande is native to a single dammed spring in the dry Chihuahuan desert of northern Mexico. Ojo Solo is one of five major springs around Ejido Rancho Nuevo in the Bolsón de los Muertos (Basin of the Dead). Ojo Solo is a spring that has been developed into a pond 150 feet (45.75 meters) in diameter. It is extremely shallow: just 3 to 4 feet (1 to 1.2 meters) deep in the center. Little aquatic vegetation is found in the pond, and the bottom is mainly sand, clay, and soft mud. The pond is drained by a small irrigation ditch, and the water is used for irrigation and water for livestock.

The fact that this small minnow is found only in one particular spring makes it vulnerable to disaster. Add to this its location in the dry Chihuahuan desert where water is scarce and of extreme importance, and all the ingredients of extinction are present. A further problem is the presence of the non-native black bullhead (*Ameiurus melas*), which preys upon the smaller shiners.

Although the sardinita bocagrande is presently protected by the Mexican government, human demands on the spring that supports it are high and continue to increase each year. Unfortunately, conservation laws are often very difficult to enforce.

This sardinita is similar in appearance to other minnows in the genus *Cyprinella*, being somewhat robust from top to bottom, although it looks rather slender from side to side.

The sardinita bocagrande's distinguishing feature is its large mouth, and the word bocagrande means big mouth.

The head of this sardinita is large and wide when compared to other shiners, and the jaws are long, extending well beyond the front of the eye. It possesses a rather wide, plum-colored lateral band along its side that is less defined near the head but is quite distinct near the tail.

Above the lateral stripe an iridescent yellow color blends to a deep violet on the back.

The breast, belly, and sides of the body below this lateral stripe are yellow, becoming a flamboyant orange at the base of the lower fins.

Fins on the underside of the fish are yellow-orange, while the dorsal fin (on the back) is clear. This rare shiner is extremely attractive and colorful.

Reproduction

Spawning is believed to begin in early spring and continues well into the fall. Females often deposit their eggs on submerged clumps of vegetation. Males develop characteristic bumps on the head (tubercles) prior to and during courtship, and these become vibrant in color.

The male sardinitas become aggressive and territorial during courtship and spend much time protecting their area.

In addition to the non-native black bullhead, the sardinita bocagrande shares its pond with another threatened shiner—the beautiful shiner (*Cyprinella formosa*)—and a small cachorrito (*Cyprinodon fontinalis*).

The diet of the sardinita bocagrande consists mainly of small aquatic insects and immature crayfish that are found in the pond at Ojo Solo.

Although this sardinita can sometimes be seen swimming near the margins of the pond, most of its time is spent in the deeper areas where the spring enters the small pond.

Sardinita Nazas
(Cyprinella nazas)

IUCN: Lower risk

Length: 2½ in. (6 cm)
Reproduction: Egg layer
Habitat: Upland and lowland streams
Range: Rio Nazas and Rio Aguanaval, Durango, Mexico

THE SARDINITA NAZAS is one of but a few species of fish found in the closed, desiccating desert basin of north-central Mexico known as the Nazas-Aguanaval Basin. Both Rio Nazas and Rio Aguanaval have no external outlet to the sea. All of the water that flows in these upland rivers empties into Laguna Mayaran. This is a fluctuating, shallow lake near the small village of El Palmito in the state of Durango, Mexico. The sardinita Nazas occurs naturally in what is truly a harsh environment. It was isolated in this closed basin many thousands of years ago, when major climatic changes reduced the annual rainfall. Prior to this, it is believed that there was enough precipitation in the Nazas-Aguanaval Basin to create a huge lake that spilled over and flowed north into the Rio Grande.

This explains the similarity in the fish species of these interior basins of central Mexico with those of the Rio Grande Basin.

Nowhere to go

The sardinita Nazas lives in rather small, fluctuating habitats in a land where each drop of water is precious. Most of the flow in the Rio Aguanaval and Rio Nazas is diverted for irrigation or human and animal consumption before it reaches Laguna Mayaran. Less water in the river channel means less available habitat for this small shiner. To make matters worse, largemouth bass (*Micropterus salmoides*) have been introduced into Laguna Mayaran. These efficient predators have apparently eliminated the sardinita Nazas from the lake itself, and are now affecting the population in the lower reaches of the Rios Aguanaval and Nazas.

The coloration of the sardinita Nazas is similar to the widely distributed red shiner (*Notropis lutrensis*). The sides of the body are silver blue, becoming a darker bluish gray on the back and much lighter on the stomach. There is a lateral stripe that is more pronounced in the tail region and faint behind the head. On the back, in diagonal rows, is a diamond-shaped pattern of pigment. Breeding males become more brilliantly colored over the body and fins, and a rectangular bar shows behind the cheek.

The head and back of the males also develop breeding tubercles at spawning time as well. Spawning is thought to occur in late May, with intermittent activity during the summer, but there is little information on the fish's ecology.

Sardinita del Pilón

(Notropis aguierrepequenoi)

ESA: Endangered

Length: 2½in. (6 cm)
Reproduction: Egg layer
Habitat: Upland streams and creeks
Range: Tamaulipas and Nuevo Leon, Mexico

SOUTH OF THE RIO GRANDE and north of Tampico, Mexico, are several rivers that drain into the Gulf of Mexico. These rivers contain an extremely diverse group of fish with a multitude of different survival strategies. One such river, the Rio Soto la Marina, is home to the sardinita del pilón. This elusive shiner was first discovered in 1973 and has continued to become increasingly rare. The Rio Soto la Marina is the second independent tributary to the Gulf of Mexico south of the Rio Grande. It drains a portion of the region known as Nuevo Leon, as well as the northern reaches of the Sierra Madre Oriental, a mountain range that predominates north-central Mexico on the Atlantic Ocean side of the Mexican continental divide.

The sardinita del pilón is found primarily in the upper portion of this basin, and much of its native habitat is disappearing. This fish is yet another victim of the declining aquatic resources in Mexico. The sardinita del pilón is extremely vulnerable because it has a very restricted range. It is the only fish of the Rio Soto la Marina that is confined exclusively to that drainage.

Home on the range

The species composition of the Rio Soto la Marina is unique. The first Gulf tributary to the north of this river, the Rio San Fernando, has a very limited fish fauna comprised mostly of lowland species that are widely distributed—fish typical of those found in the large lower Rio Grande Basin. Although the Rio Soto la Marina is just over 100 miles (160 kilometers) away from the Rio San Fernando, its waters contain species that are present in Central and South America, as well as the familiar fauna of the Rio Grande. There are nearly 40 different species present here, representing over 20 different families. Some of these fish are anadromous (they live in the ocean and spawn in the Rio Soto la Marina), some are catadromous (they live in the river and

spawn in the ocean), and some live in the estuary (the mouth of the river as it enters the ocean) near the Mexican village of La Pesca. The Rio Soto la Marina is also the southern limit of the familiar North American family of sunfishes (Centrarchidae), and is the most southern natural distribution of the largemouth bass (*Micropterus salmoides*).

The sardinita del pilón is quite typical of the genus *Notropis*. It is a small, silvery minnow, with a dark band of pigment along its side, extending from the cheek to the base of the tail fin. The back is cross-hatched with pigment, giving a diamond-shaped appearance to the scales. Males are usually more brilliant than females, and this becomes extremely pronounced during spawning season (May through August). Little is known of the food habits of this sardinita.

Sardinita de Salado

(Notropis saladonis)

IUCN: Extinct

Length: 2½ in. (6 cm)
Reproduction: Egg layer
Habitat: Upland streams and rivers
Range: Rio Salado, Mexico

THE SARDINITA DE SALADO is found in the Rio Salado. The headwaters of this river rise in the arid Coahuila province of northern Mexico. Flowing in a southeasterly direction, the Rio Salado enters the Rio Grande below Loredo. It is a relatively short river, but it contains a wide diversity of fishes. There are 32 described species of fish that are native to the Rio Salado, but only the sardinita de Salado is confined to this one drainage. There are other minnows of the genus *Notropis* present, but their range includes other rivers, especially in the Rio San Juan and Cuatro Ciénegas basins.

Scientists believe that the Cuatro Ciénegas Basin to the north once emptied into the Rio Grande by way of the Rio de Salado. Many thousands of years ago, when the climate was much wetter, and before geological uplift isolated the Cuatro Ciénegas Basin (leaving no external outlet), fish were able to move freely between the modern-day drainages. This is apparent, not only from geological evidence, but also from the similarity of certain traits of these fish that has persisted to the present day.

Two major factors have contributed to a recent population decline of the sardinita de Salado. First, water diversion has created major changes to the water flow, and this bears directly on the amount of suitable habitat in the Rio de Salado. A number of reservoirs have also had an impact by changing not only the basic structure of the river but also the water temperature. Second, introduction of non-native

The sardinita quijarrona is long and slender in form and is appropriately suited for life in a stream environment.

fish has had an impact on this minnow. Small, exotic fish compete with the sardinita Salado for resources, and larger non-native fish reduce its numbers through predation. The combined effect of non-native introduction and habitat loss has resulted in the steady decline of this Mexican shiner that was never very abundant to begin with.

The sardinita de Salado is a silvery minnow that is somewhat typical of the genus *Notropis*. It is rather brassy in color near the tail and on the back, with yellow-orange pigmentation at the base of the fins. Although not as pronounced as many other shiners, a lateral band of gray-black pigment provides a stripe from the back of the cheek to the base of the caudal (tail) fin. Males are much more colorful than females, and develop the characteristic bumps on the head during spawning periods.

The sardinita de Salado is omnivorous in its feeding habits. It consumes a wide range of aquatic insects. A smaller portion of its diet is comprised of plant material and algae. Because of the relative scarcity of this minnow, little else is known about its ecology.

Donald S. Proebstel

Sardinita Quijarrona

(Dionda mandibularis)

IUCN: Critically endangered

Length: 2½ in. (6 cm)
Reproduction: Egg layer
Habitat: Clear, quiet stream pools among vegetation and mud
Range: Rio Verde, San Luis Potosí, Mexico

THE REASONS FOR THE decline of this fish are clear. First, this species has had to vie for food with aggressive, non-native cichlids such as tilapias in the genera *Oreochromis* and *Sarotherodon*. The sardinita quijarrona is an easy target in its stream pools and backwaters. The fish has been moved out of prime river habitat areas by these aggressors.

Second, as prime habitat is destroyed and fouled by human activities such as stream modification and the discharge of domestic and industrial pollutants, the sardinita quijarrona is incapable of adapting to the new, severely degraded environment.

Appearance

The slender body of the sardinita quijarrona is accented by a pointed snout, a small mouth, and large eyes. All fins are triangular or rounded, with the exception of the tail fin, which is forked to aid swimming. This fish sports an olive-green back, golden and dark brown horizontal stripes on the sides, and a pale, lightly stippled belly. The dark side stripes run from the tip of the snout, through the eyes, and across the gill covers to the end of the tail fin between its upper and lower lobes. Fin colors conform with its body coloration for camouflage.

The sardinita quijarrona is an opportunistic feeder, consuming algae, insects and larvae, and aquatic invertebrates. It breeds in late winter and early spring, when water temperatures are on the rise and food becomes more plentiful.

Few sites within the Rio Pánuco Basin can sustain this fish. To survive, populations must be moved to more isolated areas that are free from predators. The only other solution is to prevent further destruction of its habitat and halt the introduction of competitors to sardinita quijarrona sites.

William E Manci

Sawfin

(Barbus serra)

ESA: Endangered

Class: Actinopterygii
Order: Cypriniformes
Family: Cyprinidae
Length: 22 in. (55 cm)
Reproduction: Egg layer
Habitat: Stream pools and channels
Range: Olifants River Basin, South Africa

THE SAWFIN BELONGS to a group of fishes called barbs—fish that characteristically have two fleshy barbels on each side of the mouth (but some have only one barbel and some have none at all). Barbs are small in size and exhibit bright colors. Their reproductive record in captivity is very good, which makes barbs desirable to aquarium owners. Males, are often brilliantly colored when it is spawning time, and their involved courtship behavior adds to their display value.

The sawfin and other fish are part of the large family Cyprinidae. Barbs are small fish that rarely exceed 6 inches (15 centimeters), but there are barbs that can actually grow to more than 5 feet (1.5 meters) in length and can weigh over 100 pounds (45 kilograms). All cyprinids have something called the Weberian apparatus, an internal body part that connects the fish's gas bladder to its inner ear. While the gas bladder regulates buoyancy, it also acts as an amplifier of sound to the Weberian apparatus.

The sawfin generally prefers clear water, so excessive sediments (siltation) have a detrimental effect on this fish. Unfortunately, deforestation in the part of the world this fish inhabits is increasing, causing problems such as siltation in the streams and rivers. As if that weren't enough, predatory, non-native fish like the smallmouth bass (*Micropterus dolomieu*) have taken a toll on the sawfin species.

The sawfin is important to the food chain because they breed and are eaten in large numbers. Many fish, reptiles, birds, and mammals need these fish for food. Unfortunately, when places such as the Olifants River Basin deteriorate because of human activities such as agriculture, the result can be a break in the food chain and the steady decline of uncounted species that fed on one another.

The female sawfins scatter their eggs over vegetation and a special sticky outer layer of the eggs attaches them to aquatic plants. Males fertilize these eggs by spreading their sperm (called milt) over the eggs. The small newly-hatched fry, between 200 and 300, are eaten by the parents and other fish. To avoid total disaster, the fry remain close to some cover and stay together in tight groups called schools.

Barbs have no teeth at all, but in the back of the throat they have comb-like teeth (pharyngeal teeth) that are used for the same purpose as regular teeth.

Other destructive human activities include changing the channels of streams to control flooding. When the banks are reworked by earth-moving equipment, or cemented, the habitat used by river fish for feeding and reproduction is ruined. Without familiar breeding grounds, generations are doomed.

Water diversion and flood control dams block the movement of fish up and down a stream or river, changing the seasonal water flow and chemistry that fish need for breeding cues. Only after environmental policies within South Africa and the Cape of Good Hope Province change will the sawfin be able to survive. Until then, placing this fish outside its natural range and in

similar habitat may help. The habitat would have to be protected from predatory fish that would reduce the sawfin to very low population levels.

William E. Manci

SCOPS OWLS

Class: Aves

Order: Strigiformes

There are 52 species of scops owl in the world. They are all relatively small, the largest being only 11 inches (28 centimeters) in length. These owls are widespread across much of Asia and Africa. Several species exist in the Americas, four of which are found in North America. Just one species breeds in Europe.

The range of many scops owls is limited to small islands, for example, in Southeast Asia and in the western Indian Ocean, where three of the world's endangered scops owls live.

Scops owls exhibit a variety of streaked or barred gray-brown or sandy brown colors. The different species can be distinguished from each other by subtle differences in plumage, call, and size. Scops owls have short legs and conspicuous ear tufts. These are not used for hearing but to express the mood of the bird, and to act as recognition signals at night. It is also possible that the ear tufts help to camouflage the owl by breaking up the silhouette of daytime roosting birds. As night-time hunters, scops owls have excellent hearing to help locate their prey. The facial discs around their eyes help to funnel sound waves and channel them to their real ears, which are concealed behind feathers. Another important feature is their ability to rotate their heads 270 degrees. Although the Eurasian scops owl sometimes hunts during the day, most of its relatives are nocturnal hunters, feeding mainly on moths, beetles, crickets, and caterpillars.

Scops owls live in a variety of habitats, from arid thorn-scrub and savanna in Africa to dense tropical forest. Some northern species migrate from colder areas in the autumn, in order to winter where food is more plentiful.

Anjouan Scops Owl

(Otus capnodes)

ESA: Endangered

IUCN: Critically endangered

Class: Aves
Order: Strigiformes
Family: Strigidae
Length: 8½ in. (22 cm)
Weight: Male averages 4 oz. (119 g)
Clutch size: Unknown
Incubation: Unknown
Diet: Probably insects
Habitat: Forest edge on steep mountain slopes above 1,800 ft. (550 m)
Range: Comoro islands

ANJOUAN IS ONE OF the Comoro Islands, halfway between the northern tip of Madagascar and the coast of East Africa. For more than a century after the last records, which date back to 1886, the Anjouan scops owl was thought to have been driven to extinction on the island that bears its name by the over-zealous collection of specimens. However, it was rediscovered in June 1992, and it is now thought to have been overlooked because its calls are not typical of those of other scops-owls.

Perhaps local people on Anjouan (or Ndzuani, as it is also known) should have been consulted, because apparently they have always been aware of the scops owl's presence.

This rare owl was rediscovered in fragments of upland forest in the central part of Anjouan. Although its distribution is known to be highly localized, it seems to be thriving in the right habitat: the problem is that this habitat covers only 2,500–5,000 acres (10–20 square kilometers). The Anjouan scops owl, which bears the local name *bandanga*, is restricted to primary forest on steep slopes above about 1,800 feet (550 meters). Most of the records show that the slopes are even higher, above 3,000 feet (800 meters).

There are no records from the plantations of exotic species established in the foothills in recent years. The owl perches in dense vegetation, usually at a height between 10–50 feet (3–15 meters) above the ground and this, together with its tiny range and largely nocturnal habits, makes it elusive.

Visitors intending to search for the bird usually either have to camp out or be prepared for a long night's walk. The very steep and forested slopes above Dindi and the area around Lake Dzialandze are the best areas, though even there locating the birds is still difficult. Like the Grand Comoro scops owl, it is very inquisitive and is often heard calling during the day—although that doesn't make it any easier to see. The best way to locate the owl is by playing a tape of its call to solicit a response, but this practice should always be done very sensitively, to limit disturbance. Its call is a prolonged whistled "peeooee" or "peeoo," repeated three to five times at intervals of 0.5–1.5 seconds, and it delivers a long, harsh screech.

Choose your color

Before the rediscovery of the Anjouan scops owl, it was considered by some to have been a race of the Madagascar scops owl *Otus rutilus*. However, its calls are very different, and as vocalization is often the best way to differentiate between species that are superficially similar in appearance, this is good evidence for it being a species in its own right.

It is the only small owl found on Anjouan and it occurs in two color phases, dark gray brown and rufous brown. These two forms are often seen together. The rufous birds have a dusky brown head with creamy facial discs and whitish eyebrows. Their upperparts are brown to rufous brown, with fine buff colored bars and spots. Birds of this color phase have barred flight feathers, and their paler underparts have dark streaks, finely threaded with buff and cream. Individuals of the darker color phase have no white at all in their plumage. They are dark chocolate brown to gray brown and have a finely grizzled pattern, rather than barred markings. Birds of both color phases have yellow-gray feet, gray or gray-green bills, and greenish yellow eyes. Unlike most species of scops owls, the ear tufts are very small.

Secretive lifestyle

Very little is known about this owl's lifestyle. It is thought to eat mainly insects, and it probably nests in cavities in trees—several birds have been seen perched at the entrance of such holes. The rest is speculation.

At least several tens of pairs, and probably 100 to 200, survive, but the clearance of primary forest and its replacement by exotic plantations is thought to be the biggest threat to the remaining birds. Additionally, their need to hunt for food exerts another pressure on numbers, and introduced predatory rats may reduce breeding success by taking eggs and chicks.

There are no reserves or protected areas on Anjouan and suitable habitat is getting very scarce, so urgent action is required if this small owl is to be saved. One suggested solution has been the establishment of a

ANJOUAN SCOPS OWL
Comoro Islands

captive-breeding program. This would mean capturing wild birds, and because the owls are considered a delicacy by many local people, their seizure in the name of conservation would have to be handled very carefully. Clearly, the other option is securing the long-term future of their montane forests.

Grand Comoro Scops Owl

(Otus pauliani)

IUCN: Critically endangered

Class: Aves
Order: Strigiformes
Family: Strigidae
Length: 8 in. (20 cm)
Weight: About 3 oz. (90 g) (based on similarly-sized Eurasian scops owl)
Clutch size: Unknown
Incubation: Unknown
Diet: Beetles and presumably other insects
Habitat: Forest and forest margins above 3,300 ft. (1,000 m)
Range: Slopes of Mount Karthala, Grand Comoro Island

THIS DIMINUTIVE OWL is sometimes known as the Karthala scops owl, named after the volcano on which it resides. It was discovered on the island of Grand Comoro as recently as 1958, although there was initially some debate as to whether or not it should be considered a full species. C.W. Benson, the ornithologist who first described

it after it was heard calling on the western slopes of the volcano, felt that it looked and sounded sufficiently different from its near neighbour in Madagascar to warrant separate status. For a time other ornithologists persuaded him otherwise, but after spending time studying the Madagascar scops owl (*Otus rutilus*) he concluded that his first instincts had been correct. The reason for the controversy is easy to explain: there are about 60 species of scops owl and screech owl in the large genus *Otus*; many of these are confined to single, and often small, oceanic islands (though others have very extensive continental ranges), and some look very similar.

Common ancestor

The islands of the western Indian Ocean alone account for four of the world's scops owls: in addition to the two species that have already been mentioned are the Seychelles scops owl and the

The Mindanao scops owl (*Otus mirus*), which lives in the Philippines, is another owl that is in trouble. The IUCN–World Conservation Union classifies this scops owl as vulnerable.

Anjouan scops owl. All four are closely related to each other and to those found thousands of miles away in the oceanic islands of Southeast Asia, and it seems likely that all these birds share a common Asiatic ancestor. With so much similarity, it is inevitable that opinions should sometimes be divided on how valid different species are. Plumage differences obviously count for a lot, but they are not everything: habitat preferences, songs, and calls also need to be taken into account.

A close call

The sound of a bird's call is often the truest way to tell one scops owl from another. As largely nocturnal birds that are very inconspicuous and often display similar plumage, their voices provide the safest way of telling many apart. The Grand Comoro scops owl delivers a continuous whistled toot, repeated at one-second intervals, and it was this whistle that originally gave away the bird's presence.

Although a bird was seen and collected at La Convalescence on the west side of Mount Karthala, extensive searches in other tracts of forest failed to find more, but its calls were heard again in the same area in 1981. Two years later, several were discovered to the south of the volcano.

This, the only small owl found on Grand Comoro, was at first thought to be confined to the evergreen forest of the Mount Karthala, but it is now known that its key habitat is along the margins of the forest and the adjacent scrubby montane heathland. This is one reason that it should be considered a different species from the Madagascar scops owl, which is a bird that inhabits lowland forest.

Camouflage

Not much bigger than a starling, the Grand Comoro scops owl boasts a cryptic plumage to help

GRAND COMORO SCOPS OWL
Grand Comoro Island

it blend in with its surroundings. Its facial discs and bright yellow eyes are features it shares with other scops owls, but it lacks the large head tufts of its close relative the Madagascar scops owl, and has a darker head. Its sandy-brown underparts are finely threaded with dark brown markings, and its upperparts are dark brown.

Very little is known about its lifestyle, but examination of the stomach contents of a dead bird revealed beetle remains.

Montane habitat

In November 1989, survey work found this owl at altitudes of 3,300–6,200 feet (1,000–1,900 meters) on the north, west, and south flanks of the volcano.

An estimated 259 square miles (100 square kilometers) of suitable habitat exists, and although the population could possibly be over 1,000 pairs, the Grand Comoro scops owl faces many threats.

First, any species with such a limited range must be vulnerable to any number of environmental changes. Additionally, destruction of the forest by loggers and of the heathland-forest margin by natural fires take their toll on this owl's favored habitat, and damage and disturbance from an increase in visitors to Mount Karthala could adversely affect it. Competition from the introduced common myna is also perceived as another threat.

Clearly, habitat preservation is crucial, ideally through the creation of a forest reserve on the volcano's slopes, not least because the area also holds other endemic birds such as the Comoro drongo and the Karthala white-eye.

Seychelles Scops Owl

(Otus insularis)

IUCN: Critically endangered

Class: Aves
Order: Strigiformes
Family: Strigidae
Length: 8 in. (20 cm)
Weight: About 3 oz. (90 g)
Clutch size: Thought to be 1
Incubation: Unknown
Diet: Tree-frogs, insects, lizards
Habitat: Well-forested slopes and valleys at 800–2,100 ft. (250–600 m)
Range: The island of Mahé in the Seychelles

THE SEYCHELLES scops owl holds the dubious distinction of being the rarest scops owl on the planet.

The scops owls are found in most of the world's tropical areas, although they are absent from Australasia, and some make it into temperate zones. This tribe of small owls is almost exclusively nocturnal and it prefers wooded or forested terrain. Typical features are cryptic brown or gray plumages and relatively small facial discs. Its plumage is mainly sandy brown with very fine black markings above and blackish arrow-shaped streaks on the breast and belly. Its facial discs are bordered by black blobs, and in common with most of its cousins, its eyes have bright yellow irises. However, it lacks the pronounced ear tufts of some scops owls. Its legs are unfeathered, hence the alternative name sometimes used to describe it is the bare-legged scops owl.

Back from the dead

Although discovered on the Seychelles island of Mahé in 1880 this bird was pronounced extinct in 1958. Ironically, just two years later the skin of an owl shot in 1940 was reexamined and found to be of this species. This discovery raised speculation that there may still be birds living on Mahé, and searches were carried out. By the late 1960s it was estimated that there were about 20 birds. Then in 1975–76 at least 12 pairs were logged in upland secondary forest in the Mission area. It was estimated that there were at least 80 pairs of calling birds. Because secondary forest has matured in some areas it is possible that this has enabled an increase in numbers. Surveys in 1992–93 revealed at least 80 pairs, with evidence of strong site-fidelity. Pairs remained in the same patches of forest year after year. Fortunately, much of the suitable habitat falls within the protected Morne Seychellois National Park.

Hard to see

Virtually every record of the species comes from forest at altitudes between 800–2,100 feet (250–600 meters). Forest now covers only about one-third of Mahé's surface area, but before much of it was cleared it is likely that the Seychelles scops owl ranged across the whole island. This species is harder to see than to hear, and is rarely seen at daytime roost sites. The real indicators of its presence are a persistent "waugh waugh" or a repeated "tock tock" call, both delivered at

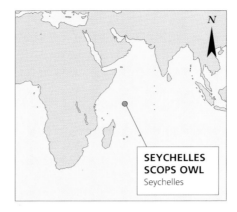

SEYCHELLES
SCOPS OWL
Seychelles

night. There have been unconfirmed reports of similar calls on other islands in the Seychelles archipelago. Some argue that the Seychelles scops owl is no more than an island race of Madagascar scops owl, but the fact that its call is so different from the latter's "broo-broo-broo," must add weight to the counterarguement that it is indeed a separate species.

This owl seems to spend much of its hunting time on the ground in boulder-strewn areas of forest, suggesting that this may be a ground-cavity nester rather than a tree nester. It needs areas of forest with water, where tree-frogs can be found. Stomach contents have revealed remains of tree-frogs as well as lizards, insects, grasshoppers, beetles, and vegetation.

Little is known about its breeding ecology, but calls of mating birds have been heard from October to April, and fledged young appear in June and November, so it may breed twice yearly.

This owl is threatened by habitat loss, mainly due to logging. As loggers reach the most remote parts of valleys, the owl's future is even less certain. However the Morne Seychellois National Park offers protection, and this and other areas must be conserved to secure its survival.

Tim Harris

The Seychelles scops owl is threatened by habitat loss. To prevent further decline, its habitat must be secured.

Sokoke Scops Owl

(Otus ireneae)

ESA: Endangered

IUCN: Vulnerable

Class: Aves
Order: Strigiformes
Family: Strigidae
Length: 6¼–7 in. (16–18 cm)
Weight: 4½–5½ oz. (126–154 g)
Clutch size: Probably 3–4 eggs
Incubation: Probably 24–25 days
Diet: Large insects
Habitat: Forest, woodland
Range: Sokoke Forest in Kenya; possibly the East Usambra Mountains in Tanzania

A MELLOW CALL RISES in the night. Sifting through the trees, the call loses direction and intensity. Minute after minute, the call continues through the night. Before sunlight breaks on the horizon, the Sokoke scops owl has ushered in another day, but it may not have many days left.

The Sokoke Forest grows in southeastern Kenya, close to the Indian Ocean coast. Four main plant communities cover the area. The dominant plant species for each community depends on soil type and rainfall. Thin forest and woodland both occur in the area, covering 160 square miles (400 square kilometers) between the villages of Sokoke on the southwest and Arabuko on the northeast. Only about 43 square miles (111 square kilometers) of the Sokoke Forest provides the kind of habitat suitable for the Sokoke scops owl.

A shy and secretive bird, the owl escaped detection until 1965. Since then, several specimens have been collected, and people report seeing it somewhat regularly. A sparrow-sized owl, it has a warm, golden-buff plumage overall, modestly patterned with slightly darker golden brown marks above. Small, white spots form neat rows over the crown, down the nape, and across the back as well as on the breast and belly. Larger white spots form a row across the shoulder. Distinct feathery tufts, or "horns," rise above bright yellow eyes.

Very little is known about the natural history of the Sokoke scops owl. The stomachs of a few specimens were examined to find out what the bird eats. The contents included all types of insects. The Sokoke scops owls apparently eat crickets, katydids, and walkingsticks, which live among the foliage and twigs of trees.

The Sokoke scops owl probably makes its living snatching insects from the trees rather than catching rodents and other small mammals on the ground.

Deliberate measures to protect the habitat of the Sokoke scops owl are necessary if this rare bird is to survive.

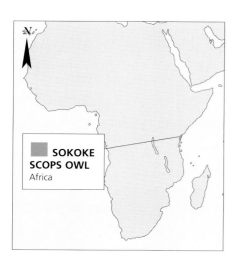

SOKOKE
SCOPS OWL
Africa

The number of trees in the Sokoke Forest has been dwindling for decades. Forests and woodlands outside the reserve have been cleared away. Much of the Sokoke has been cleared, both legally and illegally. Three sawmills once operated in the area but shut down when the supply of trees fell below a profitable level. Some parts of the forest have been cleared to make room for plantations of exotic trees. Other portions, particularly around the fringes, have been cleared to make space for agriculture. Poor soil and sparse rainfall in certain areas make traditional agriculture very risky. Still, people continue to cut the trees.

In the mid-1970s ornithologists estimated that as many as 1,500 breeding pairs of Sokoke scops owls still inhabited the Sokoke Forest. That estimate fell to about 1,000 pairs a decade later, and remains the same at the close of the 1990s. A smaller population (numbers unknown) is thought to exist in the East Usambara Mountains in Tanzania. The Kenyan government has designated a nature reserve within the Sokoke Forest, but it covers only 16½ square miles (43 square kilometers). Trees cannot be legally cut within the nature reserve. However, the government's forestry officials are not adequately supported, either with manpower or funding, and cannot protect the entire area. The Sokoke scops owl is included in CITES, and Kenya has signed the treaty. Sadly, agreement on paper concerning international trade in an endangered species means little to a species suffering habitat loss.

Larger habitat needed

Ornithologists recommended expanding the nature reserve to include more habitat for this owl and phasing out tree cutting within the Sokoke Forest. New plantations have been proposed for those areas that have already been cut, to provide local people with the firewood and fencing materials they need.

Long-term funding for forest conservation programs is in danger of being withdrawn. Without adequate measures to protect the Sokoke scops owl's habitat, this species will disappear.

People will then have neither the owl nor the trees. A little restraint and planning for future needs could allow people to produce sufficient wood and preserve the owl in their forests.

Kevin Cook

Noisy Scrub-bird
(Atrichornis clamosus)

ESA: Endangered
IUCN: Vulnerable

Class: Aves
Order: Passeriformes
Family: Atrichornithidae
Length: 8–8¼ in. (20–21 cm)
Weight: 1¼–2 oz. (34–54 g)
Clutch size: 1 egg
Incubation: 36–38 days
Diet: Insects, frogs, and lizards
Habitat: Forests and shrublands
Range: Southwestern Australia

A LITTLE FIRE CAN make a bird's habitat, but a lot of fire can destroy it. No bird proves this fact more than does the noisy scrub-bird of Australia.

The noisy scrub-bird belongs to a family that contains just two songbird species. Its cousin, the rufous scrub-bird (*Atrichornis rufescens*), lives in small but protected populations in eastern Australia. The noisy scrub-bird historically inhabited shrublands and forests from Perth to Albany in Western Australia. It was first observed in 1842. The last live noisy scrub-bird was seen 47 years later in 1889. Ornithologists feared the peculiar little bird had become extinct, and in 1949 this belief was finalized with a monument to its passing.

Remarkably, in 1961 a single male noisy scrub-bird was discovered as it sang. A nest was found in 1963. Surveys were undertaken, but the noisy scrub-bird was not found anywhere else in its historic range. The only surviving birds occupied a small patch of coastal shrubland habitat on Mount Gardner, 25 miles (40 kilometers) east of Albany.

The noisy scrub-bird uses several different plant communities. It occurs in dense shrublands, called heath, by the Australians and British. Short woody shrubs dominate the heath and, although the noisy scrub-bird lives there, it is poor habitat. No scrub-bird has ever been found nesting in the heath. It also inhabits, but does not nest in, thicket, a community of taller shrubs. The noisy scrub-bird occasionally nests in forests composed of trees under 16½ feet (5 meters) high, but its preferred habitat is forests of taller trees. The undergrowth can be very dense in these forests.

Mostly terrestrial, the scrub-bird spends most of its time searching for food in the forest litter. Rather than flying, it runs quickly through dense vegetation. It builds its nests in low shrubs and travels through the shrubbery with ease.

Royalty to the rescue

The presence of the noisy scrub-bird in poor habitat suggests that the available good habitat is already full. After decades of decline and near extinction, the noisy scrub-bird has enjoyed a small but steady recovery since the 1970s. Only 45 singing males were counted in 1970, but 157 were heard on surveys in 1985. The 1990 population was estimated at well over 300 birds, rising to 400 by 1993. This apparent recovery followed what could have been a disaster. Plans were in place for a new town to be built in the middle of the area where the noisy scrub-bird survived. During a visit to Western Australia, Britain's Prince

Philip encouraged the authorities and citizens of the area to reconsider their plans. Rather than a new town, an 11,600-acre (4,640-hectare) sanctuary was established. Two Peoples Bay Nature Reserve now harbors the largest population of scrub-birds, but this is not the bird's only population.

Beginning in 1983, Australian wildlife authorities trapped noisy scrub-birds to move them. They used techniques perfected by New Zealand ornithologists working to recover the Chatham Island robin (*Petroica traversi*). Mount Manypeaks was chosen as the site for the releases. Only 7½ miles (12 kilometers) from the population at Mount Gardner, Manypeaks offered suitable habitat close to the existing population. Thirty-two noisy scrub-birds had been moved by 1985, and 14 males had established territories. Having at least two populations, more if possible, is an essential strategy for protecting endangered species.

Ornithologists believe the noisy scrub bird evolved in the shrubby border between forests and swamps. Even today, the noisy scrub-bird selects territory that borders streams or certain kinds of wetlands. Perhaps as the climate changed over the centuries, habitat became more scarce and the noisy scrub-bird naturally declined. Some researchers fault the aborigines' practice of burning the land. Occasional fires keep burnable materials such as dead wood and leaves from accumulating. Fires also create a mosaic, or patchwork, of different kinds and ages of plants in the plant communities. Research indicates that a burned area requires four to ten years of new growth before it is suitable for the noisy scrub-bird. Some parcels of land have not been burned in 50 years and still

A brown-on-brown bird, the noisy scrub-bird wears fine, dark brown bars on a lighter brown background from its forehead to the tip of its tail.

harbor the scrub-bird. Fire, therefore, can improve habitat for the noisy scrub-bird. But modern settlers changed the pattern of fire activity.

Britain claimed Australia as a colony and opened the island continent to European immigration in the late 1700s, and settlers converted the natural landscape to agricultural uses. They cleared shrublands and forests to plant crops and developed pasture for livestock. Fire became a tool for setting back the regrowth of shrubs and stimulating plants useful to cattle and sheep. The burning may have destroyed the habitat needed by the noisy scrub-bird. Most likely, the burning destroyed the accumulation of litter in which the noisy scrub-bird finds its food.

Plans for protecting the noisy scrub-bird do not exclude fire as a way to maintain habitat, but the plans do call for controlling what habitat is burned and when.

The noisy scrub-bird probably survived in the Mount Gardner area because there are natural rock formations that interrupt the landscape. These rock formations prevented local fires from spreading and left pockets of suitable habitat unburned for decades. The poor soil and rugged landscape discouraged agriculture.

The noisy scrub-bird has helped ornithologists understand about the anatomy and behavior of songbirds For science as well as ethics, it is important that the habitat of the noisy scrub-bird be allowed to continue.

Kevin Cook

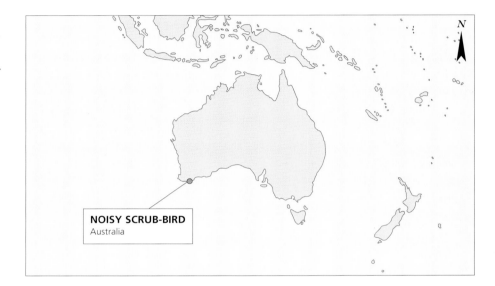

NOISY SCRUB-BIRD
Australia

SCRUBFOWLS

Class: Aves

Order: Galliformes

Family: Megapodiidae

Scrubfowls learned in ancient times to use natural processes for warming their eggs. Embryos—the young birds developing inside their eggs—need constant heat to develop properly. Incubation is the application of heat to an egg. Most parent birds use their own bodies to provide that vital heat to the egg.

However, the scrubfowls and their relatives do not. They use solar radiation, volcanic steam, and compost to provide the necessary heat for the egg.

The family Megapodiidae includes 13 species in seven genera. Birds in the family are generally known as megapodes, which means "large feet." They closely resemble each other and form a natural grouping as a family. In many respects they also resemble pheasants and chickens, so the family is placed in the order Galliformes. Their most unifying trait may be their unique method of incubation.

All the megapodes bury their eggs. Some bury the eggs in loose sand, some in soil, some in special mounds. At least one species lays its eggs in rock fissures, where they are warmed by volcanic steam. Those species that lay in mounds make the largest nests of any bird, measuring up to 32 feet (11 meters) across and 16 feet (5 meters) high.

Such huge nests are not built anew each season but are added to a little each year for decades. The males scratch vegetation into a heap and onto the mound. Females lay their eggs, one per hole, within the mound.

The process of decay releases heat that warms the eggs buried within the mound. Males guard the nest mound and monitor the heat. They take mound material into their mouths to sense the heat level. If it is too cool, they heap up more nest debris. If it is too hot, they scrape some off.

Scrubfowls do not work so hard. They bury their eggs and leave them. Their nesting habits have left them vulnerable, and some of them are suffering population losses.

Polynesian Scrubfowl

(Megapodius pritchardii)

IUCN: Endangered

Length: 15 in. (38.1 cm)
Weight: Unknown
Clutch size: 1–12 eggs
Incubation: Probably 2–3 months
Diet: Fruits, seeds, insects
Habitat: Forest
Range: Niuafo'ou Island, southwestern Pacific Ocean

MILLIONS OF YEARS ago, enormous forces pushed molten rock through holes in the ocean's floor. Before the energy was spent, a mountain had formed. Its top peeked above the ocean's surface. From the day of its birth, the island was set upon by other forces. Wind and waves immediately began the tedious process of erosion. Bits of plants drifting on the waves and seeds floating in the air settled on the island and created a garden where none had been before. Slowly, century by century, millennium by millennium, birds and insects arrived. One of them was a chickenlike bird. One day, people found the island. Eventually, the island became known as Niuafo'ou and the bird was named the Polynesian scrubfowl.

Niuafo'ou is just one of 169 islands in the Kingdom of Tonga. People live on only a fourth of the islands in this kingdom. The islands were originally settled by Melanesians spreading eastward into the Pacific Ocean. Dutch sailors discovered the Tongan islands in the 1600s. Other Europeans also visited them.

These islands follow a roughly north-to-south alignment south of Samoa, east of the Fiji Islands, and west of the Cook Islands. After much political strife throughout the 1800s, Tonga came under British control in 1900, but it was never actually settled as a British colony.

Independence was granted in 1970, and Tonga remains a part of the British Commonwealth. Just over 100,000 people live in Tonga, 20,000 of them on the main island of Nuku'alofa. Tourism, coconuts, and bananas provide the primary livelihood for most of the citizens around the kingdom.

A circular island, Niuafo'ou covers 13½ square miles (35 square kilometers). In the early 1970s only 800 people lived there. Recent lava fields cover a small portion of the island, and that area does not support Polynesian scrubfowls. The human settlements require a little more habitat. One researcher in the early 1970s suggested the population might exceed 2,000 and that the population was at its maximum level for the size of the island. Nothing in his report indicated how he arrived at that estimate. The population is now estimated to be less than 1,000 individuals. Feral house cats (*Felis sylvestris*) and egg-collectors currently pose the greatest hazards to the scrubfowl.

No natural predators

The Polynesian scrubfowl and its relatives evolved on islands that were free of significant predators. Niuafo'ou has no native snakes, lizards, or mammals capable of eating an egg or chick. The scrubfowl found an ingenious way to lay its eggs and keep them warm without having to attend to them. It tunnels into soil of fine, crushed lava, lays its eggs, then buries them. Two possibilities explain the habit. The fine black particles absorb the heat of the

Like many tropical species, the Polynesian scrubfowl's severest threat is its own isolated island range.

1247

sun to keep the eggs warm, and heat from volcanic vents can accomplish the same thing. Most ornithologists accept the volcanic heat explanation.

Eggs laid in tunnels

Only the females excavate the tunnels. They apparently lay one egg each day they visit the tunnel, but up to a dozen eggs may eventually be laid in a single tunnel. Such a high number of eggs may be from more than one female laying in the same tunnel. The embryos take many weeks to develop, perhaps as long as three months. After hatching, the little birds claw their way to the surface. They can fly within hours, but need several days to learn how to find food. They are on their own from the day their egg is laid, and they have no parental guidance once they hatch.

These scrubfowl tunnels are easy to find and people, unfortunately, have developed a taste for scrubfowl eggs. The birds lay year-round, so the supply is fairly constant. Thankfully, Niuafo'ou is a rugged island, and many of the areas where the scrubfowls bury their eggs are extremely difficult, if not impossible, for people to reach.

But where people cannot go, cats often can. Young scrubfowls are vulnerable to cats. Egg-collecting is illegal, but the laws are not strictly enforced.

The Polynesian scrubfowl is a plain bird, uniformly gray about the body with brownish wings. A small crest gives the head a squarish look. The golden yellow toe and foot are very large and stout. The bird lives throughout the island, but only a few sites are suitable for nesting. If the human

or cat populations grow much beyond 1990 levels, the Polynesian scrubfowl could be seriously jeopardized. To help save this bird, eggs and chicks have been placed on the predator-free islands of Late and Fonualei.

Sula Scrubfowl
(Megapodius bernsteinii)

IUCN: Lower risk

Length: Probably 15–17 in. (38.1–43.2 cm)
Weight: Unknown
Clutch size: Unknown
Diet: Probably fruits, seeds, and insects as in related species
Habitat: Forests
Range: Banggai and Sula Islands of Indonesia

THOUSANDS OF ISLANDS and islets make up the East Indian nation of Indonesia. Islands are places that always present the opportunity for isolation. However, in turn, isolation offers the potential for an organism to specialize—and specialization can lead to new species.

The dusky scrubfowl (*Megapodius freycinet*) poses an interesting challenge for ornithologists. The bird is either a very widespread species through northern Australia, Indonesia, and many Pacific islands, or it is one in a complex of species that long ago began specializing on the islands of this region. Traditionally, ornithologists recognized three to five species in the genus *Megapodius*. A more recent interpretation of the scrubfowl group recognizes

11 species. The Sula scrubfowl ranks among them.

According to criteria established by the Convention on International Trade in Endangered Species of Wild Fauna and Flora (CITES), a species may be regarded as extinct if not documented for 50 years. However, the cahow (*Pterodroma cahow*) was believed extinct for almost 300 years before it was rediscovered. The vital question is, who studies birds on Sula?

A rather plainly colored bird, the Sula scrubfowl is dull gray-brown overall. The lower back and rump are deeper brown, and the lower breast and belly take on a more rufous hue. The foot and toe are orangish red. Very little else is known about the Sula scrubfowl, other than assumptions drawn from what is known about related species. At least one published account says the Sula scrubfowl has not been seen since 1938.

Off the beaten path

The Banggai and Sula Islands lie due east of Sulawesi in the Molucca Sea. They are seldom visited by tourists or scientific investigators. In fact, considerable effort must be expended just to reach these islands. No specific recent information about the islands clarifies conditions there, but general impressions are that the islands are being heavily cut for lumber production. Severe cutting would destroy the Sula scrubfowl's feeding habitat and basic cover. The species lays its eggs in soil tunnels that would be extremely vulnerable to livestock such as pigs (*Sus scrofa*). Either domestic or feral pigs can easily sniff out the nests and root

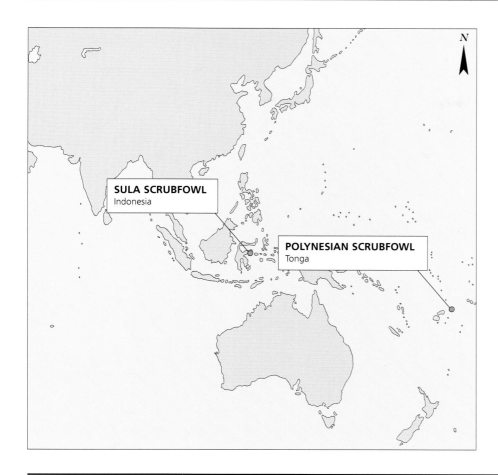

around for the eggs. House cats (*Felis sylvestris*) and dogs (*Canis familiaris*) both pose a significant threat to chicks and possibly adults. Erosion, an inevitable consequence of excessive timber cutting, could jeopardize vital nesting grounds.

Island search

These possibilities are largely speculative, but they explain why the species has not been seen in half a century. The islands are very small. Human activity such as forest cutting would not have to progress very long before the Sula scrubfowl would feel the impact. A specific search of the islands needs to be completed before a useful assessment of the scrubfowl's endangerment status can be accurately made.

Kevin Cook

Grauer's Scrub-warbler

(Bradypterus graueri)

IUCN: Vulnerable

Order: Passeriformes
Family: Muscicapidae
Subfamily: Sylviinae
Length: Unknown
Weight: Unknown
Clutch size: Unknown
Incubation: Unknown
Diet: Insects
Habitat: Montane wetlands
Range: Eastern Democratic Republic of Congo, Uganda, Rwanda, and Burundi

SWAMPS AND MARSHES can be both beautiful and ugly places. The stench of rotting vegetation and decaying animal corpses can reek strongly enough to foul the nose. Despite the aroma of decay, wetlands can offer much beauty. This beauty can be found in the color of a blossom, the glint of a dragonfly's wing, or the song of a bird. Although the Grauer's scrub-warbler's song may not be melodious, any song in a swamp can be a cheery thing.

Grauer's scrub warbler ranges between 6,232 and 8,528 feet (1,900 and 2,600 meters) in elevation. Within this altitude range, the bird occupies both shrubby swamps that are surrounded by forests, and roams over marshes far removed from forests.

The usual plants that dominate the bird's habitat include reeds (*Miscanthidium* sp.), sedges (*Cyperus* sp.), rushes (*Juncus* sp.), and mosses (*Sphagnum* sp.). The male Grauer's scrub-warbler perches above the wetland vegetation when it is singing its territorial song. It follows its song with a short display flight before returning to the safety of the plant life. When feeding, the bird picks its way among the plants and gleans insects and probably other small invertebrates from the leaves and stems.

Almost nothing is known about the natural history of the Grauer's scrub-warbler. Some ornithologists have traditionally counted the Grauer's scrub-warbler and the white-winged warbler (*Bradypterus carpalis*) as being the same species as the large rush warbler (*Bradypterus grandis*). However, they sing very differently, and the Grauer's scrub-warbler has only 10 tail feathers, while the white-winged warbler has 12. Based on these traits, the two birds are now considered distinct species.

The warblers in the genus *Bradypterus* include nine species in Africa and another nine species in Asia. These species are part of the Old World warbler subfamily (Sylviinae), which, in turn, belongs to the Old World flycatcher family (Muscicapidae). This subfamily does not include the wood warblers of the New World, but it does contain the kinglets (*Regulus* sp.), which are familiar to bird enthusiasts in the United States.

Wetland habitat

Where the species occurs, the Grauer's scrub-warbler can be quite abundant. The problem lies in the extent of its habitat. The Rugezi Swamp in Rwanda covers 21,250 acres (8,500 hectares), or about 33 square miles (86 square kilometers). The Kamiranzovu Swamp, also in Rwanda, offers only 500 acres (200 hectares) or less. Habitat in Burundi may amount to fewer than 250 acres (100 hectares). The amount of habitat available in the Democratic Republic of Congo and southwestern Uganda has not been estimated. The bird occurs only in a small strip of montane

GRAUER'S SCRUB-WARBLER
Africa

wetlands in the heart of Africa. Its total population is not known, however it is estimated that the Kamiranzovu marsh, which is now protected from drainage and gold mining pollution, has about 3,000 individuals. Curiously, it does not inhabit all the wetland habitats that appear suitable for it. The only way to solve this puzzle is to study the bird's natural history.

The Grauer's scrub-warbler has been found in the Kahuzi Swamp in Kahuzi-Biega National Park, which sits west of Lake Kivu in eastern Democratic Republic of Congo. It also occurs in Rwanda's Virunga Volcano National Park. Not all national parks are equally protected. Political rebels in Rwanda use their country's national parks as hideouts. The status of wildlife in such parks is always doubtful, and habitat outside the parks is even more in jeopardy. Rwanda's

The Grauer's scrub-warbler inhabits wetlands in the high country of eastern Democratic Republic of Congo and adjoining portions of Uganda, Rwanda, and Burundi.

Rugezi Swamp faces an uncertain future, as people eye it for plantations and croplands. Other wetlands are threatened by mining and water consumption. Grauer's scrub-warbler depends on swamps and marshes for its existence. Swamps and marshes have long been viewed as soggy wastelands that produce foul odors and disease-carrying mosquitos, but they do support enormous numbers and varieties of plants and animals.

Those who wish to use the bird's habitat for their own interests need to look at wetlands habitats in the entire region, not just within the artificial boundaries of dotted lines on maps.

Kevin Cook

SCULPINS

Class: Actinopterygii

Order: Scorpaeniformes

Family: Cottidae

While most members of the family Cottidae (sculpins) live in marine environments, the fish listed here all can be found in fresh water. Over 300 members of the family are scattered over the seas and oceans at northern latitudes, and across northern Eurasia and North America. Two species of sculpin also can be found in waters off New Zealand and Argentina in the Southern Hemisphere.

Sculpins are bottom-dwelling fish, with spines on the gill covers and fins for protection from predators. This is needed because many other fish prefer sculpins for food. In North America, trout and other salmonids are particularly fond of sculpins. In fact, trout fly fishermen tie sculpin lures to outsmart and capture their prey.

Sculpins lack an organ called the swim bladder. This organ is used to maintain neutral buoyancy in the water and minimize a fish's need to swim just to stay in place. Imagine the amount of energy that would otherwise be required for a fish to maintain its position in rushing water without such an organ. Because sculpins live on the bottom, they do not require a swim bladder. For sculpins that live in streams, this adaptation is particularly advantageous; their own weight and lack of buoyancy helps "glue" them to the bottom.

Many other river fish (for example, darters) use this same adaptation in conserving precious energy for other purposes.

Other common physical features of sculpins include a large head, high-set eyes, and large pectoral fins for better maneuverability.

Because of their preference for streams, freshwater sculpins are more likely to come in conflict with human activities than are their saltwater relatives. As streams are dammed and water is diverted, it is likely that other sculpins will become threatened or endangered. Because of their importance to the food chain and as unique creatures that offer clues to the evolutionary puzzle, sculpins deserve as much protection as people can offer.

Deepwater Sculpin

(Myoxocephalus thompsoni)

IUCN: Vulnerable

Length: 2¾ in. (7 cm)

Reproduction: Egg layer

Habitat: Bottoms of deep freshwater lakes

Range: Great Lakes and Canada

THE DEEPWATER SCULPIN can be found in a variety of freshwater environments. It lives in cold, temperate, and polar waters, and in freshwater lakes across a wide range of latitudes.

This species can be found from the Arctic Ocean to southern Canada, where it lives as far south as the Great Lakes.

Given this large range, it may seem strange that this fish is listed as vulnerable. The designation is rather misleading. At many locations populations are relatively healthy, but in Canada total numbers of this sculpin have fallen dramatically and some populations have been entirely eliminated.

Poisoned water

The reasons for this decline are not entirely clear. In the early 1900s, the deepwater sculpin was found in large numbers. Fishers on Lake Ontario at the U.S.-Canadian border considered this fish a pest because gill nets set for lake trout were consistently clogged with deepwater sculpin. Then, around the late 1950s, the sculpin's numbers began to drop substantially. Fisheries biologists speculate that the drop was caused by the widespread use of the pesticide DDT and other water pollutants that were less regulated at the time. Today it is rare that a deepwater sculpin is captured by a fisherman. While the concentrations of pesticides like DDT have fallen significantly, recovery for this fish in the southern latitudes of Canada will not be rapid. Changes in the community structure and overall ecology of these lakes, as a result of past pollution, are unlikely to reverse themselves. That means the deepwater sculpin may have to settle for a somewhat reduced natural range.

The deepwater sculpin is closely related to the fourhorn sculpin (*Myoxocephalus quadricornis*—primarily a marine species), and used to be classified under the same scientific name. The species name *quadricornis* (meaning "four horns") originally was assigned to these fishes because of the two pairs of spines on their gill covers. The deepwater sculpin has other numerous protective spines on both dorsal fins on the back and on the anal fin.

Despite its protection, the deep-water sculpin is a favorite food of the lake trout (*Salvelinus namaycush*). While defensive spines may appear to be a formidable type of protection, predators like the lake trout have learned to eat spiny fishes in a "head first" position to force the spines to flatten to the sculpin's side as it is swallowed.

The back and sides of this small fish are gray-brown with lighter tones on the belly. Additionally, the back and sides are lined with a row of saddle-like blotches. The pectoral fins just behind the gills, as well as the second dorsal fin, are quite large relative to the body, and they carry broken bands of dark pigmentation. Bands on the round-tipped tail and anal fins are less pronounced. The deep-water sculpin has a shape that is very slender, particularly toward the tail. The majority of the fish's weight is forward. The head is large, but the snout is quite pointed. The eyes of this bottom-dweller are set high on the head for good upward visibility.

In the depths

True to its name, this fish commonly lives at depths below 600 feet (183 meters), which has made the collection of information about its life history difficult. The deepwater sculpin probably spawns in summer and early fall, but some populations may spawn year-round. Females deposit large eggs and, after fertilization, one or both of the parents may guard the eggs until they hatch.

The deepwater sculpin consumes a variety of foods, including freshwater shrimp, insect larvae, and other small aquatic invertebrate animals.

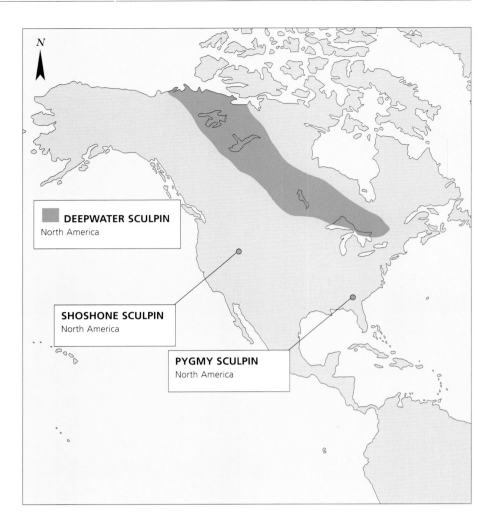

Pygmy Sculpin

(Cottus pygmaeus)

ESA: Threatened

IUCN: Critically endangered

Length: 1½ in. (4 cm)
Reproduction: Egg layer
Habitat: Spring pools and outflow
Range: Coldwater Spring, Alabama

THE SMALL AND unassuming pygmy sculpin makes its home at a single large spring in northeastern Alabama. Located in Calhoun County, Coldwater Spring produces over 30 million gallons of water per day. The spring outflow is dammed near its source, forming a large pool. Water then flows into Coldwater Creek after a 500-foot (152.5-meter) run. The spring pool and the adjacent outflow support this sculpin and its fragile existence.

Calhoun County is primarily rural in nature, and a water supply the size of Coldwater Spring is understandably viewed as a valuable resource. As a result, the spring and its nearby waterways have been modified to serve human needs. Unfortunately for the pygmy sculpin, this work destroyed or altered habitat in its limited range. This fish survives under a fragile set of circumstances. A single catastrophic event could eliminate the entire spring population. Pollution of the water supply, spring failure caused by demand on the underground water supply from nearby wells, or other artificial changes could spell the end for this species.

If the pygmy sculpin is to survive, additional modification of the spring and its waterways must be avoided. In addition, the establishment of another pygmy sculpin population at some other secure site must be a conservation priority in the near future.

True to its name, the pygmy sculpin is among the smallest of the fish in its family. It has an odd shape, with a large head relative to its body and most of its weight forward of the body's midpoint. Viewed from the side, only the large second dorsal fin on the back and the anal fin tend to offset the unbalanced appearance of the body. Typical of all sculpins, this fish has a blunt face and high-set eyes. Of the two dorsal fins, the first is by far the smallest, but it does carry defensive spines. The pectoral fins just behind the gills are quite large,

which makes the pygmy sculpin quite maneuverable when it searches for food or performs other tasks. This fish is handsomely camouflaged, with a dark face and dark vertical bars and large blotches over a light-colored background; the fins follow the characteristic coloration and patterning of the body.

Year round offspring

Because of the constant water temperature provided by Coldwater Spring, reproduction takes place all year. However, peak months appear to be from April to August. As a means to protect future offspring from predators, eggs are laid under flat rocks over a gravel bottom. Both newly hatched young and adults feed on insect larvae, adult insects, and other aquatic invertebrates, but the offspring also prey on microscopic plankton in the water column, which is a meal appropriate for their size.

With their striking coloration and markings, large heads, and high-set eyes, sculpins look unusual. They are well adapted to life on the bottom of rivers, lakes, and oceans.

Shoshone Sculpin
(Cottus greenei)

IUCN: Vulnerable

Length: 3 in. (8 cm)
Reproduction: Egg layer
Habitat: Headwaters of small spring-fed streams
Range: Hagerman Valley, Idaho

IDAHO IS A STATE not only known for potatoes, but also as the largest producer of rainbow trout for food in the United States. The southern part of Idaho, in the Snake River Valley, is a virtual fish farmer's paradise, with large quantities of cool spring water literally gushing from the valley walls. Millions of pounds of rainbow trout are produced each year at several large facilities near the towns of Twin Falls and Hagerman. The economic impact on the region is enormous.

In the midst of all this activity lies the only remaining habitat of the threatened Shoshone sculpin. Some streams within the nearby Thousand Springs area of Hagerman Valley have produced a tug-of-war between the trout producers who want to expand their operations and conservationists who are trying to save this small river fish.

Traditional trout farming, also known as aquaculture, requires enormous amounts of flowing water to maintain the large crops of fish at these facilities. This water can be obtained by diverting it from other areas or by pumping ground water sources to bring water to the surface more quickly. All of this human

demand for water makes it increasingly difficult for the Shoshone sculpin to survive. As stream diversions sap water from the area and direct it toward farming interests, this has the effect of shrinking the available habitat for the Shoshone sculpin, and competition for that habitat increases all the time.

The Shoshone sculpin is an odd-looking character, but is typical of the family Cottidae, with a large head and tapered body. This bottom dweller has a large mouth and "lips," and eyes that are set high on the head and forward. Despite having numerous protective spines on the dorsal fins on the back, on the anal fin on the belly, and on the large pectoral fins just behind the gills, this fish often becomes a meal for hungry predators such as trout. Body coloration serves to camouflage this fish; overall it is brown-gray and has darker vertical bars and stripes.

The fins are spotted and banded with dark pigment as well. The tail fin is relatively small with a rounded tip.

The life history of the Shoshone sculpin has not been well studied, but it probably spawns in the spring and consumes insects and other aquatic invertebrates that inhabit its spring-fed streams.

Given the high probability that demand on local water supplies by business interests will continue to increase, the most reasonable course of action to save the Shoshone sculpin might be to transplant this fish to a more secure part of the state.

William E. Manci

SEAHORSES

Class: Actinopterygii

Order: Syngnathiformes

Family: Syngnathidae

All seahorses belong to a single genus *Hippocampus*, which comes from two Greek words meaning "horse monster." With the head of a horse, an armor-plated body, the grasping tail of a monkey, the independently moving eyes and color-changing abilities of a chameleon, a seahorse is an unusual creature. Yet it possesses fins, breathes through gills, and has a swim bladder, thus making it a true fish. Uniquely, it is the male that becomes pregnant, fertilizing the female's eggs within his body and giving birth to as many as 1,500 live babies after a period of labor and contractions.

There are thought to be around 30 species worldwide, ranging from the tiny *Hippocampus bargibanti* at less than ¾ inch (2 centimeters), up to the giant seahorses such as *H. ingens* at almost 8 inches (20 centimeters) long.

Giant Seahorse
(Hippocampus ingens)

IUCN: Vulnerable

Length: Up to 8 in. (20 cm)
Reproduction: Egg layer
Habitat: Seabed among gorgonians and black coral
Range: Gulf of Mexico, Florida, Venezuela, and Brazil

ALSO KNOWN AS the Pacific seahorse, the giant seahorse is the only species to be found in the eastern Pacific Ocean. It is thought to have evolved into a distinct species since continental drift and its accompanying tectonics separated it from the closely related slender seahorse (*Hippocampus reidi*) after the formation of the Isthmus of Panama.

The giant seahorse deserves its name and can grow to almost 8 inches (20 centimeters) long. The rings around the body, formed from the armor-plated covering, number 11 in the trunk region and a further 39 in the tail. The head is well proportioned, with the snout taking up about half the length. The large size of this seahorse permits clear views of the tubular snout through which food is drawn with such suction that it disintegrates as it passes through. This method of breaking down food is necessary because seahorses possess no teeth. The head is adorned with prominent eye spines and an obvious long, drooping spine on each cheek. The head is topped by a high coronet. Males are distinguished from females by a keel on the front of the trunk; females often show a dark patch under the anal fin when mature.

Color change
All seahorses can change color to a greater or lesser extent. The giant seahorse may be dark red through yellow to various shades of gray and brown. It is covered with numerous small brown spots and speckled with silvery white dots, which join up to form fine streaks over most of the head, body, and tail.

Like all seahorses, the giant seahorse possesses a prehensile tail, which it uses to cling to plants.

Color is important for camouflage against the black corals and gorgonians among which the giant seahorse lives. Ambush attack is the method of capturing prey for seahorses. They cling with their prehensile tails, awaiting the tiny shrimplike creatures that make up their prey.

Even as youngsters, they possess large eyes; seahorses seem to rely upon sight for detecting prey as well as potential predators. The eyes are able to move independently, allowing them to survey their surroundings while still focusing on food.

Giant seahorses are thought to be mainly nocturnal, a possible adaptation to their large size, which would make them more obvious to predators during daylight. Although most seahorses present an unpalatable mouthful, this seahorse is known to be eaten by some tuna species.

Male gives birth

Observation of captive giant seahorses indicate that they become sexually mature at about 12 months. The male broods the eggs within the brood pouch in his body for about two weeks before giving birth to about 400 babies, each about ½ inch (1 centimeter) long. Following the birth, the male takes no further part in their care.

Like most species of seahorses worldwide, the giant seahorse is regarded as vulnerable. The major threats appear to come from an increase in shrimp fishing in the seahorse habitat when the giant seahorse becomes part of the by-catch. Giant seahorses are also dried for export to supply the trade in traditional Chinese medicine.

Kelvin Boot

GIANT SEAHORSE
North and South America

Knysna Seahorse

(Hippocampus capensis)

IUCN: Vulnerable

Length: 3 in. (8 cm)
Reproduction: Egg layer
Habitat: Estuaries and other coastal zones
Range: Southern coast of South Africa

THE KNYSNA SEAHORSE belongs to one of the most unusual families in the world, Syngnathidae, which includes pipefishes and seahorses. Most people are familiar with seahorses and their upright posture, finless prehensile (or grasping) tail, and 90-degree bend in the head. Pipefishes are long and slender like seahorses, but they swim in a horizontal position and lack the prehensile tail and bend in the head; the tip of the tail actually has a small fin.

The pipefish and the seahorse display reproductive behavior that is quite different from other fish. After eggs are laid by the female and fertilized by the male, it is the male that protects the future generation in a kangaroo-like brood pouch on its belly. Males of other species are known to protect eggs in a nest or even within their mouths, but an adaptation such as the brood pouch displayed by the syngnathids is, indeed, rare. Very few biological studies have been undertaken on seahorses. They have very good camouflage, which enables them to blend in with their surroundings; this makes them very difficult to see and study.

Pollution and exploitation

The Knysna seahorse can be found in the coastal estuaries and along the southern coastline of South Africa. Chemical pollution from cities has hurt the estuarine and coastal habitats of this fish. Deforestation is another problem. Trees stabilize soil and prevent erosion. When trees are cut and removed, the soil loses its stability and erodes into rivers. As this sediment moves downstream and ultimately into estuaries and into the ocean, it covers the clean-bottom habitat and smothers food items. This process has a detrimental effect on fish populations and radically changes the entire structure of aquatic communities.

Seahorses are globally exploited; many millions are taken from the wild for use in traditional Asian medicines and as aquarium fish and curios.

The Knysna seahorse is one of the most unusual fish on earth.

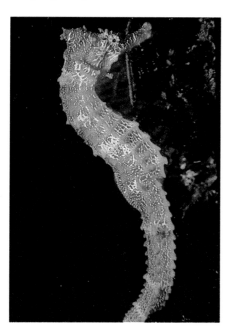

Swimming upright is no problem at all for the Knysna seahorse.

Most striking is its upright posture and its ability to seemingly "swim on its tail." This fish has a large head relative to the rest of the body and a tube-like snout. The texture of the skin is strange, consisting of a series of peaked ridges. The Knysna seahorse uses its dorsal fin for propulsion and its pectoral fins for steering. Its tail is used primarily for grasping.

William E. Manci

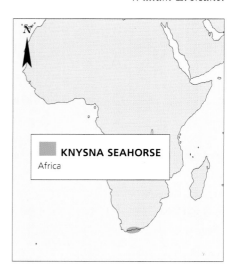

KNYSNA SEAHORSE
Africa

Slender Seahorse

(Hippocampus reidi)

IUCN: Vulnerable

Length: 6½ in. (16.5 cm)
Reproduction: Egg layer
Habitat: Seagrass beds and among gorgonians, sometimes within floating sargassum weed rafts
Range: Gulf of Mexico and off the coasts of southwestern Florida, Venezuela, and Brazil. Also recorded off Cape Hatteras, and North Carolina

ONE OF THE LARGER species of seahorse, the slender, or longsnout, seahorse is a slimmer version of the giant seahorse, *Hippocampus ingens,* from which it became separated by the formation of the Isthmus of Panama. It certainly merits the name of slender seahorse; its narrow body is characteristic, as is the long snout that occupies about half the head length.

The slender seahorse possesses 11 trunk rings and a further 35 rings around the tail. These rings have low, rounded spines. The facial spines on the cheeks and near the eyes are broad; the coronet on the head is large, low, and rounded with a convoluted texture. The spotted coloration—brown and white on a base of yellow to red—is very variable and may alter with background to enable efficient camouflage or with mood when

This slender seahorse shows its ability to change color to match its surroundings.

two individuals meet. The slender seahorse is known to pair bond in the wild; that is, males and females remain together from one year to the next and only mate with their partner, even if another suitable member of the opposite sex is available. Males appear to develop their brood pouch when about half grown and are sexually mature at about 12 months.

Life cycle

Almost nothing is known about the biology of most seahorses, and rare species like the slender seahorse are shrouded in even more mystery. They probably live for up to five years, during which time they will produce many offspring during each eight-month breeding season. Courtship in seahorses may last many hours, during which the male and female may change color, normally lightening. They grasp with their tails to a holdfast: a rock, piece of coral, or weed. Their tails become entwined as they perform a nodding dance. Upward snout-pointing appears to be the trigger for the male to flush out his brood pouch with jerking motions prior to the female inserting her ovipositor and depositing her eggs. There may be many attempts before the pair is successful and separates, the male rocking gently to settle the eggs within his body. He bathes the eggs in a placental fluid and controls its composition, altering it to be more like seawater as the eggs become ready to hatch. Gestation lasts about two weeks, and the male may give birth to as

SLENDER SEAHORSE
North and South America

many as 1,600 tiny but perfect replicas of the adult. Populations of the slender seahorse exist in the eastern Gulf of Mexico and off the coasts of southwestern Florida, North Carolina, Venezuela, and Brazil. This species is rare where it occurs and its vulnerable status might not truly reflect its scarcity. It occurs in seagrass beds, among gorgonians, and sometimes within sargassum weed rafts.

Seahorses are largely slow-moving and restricted in distribution, so they are extremely vulnerable to isolation as their habitats deteriorate and fragment. Due to the variability in color and size within species of seahorses, it is often difficult to be certain exactly what constitutes a species. There is still a question as to the exact status of some populations of the slender seahorse, and urgent study is needed to establish whether the southwestern Florida populations deserve more specific conservation status.

Kelvin Boot

SEA LIONS AND SEALS

Class: Mammalia

Order: Pinnipedia

Seals constitute a group of mammals called the pinnipeds. These mammals are semiaquatic, which means they spend time both on land and in the water. For this adaptation, pinnipeds have a body type that is a compromise between structures needed for land and those needed for the water.

All pinnipeds have a fusiform, or torpedo-shaped, body. This shape allows pinnipeds to move quickly and efficiently through the water without suffering excessive drag (any object in water experiences some drag while in motion).

Pinnipeds also have flippers instead of feet, which help propel them through the water. The ears and nose can be closed to prevent water from entering during a dive, and pinnipeds have a protective, buoyant, and warming layer of fat, or blubber. However, because pinnipeds need to come ashore to breed and bear their young, their flippers must also offer support and help them move about on land. A coat of hair protects their skin from rocks and sand abrasion.

The pinnipeds can be divided into three groups. One group, which includes the sea lions and fur seals, is notable for having external ears and a comparatively thick fur coat. The second group, which includes most other seals, does not have external ears, and their flippers have a different structure from the fur seals and sea lions. The third group contains only one species—walruses. Walruses are notable for having long upper canine tusks that are used in aggressive encounters with other walruses, as defensive weapons. The tusks are also used as aids to help them climb out of the water or to help to dig for organisms along the ocean bottom.

Fossils indicate that some of the earliest pinniped ancestors were evolving more than 35 million years ago, during the Oligocene period. Yet it has taken just a few hundred years to jeopardize this great order Pinnipedia. Ever since the colonizing of North America, seals and sea lions have been the victims of overhunting. Some of the earliest European settlers found pinnipeds to be excellent providers of fur, oil, and ivory. Hunting of these species was relentless, devastating breeding grounds and destroying millions of individuals.

The Marine Mammal Protection Act of 1972 was finally enacted by the United States government to prohibit the taking of any pinnipeds in U.S. territorial waters (with certain specific exceptions).

Steller's Sea Lion

(Eumetopias jubatus)

ESA: (eastern population) Threatened

ESA: (western population) Endangered

IUCN: Endangered

Weight: 550–2,200 lb. (250–1,000 kg)
Length: 8–10 ft. (25–30 m)
Diet: Fish, squid, mollusks, and crustaceans
Gestation period: 345 days
Longevity: Up to 30 years
Habitat: Coastal waters near rocky shores and islands
Range: Pacific Ocean from southern California up through the Bering Sea to Japan

STELLER'S SEA LION belongs to the group of eared seals from the family Otariidae, the same family that includes the California sea lion and the fur seals. All members of this species have small external ears. This feature separates them from the true, earless seals of the family Phocidae, which have only a small hole or wrinkle forming an external ear.

The Steller's sea lion, like other members of its family, has a pair of long, strong, front flippers that it uses to propel itself through the water and to lift and

The Steller's sea lion does fall prey to such predators as sharks and killer whales, but the major threat to this mammal has always come from people. Humans have hunted sea lions for centuries, and over time this has greatly reduced populations.

carry itself on land. The hind flippers have a range of motion that allows them to work almost like feet. When this action is combined with that of their powerful front flippers, sea lions can virtually "run" on land.

True seals cannot use either their fore or hind flippers well on land, and they propel themselves through the water mostly with their hind flippers.

Biggest sea lion

The Steller's sea lion is the largest of the 14 species of eared seals. Its range overlaps that of its close relative, the California sea lion (*Zalophus californianus*), but the two species are easily differentiated by size: a Steller's sea lion is up to three times the size of a California sea lion.

The Steller's sea lion has a range that extends from southern California, up the Pacific Coast to Alaska, throughout the Bering Sea, and along the coast of the former Soviet Union to the Kuril Islands and Hokkaido (Japan). The California sea lion ranges from northern Mexico up the Pacific Coast to Vancouver Island. A subspecies of the California sea lion from the Sea of Japan may now be extinct.

An adult male Steller's sea lion looks dramatically different from an adult female. For one thing, the male outweighs the female by a ratio of almost three to one; a female averages about 660 pounds (300 kilograms), while a male might weigh more than a ton (1,000 kilograms).

Although the female has a rather sleek, streamlined look, the male has a massive neck and a fairly thick mane of hair around the neck area. This which tends

to dramatize the size difference. This sexual dimorphism, or physical difference between the sexes, holds true to some extent for all the species of eared seals.

The dramatic size difference between the male and female of this species is related to their mating behavior. Males arrive at mating beaches before the females and spend the next few months fighting each other for territories—and for rights to the females, once they arrive.

The thick neck and mane is used both for display and as the focus of attack during the occasional but vicious fights between males. The skin of the neck is thick enough to provide a measure of protection from the bites of rivals.

After mating territories are established, the resulting male-to-female ratio is about 20 females for each successful territorial male. Therefore, there is a strong evolutionary compulsion for males to grow as large as possible. Small males cannot hold a territory and, therefore, cannot mate with a large number of females. Small males must rely on chance encounters with females as they move up and down the beaches because they are constantly being harassed by larger males.

Unexplained decline

Steller's sea lions are preyed upon by great white sharks and killer whales. However, as with other seal species, the major cause of decline for the Steller's sea lion has been hunting by humans. The native people of the Pacific coasts of North America and Asia have captured Steller's sea lions for centuries without

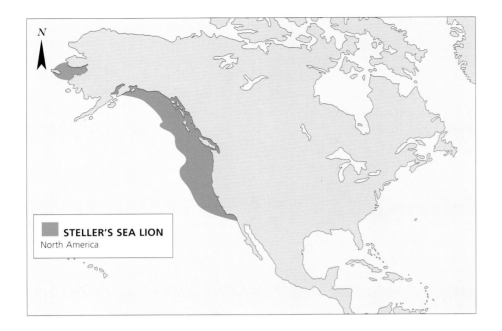

STELLER'S SEA LION
North America

Guadalupe Fur Seal

(Arctocephalus townsendi)

ESA: Threatened

IUCN: Vulnerable

Weight: 110–300 lb. (50–140 kg)
Length: 4–6½ ft. (12–20 m)
Diet: Squid and fish
Gestation period: 330–365 days
Longevity: Unknown
Habitat: Coastal waters near rocky coasts or cliffs
Range: Guadalupe Island and neighboring islands off the west coast of Mexico

adversely affecting the population, but the intensive harvesting that occurred during the 19th century, when seals were hunted for their oil, meat, and fur, severely diminished the numbers of Steller's sea lions on both coasts. Populations seemed to recover over much of the original range of the sea lion during the early 1900s, but recent declines have been serious enough to warrant the classification of this species as endangered.

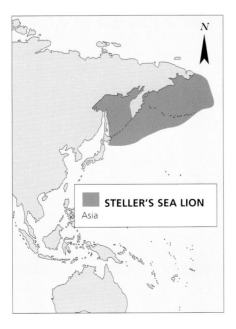

STELLER'S SEA LION
Asia

A number of causes have been suggested to explain the recent decline of Steller's sea lions, including entanglement with fishing nets and persecution by fishers (whose catch is often raided by sea lions). Disease also may be a contributing factor. Another culprit may be the decline in fish stocks, such as various species of Pacific salmon, on which the Steller's sea lion depends for food.

Diminished numbers

The Steller's sea lion population has now declined to only a third of what it was 30 years ago. While it is still not known exactly what has caused the Steller's sea lion population to crash, it is important to determine which cause is having the greatest impact, and whether the cause is the same for all populations of this sea lion. Otherwise, it may be necessary to take a case-by-case approach to conservation management of this species. The most important step people can take is to increase their awareness of these wonderful creatures.

THE GUADALUPE FUR seals are members of the eared seal family (Otariidae). The fur seals and sea lions that make up this group have small external ears, separating them from the true, or earless, seals of the family Phocidae. True seals have only a small hole or wrinkle where an external ear would be positioned.

Sea lions and fur seals also have long, strong, front flippers that are excellent for both swimming swiftly in water and running on land.

Like the other species of fur seals, the Guadalupe fur seal has a layer of underfur, as well as the outer guard hairs found in all seals. The guard hairs help protect the seal when it is moving along on the sharp rocks of its

The Guadalupe seal was once found on a number of islands off the coast of southern California, but today the only known breeding colony is found on the island from which this mammal gets its name: Guadalupe Island.

coastal home, and the undercoat helps to keep the skin dry by trapping bubbles of air.

Northern-southern seal

The Guadalupe fur seal belongs to the group of eight species known as the southern fur seals. Unlike all other fur seals except for the Juan Fernandez fur seal (*Arctocephalus philipii*) from off the coast of Chile, the Guadalupe fur seal has a much longer and sharper snout. The Guadalupe fur seal is also the most northern seal in this group—most others are found to the south of the equator. Guadalupe Island, the main location where this seal is found, is approximately 150 miles (250 kilometers) off the coast of southern California.

The Guadalupe fur seal was once found on a number of islands around this area, and even today may wander widely at sea, occasionally showing up on the California coast or on the Channel Islands. However, most of the population today is limited to Guadalupe Island.

The Guadalupe fur seals are one of the few seals to spend all year based at a single site on land. Males are strongly territorial and defend both their area and a small group of females from other males.

The seals tend to spend their time on rocky shorelines in and around cliffs and caves, rather than on smooth sandy beaches.

It seems probable that this behavior may have evolved as a means of avoiding the extensive hunting that once almost destroyed their populations. It is not likely that these fur seals would naturally prefer inaccessible shorelines.

Fur coats

Most species of pinnipeds have coexisted with humans for thousands of years. They were hunted in small numbers by coastal people who often could depend on just a few of these large mammals to provide adequate meat, hides, and bones for tools. However, all pinnipeds suffered greatly at the hands of commercial hunters during the 1800s. The interest in seal fur, as well as the need for oil for lamps, created a massive seal-hunting industry. Since seals tend to congregate in large numbers on land or ice, especially during the breeding season, and since they cannot move quickly, it was fairly simple for a group of sealers to kill thousands of seals in one trip.

All eight species of southern fur seals were severely affected by commercial seal hunting during the 1800s. The Galapagos fur seal (*Arctocephalus galapagoensis*), found only on the Galapagos Islands, was thought to have been driven to extinction during this time, however, it still survives today, as was the Juan Fernandez fur seal. Other species of southern fur seals suffered local extinctions as sealers moved from one breeding area to another.

Once thought to number up to about 100,000 animals, the Guadalupe fur seal was another victim of overhunting for seal fur and meat. Extremely heavy exploitation by professional sealers wiped out most of these fur seals in only a few decades. By 1920 the Guadalupe fur seal was thought to be extinct, and it was not until 1954 that a few seals were again discovered on Guadalupe Island. Most other southern fur seal species have recovered in suitable numbers so that they are no longer in danger of extinction, and the Guadalupe fur seal has managed to survive. It is estimated that the present population ranges from 3,000 to 6,000 seals.

Protection

Although the Guadalupe fur seal population is legally protected from hunting and disturbance, and even appears to be recovering its numbers slowly, there are still threats to its existence.

Probably the biggest threat to the seal is oil and gas exploration and drilling along the coast of California and Mexico. This present a potential hazard in terms of habitat disturbance and destruction, should a major leak or spill occur near the seal's range. Also, excessive activity around the breeding grounds may lead to female seals abandoning their young.

The population of the Guadalupe fur seal is so low and so localized that any major disaster such as a large oil spill could essentially wipe out the species. Careful consideration should be given to any new offshore oil projects, especially those closest to this fur seal's breeding ground.

Oil can be found in many areas of the world, but this species is irreplaceable.

GUADALUPE FUR SEAL
North America

Juan Fernandez Fur Seal

(Arctocephalus philippii)

IUCN: Vulnerable

Weight: 110–300 lb. (50–140 kg)
Length: 4–6½ ft. (1.2–2 m)
Diet: Fish, cephalopods, and crustaceans
Gestation period: Probably 352 days
Longevity: Unknown
Habitat: Coastal waters near rocky coasts or cliffs
Range: Islands off the Pacific coast of Chile

THE JUAN FERNANDEZ fur seal is another member of the eared seals of the family (Otariidae). All seals have the typical mammalian internal ear structure, and their hearing is excellent. However, eared seals, such as fur seals and sea lions, also have an external ear that earless seals lack.

The Juan Fernandez fur seal belongs to a group of eight southern fur seals. It is probably most closely related to the rare Guadalupe fur seal (*Arctocephalus townsendi*), from the coast of California, with whom it shares a characteristic long snout. Like other members of its family, the Juan Fernandez fur seal shows a marked difference in size between the sexes, with the males frequently reaching three times the size of females. The males fight each other for territories and harems of females. All fur seals have a layer of underfur, as well as the outer guard hairs found in all seals. Their thick coat of fur is what caused the Juan

Fernandez fur seal to be driven almost to extinction.

The Juan Fernandez fur seal is found only on a few small islands off the coast of central and northern Chile—specifically, Juan Fernandez, San Felix, and San Ambrosio Islands. These islands are approximately 400 miles (600 kilometers) from mainland Chile. Here the seal frequently wanders out into the cold Humboldt current that runs from the Antarctic up along the Pacific coast of South America. This current is an extremely fertile hunting ground for seals, because the mixing of cold and warm water causes an upwelling that brings nutrients to the surface. This mixing creates an explosion of marine life that provides the seals with an abundant supply of fish and squid. The Humboldt current can sometimes be unpredictable, however. An atmospheric event called El Niño can affect the Humboldt. El Niño results when a change in the direction of Earth's jet stream changes the direction and flow of ocean currents. One result of an El Niño is that an area once awash with the food supply from the Humboldt current's cold waters may suddenly change to warm, unproductive waters. While periodic fluctuations in ocean currents may cause brief declines in seal populations, they do not present a real hazard unless other factors are also acting to depress numbers. For this seal, that pressure has come from human activities.

There were once probably more than 4 million Juan Fernandez fur seals around the archipelago. The isolation of these islands provided the fur

JUAN FERNANDEZ FUR SEAL
South America

seals with a measure of protection. However, the uncontrolled hunting of seals during the 1800s led seal hunters to search out isolated seal populations. Sealers found and almost destroyed the Juan Fernandez fur seal population. The isolation of the fur seals' islands meant there was no place to which they could escape. By the mid-1800s, the slaughter was so intensive that this species was considered to be extinct.

It was not until 1965 that the few surviving members of the Juan Fernandez fur seal were discovered. Protection by the Chilean government and the creation of the Juan Fernandez National Park gave the seal an opportunity to revive, and by the mid-1980s the population was about 6,000 individuals. Between 1990 and 1991 the population rose to about 12,000 individuals. However, because the islands are such a distance from the mainland, active protection of the seals is difficult, and poaching still happens. Disturbance of the seal's breeding grounds by fishers is also a hazard. Another problem is discarded plastic waste, which can wrap round a seal's neck and slowly strangle it, or prevent it feeding so that it starves to death.

Hawaiian Monk Seal

(Monachus schauinslandi)

ESA: Endangered

IUCN: Endangered

Weight: 375–600 lb. (170–270 kg)
Length: 6½–7½ ft. (20–23 m)
Diet: Fish, cephalopods, and crustaceans
Longevity: 20–25 years
Habitat: Shallow water near small islands
Range: Leeward and other western Hawaiian Islands

A NUMBER OF taxonomists believe that the Hawaiian monk seal is different enough to warrant being placed in its own genus, separate from the two other monk seals.

Various skeletal features of the Hawaiian monk seal resemble certain primitive seals. This suggests that the Hawaiian monk seal may have branched off from other monk seals as long ago as 14 million years, when there was no land bridge in Central America separating the Atlantic from the Pacific Ocean. The other monk seal species are found in the Atlantic and adjacent waters, and this strongly suggests a long period of isolation for the Hawaiian species.

Hawaiian monk seals have thick blubber like their northern seal cousins. Since they live in much more temperate waters, they need to find ways to remain cool. They often choose to lie close to the water or in wet sand, or they find beaches near cliffs, where the shade can protect them from the midday sun.

Hawaiian monk seals have a fairly unusual breeding system for pinnipeds. Although the females frequently lie together on shore in fairly large congregations like other seal species, the males do not develop specific territories or harems. This is because the warm climate allows for a long breeding season, and at any one time only a few females are prepared to mate. Males tend to wander in search of females that are in estrus, and compete over these individual females instead of over a group of females or a piece of shoreline.

The females tend to be somewhat larger than the males, which is the reverse of most other species of seal. Another interesting behavior of these seals is that there appears to be a surprising amount of foster care among females; they do not seem to mind nursing other females' pups as well as their own.

Extinct cousin

Perhaps the saddest story in human-seal interactions involves the West Indian or Caribbean monk seal (*Monachus tropicalis*). Apparently this species was once common over a wide area of the Caribbean basin from Florida to Central America. It came ashore on isolated coasts and on the many islands to breed. However, this species was hunted relentlessly during the last 200 years for both its meat and fur and because it was viewed as a competitor by fishermen. The last known member of this species was taken in the early 1950s, and the animal is now listed as extinct. At this point in time, the Caribbean monk seal is the only seal to have been driven to extinction by humans.

Unfortunately, the Hawaiian monk seal may soon by following in its Caribbean cousin's footsteps. A 1987 census determined

The Hawaiian monk seal, unlike the Mediterranean monk seal, tends to use sandy beaches for breeding grounds.

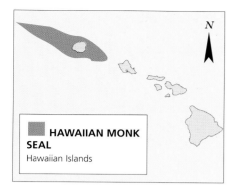

HAWAIIAN MONK SEAL
Hawaiian Islands

that that there were 500 to 1,500 of these seals, however, the population is currently estimated at 1,300 to 1,400 individuals. Between 1958 to 1996 the number of seals counted on beaches declined by 60 percent.

This species was probably once extremely common on all the Hawaiian islands. The range of islands and atolls where they were found stretches for over 1,550 miles (2,500 kilometers). The threats to this seal are female seal mortality due to mobbing by males in breeding areas; entanglement in discarded fishing gear; incidental catch by fishers, disease, and attacks by sharks.

When the Polynesian people first came to the islands some 2,000 years ago they drove the seals from the larger islands as permanent human settlements were developed. However, it was not until commercial hunting began in the early 1800s that the population of Hawaiian monk seals began to be put at serious risk. The hunting pressure was so intense that the seal was thought to have been driven to extinction by 1824. A few did survive on the western islands and atolls of the Hawaiian chain.

World War II produced more problems for the few remaining seals, as military installations were built on the more isolated islands that had once provided a safe refuge for the seals.

Monk seals do not adapt well to the presence of humans, and pups are frequently abandoned for long periods if the mothers are disturbed, leading to pup mortality from starvation. Since many of these islands were heavily used by the military during World War II, the population of seals suffered another setback. A number of monk seals have also died from the disease ciguatera, outbreaks of which have been linked to disturbed coral reefs.

Benign intervention

A large proportion of the seal's range was made into a national wildlife refuge in 1940, and when the war ended much of the activity around the western islands decreased. Further protection was afforded to the area when it was named a Research Natural Area in 1967. This has limited access to the more remote areas where the seals live and breed. Unfortunately, the Hawaiian monk seal has an extremely low rate of reproduction, and pup mortality is fairly high even under the best conditions.

This seal is listed under Appendix I of CITES. Government and environmental groups are closely monitoring the remaining breeding colonies, and management plans are being developed to help this seal increase its numbers.

Coastal development on the eastern islands make it unlikely that the seals will be able to recolonize them, but if the breeding colonies on the western islands are left undisturbed, there is a chance that they will manage to survive.

Mediterranean Monk Seal
(Monachus monachus)

ESA: Endangered

IUCN: Critically endangered

Weight: 550–900 lb. (250–400 kg)
Length: 7½–9 ft. (23–27.5 m)
Diet: Fish and octopus
Gestation period: 330 days
Longevity: More than 20 years
Habitat: Coastal waters near small rocky islands
Range: Mediterranean and Aegean Seas, Madeira, and Atlantic coast of northwest Africa

ORIGINALLY DESCRIBED in works by Plato, Homer, and Aristotle, the Mediterranean monk seal may well have the longest written history of any of the pinnipeds. The name monk seal does not refer to a hood or cowl like a monk might wear (a separate species, the hooded seal, has an inflatable nasal cavity in the males that earns it that name). It refers instead to the coloration of these seals, which is a dull gray or brown, colors that resemble the robes of a monk.

The Mediterranean monk seal is a member of the family Phocidae, which are also called the true or earless seals. Unlike the other members of the order Pinnipedia (the Otariidae or eared seals), phocids have only small openings and no external structure to their ears.

However, Mediterranean monk seals are perfectly capable

of hearing, having the same basic internal ear structure as the otariids and other mammals.

Another difference between the earless and eared seals is the structure and function of the flippers. Earless seals mainly use their hind flippers to propel themselves through the water. They have smaller front flippers than the eared seals, which use their large front flippers as oars to swim. Because the front flippers of earless seals are weak and their strong, fluke-like hind flippers are clumsy out of water, these seals are much less mobile on land than their eared cousins. Earless seals are unable to support themselves well with their front flippers and must move with a wiggling motion.

Historic cohabitation

The Mediterranean monk seal is thought to have once occured throughout the Mediterranean Sea, occupying beaches that had extensive cliffs or other protection from predators. However, human interference and hunting restricted Mediterranean monk seals to living on inaccessible rocky islands. Luckily, the range of this seal encompassed an area bursting with tiny barren islands, so despite the heavy use of this area by humans for thousands of years, the seal managed to survive, if not prosper.

Unfortunately, increased tourism, fishing, and pollution have driven this seal from the coasts of France and Spain, as well as from much of the coastline of the Middle East. There now appear to be only two major populations of Mediterranean monk seals, one in the eastern Mediterranean, and one off the coast of the west-

ern Sahara at the Côte des Phoques (Bay of Seals). In 1997 the western Sahara population was reduced by more than 60 percent, although scientists are not sure what caused this decline.

Historically, the largest population has existed around Greece, but there may now be less than 200 seals in that area. The world population is estimated at 300 to 400 individuals. The range of this seal involves the borders of at least ten countries, and international cooperation will be needed to help save it from extinction.

Uncertain future

The breeding habitat for the monk seal is the deep caves that riddle the tiny islands of the Mediterranean. These caves often have underwater entrances. Here the seals are safe from human persecution and disturbance. Unfortunately, this is not always a safe location to raise a pup, and many pups may drown when storms flood the caves. The monk seals do not breed every year and produce only one pup at a time, so the population is very slow to recover.

Another major problem associated with the decline of this seal is the breakup of the population into small, separated, or relic, groups. This separation makes it more difficult for adult seals to find breeding partners and the chance of inbreeding is thus increased. Inbreeding can lower an animal's ability to fight disease or adapt to changes in the environment.

Water pollution

Semiaquatic animals are strongly affected by water pollution, and the Mediterranean monk seal is no exception. Many European,

North African, and Middle Eastern countries are using the Mediterranean as a drainage catchment (or, more bluntly, a sewer). Laws concerning sewage, pesticides, and pollutants from agriculture and industry vary among these countries. Many of them purposefully dump wastes or do nothing to prevent the runoff of pollutants into rivers emptying into the Mediterranean.

There have also been a number of large oil spills that have severely affected coastlines along the Mediterranean. Areas of this sea have become comparatively barren of life from the damaging affects of pollution, and this has had an affect on the monk seals, that depend on the fish and other marine life for food.

A number of dead and sick monk seals were found in 1991 during a morbillivirus epidemic that killed hundreds of dolphins in the Mediterranean. This disease has also killed thousands of harbor and gray seals in Europe in the past few years. It has been suggested that the disease is linked to water pollution, which can increase an animal's suscep-

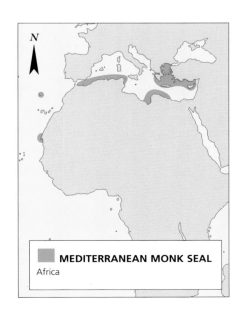

MEDITERRANEAN MONK SEAL
Africa

tibility to disease by harming their immune system.

While a direct link between pollution and morbillivirus outbreaks has yet to be proven, there is no argument that the Mediterranean has become extremely polluted and that pollution is seriously affecting a wide spectrum of species in the sea.

There is no doubt that a severe morbillivirus outbreak affecting the few surviving Mediterranean monk seal populations would threaten the species as a whole.

The fishing threat

The fishing industry also threatens the Mediterranean monk seal's survival in four different ways. Overfishing throughout the Mediterranean has combined with the effects of pollution to deplete fish stocks that this monk seal depends on for food. The heavy fishing means that many areas that this shy seal still inhabits are visited regularly by fishers, and the disturbance they cause can make the seals abandon an area. If they are nursing, female seals may even abandon their young. Monk seals also occasionally tangle themselves in nets set by fishers and they drown.

Finally, people fishing in the area consider the monk seal as a competitor for their catch and a nuisance, and they will often kill monk seals when they find them. This attitude must be changed through reeducation, and better care must be taken of the entire ecology of the Mediterranean, if this critically endangered seal is to have any chance of surviving the decline it is now experiencing. This monk seal is listed under Appendix I of CITES.

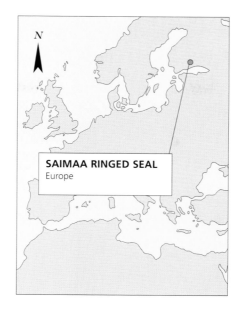

SAIMAA RINGED SEAL
Europe

Saimaa Ringed Seal
(Phoca hispida saimensis)

ESA: Endangered

IUCN: Endangered

Weight: 110–220 lb. (50–100 kg)
Length: 3½–5 ft. (10–15 m)
Diet: Fish
Gestation period: 330 days
Longevity: Over 40 years
Habitat: Freshwater lakes
Range: Lake Saimaa, Finland

Most people think seals are ocean-going creatures that are to be found around sandy beaches, rocky ocean islands, or near Arctic or Antarctic ice floes. However, a number of seal species are known to occasionally venture up freshwater rivers, and even to spend part of the year in freshwater lakes. A few seal populations even spend all year in freshwater lakes and rivers. Rarer still are the seals that are only found in fresh water.

The Lake Baikal seal may be the best known species of freshwater seal. It is found in the enormous Lake Baikal in central Russia, a deep body of water that is thought to contain 20 percent of all the unfrozen fresh water in the world. The Caspian seal lives only in the Caspian Sea, which is actually not a sea but another huge lake, although the salt content in the Caspian is higher than in normal fresh water.

The Saimaa ringed seal is another of the seals that live out their lives in a freshwater habitat. It is restricted to Lake Saimaa, a seemingly landlocked body of fresh water in Finland. Lake Saimaa is not in fact landlocked, however. A swift stream connects the lake with Lake Ladoga in Russia, where a separate subspecies of ringed seal lives. A canal also connects Lake Saimaa with the Gulf of Finland in the south. However, the Lake Saimaa seal appears to avoid the southern part of the lake, perhaps due to heavy industrialization and water pollution, and it has never been known to enter the sea.

Lake Saimaa is not an ordinary lake. It is actually a series of lakes connected by natural canals. The lake system stretches for 185 miles (300 kilometers) and covers 680 square miles (1,760 square kilometers) in total. It is an important lake in terms of providing a transportation route through the difficult terrain of central Finland. It also sustains a wide variety of commercial activities such as fishing, recreation, creating hydroelectric power, and transporting timber.

When ice covers much of the water, northern seals cut open small holes in the ice in order to breathe. They use their long claws to keep the holes from freezing over. While the ringed seal tends to spend from a few seconds to ten minutes below the surface during a dive, it can stay underwater for over an hour.

Most ringed seals found at sea build lairs of snow and ice, usually with an entrance into the water from within the lair. These lairs provide protection from the weather and from predators while the female gives birth and nurses her young. Interestingly, the Lake Saimaa ringed seal also builds lairs, but tends to do so along the shoreline, so that the lairs are partly over land. Unlike many other seal species, the ringed seal does not usually gather in large groups, even during the breeding season.

Hunting and poisoning

The ringed seal may well be the most numerically common northern seal, with numbers estimated at over six million. While hunting of the ringed seal has caused the population to decline throughout its range, the fact that the ringed seal does not gather in large groups has kept it from suffering the high mortality from hunting that other more social species have experienced.

However, some populations of this seal have undergone dramatic numerical declines. This is especially true in the Baltic Sea area, where the population of ringed seals is estimated to be less than a tenth of what it was only a century ago.

Commercial fishing has had a detrimental effect on these seals as they become entangled, and drown in the nets, or are killed by fishers who resent the competition. The accidental drowning of young seals in commercial fishing nets is thought to be the major reason for the decline of the Saimaa ringed seal.

Polluted waters

Another problem facing ringed seals throughout the Baltic is that they have been found to be suffering from the effects of pollution such as PCBs. These pollutants tend to accumulate in organisms as they move up the food chain; while only trace amounts may occur in an aquatic

Like other northern seals, the Saimaa ringed seal has a deep layer of blubber that keeps it warm even in freezing temperatures and ice-covered waters.

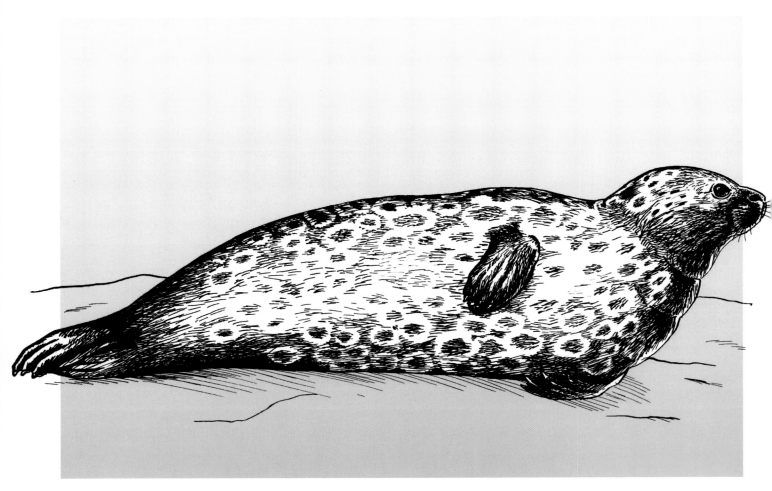

insect, a small fish that eats many of the insects will accumulate higher levels of the toxin. A larger fish that eats smaller fish will accumulate still higher levels. Seals are at or near the top of any aquatic food chain and tend to have the highest levels of these toxic compounds in their bodies. Not surprisingly, they suffer the most from the toxic effects. Ringed seals have been found to have high levels of PCBs in their system, and this is thought to be linked to a dramatic decrease in fertility among Baltic ringed seal females. Lake Saimaa ringed seals have been found to contain not only PCBs but DDT, chlor-

dane, chlorophenols, and mercury—all compounds with strong toxic effects on wildlife.

Any conservation plan for the Saimaa ringed seal will have to include the improvement of water quality in Lake Saimaa. Stricter laws concerning industrial and agricultural waste disposal and better enforcement of existing laws are needed to stop the slow poisoning of the waters. While large areas of shore along Lake Saimaa are still fairly pristine, the increase in shoreline development and the increase in recreational use of the lake is bound to adversely affect the Lake Saimaa seals, especially

during the breeding season. Luckily the seal's main breeding period, April and early May, corresponds with the times when the lake's waters are still frigid and fewer people are around.

However, the main areas where the seals breed must be pinpointed, and rules concerning the use of that part of the lake system must be made.

Of special concern is the threat from the use of commercial fish nets during the baby seals' weaning period in June.

Estimates made in the 1990s indicate that there is a population of approximately 200 seals.

Peter Zahler

SEROWS

Class: Mammalia

Order: Artiodactyla

Family: Bovidae

Subfamily: Caprinae

Tribe: Rupicaprini

Serows are small bovines that are related to goats, gorals, and chamois. They are found in parts of Asia, including China and Japan.

They range in montane forests or on ridges that have thick brush. Serows, like goats, are quite good at moving along precarious, rocky slopes—rugged terrain is no problem for them. But they are not swift-moving like their cousins the antelopes.

These animals prefer to range by themselves but can be found in small groups of less than 10 individuals.

Mating in late fall usually produces a single kid, which comes to sexual maturity after about three years.

Formosan Serow

(Capricornis swinhoei)

IUCN: Vulnerable

Weight: 75–100 lb. (34–45 kg)
Shoulder height: 28–35 in. (71–89 cm)
Diet: Leaves, shoots, and grass
Gestation period: 230–240 days
Longevity: Probably 15 years
Habitat: Mountainous regions
Range: Taiwan (formerly Formosa)

THE ISLAND OF TAIWAN is roughly the size of Connecticut and Massachusetts combined. It lies about 100 miles (161 kilometers) offshore of mainland China and is 20 million people live there. The Republic of China, as the government on Taiwan is known, claims to be the only true government of China, instead of

the People's Republic of China. This political dispute has created many diplomatic and military tensions over the decades, but none of this helps the serow.

Serows are found in China, Southeast Asia, Malaysia, Indonesia, and Japan, indicating that during the Pleistocene epoch (some three million years ago), islands such as Taiwan and Japan were part of the same land mass. The Formosan variety lives amid the mountains that run north to south along this island.

The Formosan serow is the smallest of all the serows, sporting a soft, milk chocolate-colored coat, with a yellow patch underneath its chin. It has small, recurved, shiny horns and large, alert eyes. Overall this serow has a compact appearance. Little is known about the natural history of the Formosan serow, and it is difficult to learn about island species when captive specimens are unavailable.

Serows are found in China, Southeast Asia, Malaysia, Indonesia, and Japan, but the animals found in many of these places are considered subspecies due to significant differences in their physical characteristics.

Why the decline?

Serows were once quite common over the more rugged parts of Taiwan. Due to uncontrolled hunting, their numbers have plummeted. The locals used dogs, pits, and snares to trap these animals—presumably for food, although some experts claim the flesh is not tasty. Parts of this serow have been used in folk medicine, however. Despite its small size, hunting the serow is not necessarily easy, for this little bovine will defend itself aggressively with its 6-inch (15-centimeter) horns. Aside from hunting, habitat loss is the most obvious problem. With so many people living on this island, the serow's range is shrinking at an alarming rate.

Captive population needed

There have been numerous attempts to establish captive populations in the government zoo in the capital city of Taipei, where a small group is maintained. A few animals were even sent to Japan, but none of these efforts were successful. This serow is now classified as vulnerable, which means that if hunting continues unrestricted and habitat is further degraded, this animal could easily be reclassified as endangered. More field studies are badly needed to understand and determine this bovine's needs.

There appears to be no reason why a captive population could not be successfully established, under the proper conditions.

Sumatran Serow

(Capricornis sumatraensis sumatraensis)

IUCN: Endangered

Weight: 250–300 lb. (115–140 kg)
Shoulder height: 36–42 in. (90–105 cm)
Diet: Leaves, grass, and shoots
Gestation period: 210–225 days
Longevity: 15 years
Habitat: Mountain forests
Range: Sumatra, Indonesia

SEROWS ARE FOUND over most of the mountainous portions of Southeast Asia, ranging north into China and east onto some of the Indonesian islands. The subspecies *Capricornis sumatraensis sumatraensis* is now highly endangered in part because of its isolation on just one Indonesian island, Sumatra.

Like many islands, Sumatra has seen many changes in recent decades. As the human population of this island has increased, the wildlife, from tigers to crocodiles, has been victimized by habitat destruction and hunting. The serow is no exception.

Shy and solitary

Sumatran serows, like their genetic cousins, are solitary creatures, occasionally found in pairs in the wild. They are shy and difficult to see in their natural

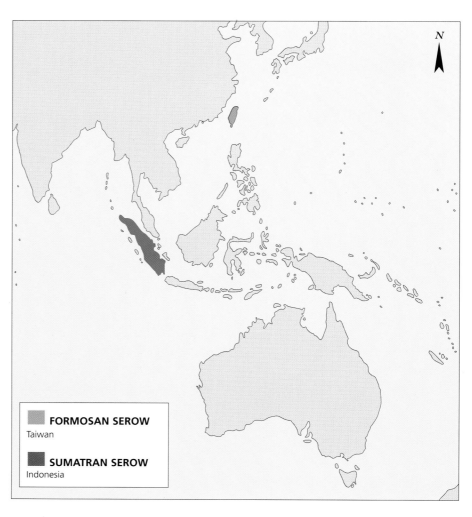

FORMOSAN SEROW
Taiwan

SUMATRAN SEROW
Indonesia

habitat. Both sexes are armed with short, recurved horns, but they primarily depend on escape from danger for survival.

The Sumatran serow is mostly black, although it does have some whitish markings. The horns are gray and are framed by ears that are both long and wide when viewed from the front. The head and shoulders stand taller than the rump.

Territorial marking

Serows use what are called preorbital glands to secrete a substance with which they mark their territory. These are located in front of the eyes on either side of the animal's face, but there are also glands in the hooves that accomplish the same thing. These bovines are generally silent by nature, but when surprised, will quickly emit a honking snort as they flee into the underbrush. Up close they have a strong, penetrating body odor.

Although the serows' natural predators are leopards and tigers, they are an endangered species due to the destruction of their habitat by people. Steady, relentless hunting is also a major problem. Serows are commonly hunted and stalked by using dogs, snares, and pitfalls. With the increasing human population on the island of Sumatra—both the indigenous population and a translocated population moved there by the Indonesian government—the hunting pressure is on the rise. No attempt to increase the serow population through captive breeding has been successful. A few pairs have been kept in Indonesian zoos, but unless the animals are young when brought into captivity they do not adjust well. A pair in the zoo in Hô Chi Minh City, Vietnam, did produce one offspring.

Warren D. Thomas

Madagascar Serpent-eagle

(Eutriorchis astur)

ESA: Endangered

IUCN: Critically endangered

Class: Aves
Order: Falconiformes
Family: Accipitridae
Length: Estimated at 21–23 in. (53.3–58.4 cm)
Weight: Unknown
Clutch size: Unknown
Incubation: Unknown
Diet: Chameleons, poultry, lemurs; probably other small mammals
Habitat: Forests
Range: Northeastern Madagascar

MALAYSIAN PEOPLE arrived in Madagascar about 2,000 years ago. Crossing the Indian Ocean in boats, they settled on the world's fourth largest island. Like all those who would eventually follow them, they found an island full of creatures unlike any others in the world. The Madagascar serpent-eagle no doubt watched them land and witnessed their spread across the island. No historical records of any kind indicate that the ancient people knew of the serpent-eagle, but the bird was there. Two thousand years later, much has changed on Madagascar, and little evidence survives to prove the Madagascar serpent-eagle ever existed.

A mountain range runs north to south like a spine along the island's midsection. Dense rain forests cover the mountains' eastern flanks. Mountain valleys hold fertile soil, and the mountains themselves harbor precious minerals. In this setting the Malagasy people, descendants of the early Malaysian pioneers, developed their own culture and society. They were probably the last people to see the giant elephant bird (*Aepyornis maximus*) alive. Scant

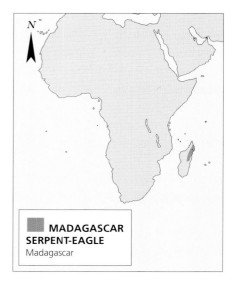

MADAGASCAR SERPENT-EAGLE
Madagascar

but convincing evidence suggests these people probably killed the giant elephant birds for food and probably collected their huge eggs as well. The consequence of relentless hunting was extinction for a bird that stood at least 10 feet (3 meters) tall and weighed several hundred pounds.

The fate of the giant elephant bird was not an isolated event. The human presence on Madagascar has caused a string of extinctions. The rate of extinctions and the number of victim species have increased in modern times. The Madagascar serpent-eagle may be among them.

Appearance

Slightly larger than most hawks but smaller than most eagles, the Madagascar serpent-eagle is a medium-sized bird of prey. Dark brown covers the back and tail. The back is barred, and the tail is conspicuously banded. The wing shows a paler brown with fine, dark barring. Thin black streaks pattern the dingy white to gray chin and throat. The breast and belly are very pale rufous, and heavily barred with dark brown. The most distinguishing feature of the Madagascar serpent-eagle is its head. The crown and nape feathers are dramatically elongated. Even when relaxed, these feathers give the bird a shaggy-headed look. When erected, the crest looks like a great feathery bonnet.

The serpent-eagle's short, rounded wings and long, narrow tail follow the typical physique of forest birds. Short, rounded wings give a bird strong flight but also allow it considerable maneuverability in the tangle of limbs and branches. This bird needs to be able to maneuver quickly and accurately as it pursues small mammals, birds, and lizards. Snakes have never been proved to be a part of this bird's diet.

Ornithologists classify the Madagascar serpent-eagle in a genus of its own (*Eutriorchis*). The basis for classification is slight, as only eight specimens of the Madagascar serpent-eagle have ever been collected and no ornithologist has ever studied it in the field. The specimens were

all collected between 1874 and 1930. All specimens and all verified sightings of the serpent-eagle came from the primary rain forests in the northern two-thirds of Madagascar's eastern foothills. Apparently, it once ranged from the coastal forests up to about 1,800 feet (549 meters). Since the last specimen was collected in May of 1930, a few sightings have been reported. All sightings were in the Marojejy Reserve between 1964 and 1977, but none were ever supported by a skilled bird observer. Essentially, the Madagascar serpent-eagle has not been verifiably seen since 1930. Forest destruction explains why.

Most birds of prey seem majestic in flight and at rest. The critically endangered Madagascar serpent-eagle may no longer be seen in the skies.

During the last decades of the 1900s, Madagascar emerged from its status as a French colony into an independent nation of ten million people. Politics within the country have been somewhat unstable, and the economy has suffered. Hungry people have desperately sought answers from the land. In order to produce more food, they have cut and burned their forests to convert them to croplands. Swamps and other wetlands have been converted to rice paddies. Forests and woodlands have also been cleared to make way for plantations of coffee, sugarcane, and tobacco, among other crops. Mining for graphite and chromium has expanded. The collective result has been the drastic loss of primary forests, especially the rain forests where the Madagascar serpent-eagle once lived.

Only 14 species of birds of prey nest on Madagascar. Eight of them are unique to the island, including the Madagascar serpent-eagle. Several efforts have been made to find the serpent-eagle, but only one has been successful. In September 1988 two observers, specifically searching for the serpent-eagle, found a single bird that they studied for 25 minutes before it disappeared. Their report is con-

vincing, but not all ornithologists accept it as conclusive.

Traditionally, field observations of rare birds, without supporting photographs or specimens, are always considered suspect. After 60 years without a sighting, some ornithologists now consider the bird extinct. Others are not so willing to admit extinction, and the 1988 sighting gives them hope.

The Marojejy Reserve where the sightings from the 1960s and 1970s were reported covers 150,375 acres (60,150 hectares), or about 235 square miles (611 square kilometers). Only a portion of the lower reserve still offers adequate habitat for a Madagascar serpent-eagle, but the possibility exists that a few of them yet survive there. At present, the only solution to the

threat of extinction is to protect the reserve, which raises the issue of priorities. No present-day ornithologist has ever seen a live Madagascar serpent-eagle.

By some standards, such as those of the Convention on International Trade in Endangered Species of Wild Fauna and Flora (CITES), and after 50 years of no reports and failed attempts to find a species, this species may truly be extinct. Why preserve a forest for a species that may no longer exist? The answer is that the Marojejy Reserve harbors many other rare and endangered species besides, potentially, the Madagascar serpent-eagle.

Preserving the rain forest for them may give the Madagascar serpent-eagle its last chance in its fight against total decline.

Kevin Cook

Black Shama

(Copsychus cebuensis)

ESA: Endangered

IUCN: Endangered

Class: Aves
Order: Passeriformes
Family: Muscicapidae
Subfamily: Turdinae
Length: 7¾–8 in. (19.5–20.5 cm)
Weight: Unknown
Clutch size: Unknown
Incubation: Unknown
Diet: Probably insects
Habitat: Primary forests
Range: Cebu Island, Philippines

THE BLACK SHAMA is a bird desperately in need of habitat that no longer exists. If the black

shama manages to survive it will do so because it learns to adapt to different habitats.

Of the eight species in the genus *Copsychus*, five are called shamas, and three are called magpie robins. All are part of the thrush subfamily (Turdinae) in the Old World flycatcher family (Muscicapidae). The various species range from Madagascar through the Seychelles into southern Asia and eastward into Malaysia and the Philippines. The black shama lives nowhere else in the world except on Cebu Island of the Philippines. It is an all-black bird with a conspicuous blue sheen to its feathers and a small blue wattle around its eye. The species' habitat on Cebu was nearly gone by the early 1960s.

The word "habitat" is routinely used, but the full meaning

of the term is not always clearly understood. Habitat describes the complete set of conditions that a creature needs for living. Plants often get overlooked in habitat discussions. They form a major part of an animal's habitat, but they also have habitat requirements of their own. Anything that disturbs the plants' habitat obviously has an affect on the habitats available to animals.

The need for cover

Wildlife biologists usually divide habitat requirements for animals into three parts: food, water, and cover. Food and water requirements are simple enough, but cover is more complicated. Cover includes all the other needs of an animal. Shelter from weather and predators obviously qualifies as cover. Less obvious are the little

BLACK SHAMA
Philippines

island. Nearly the whole island was developed to provide dwellings for humans, farm plots, and plantations. Ornithologists feared the black shama would quickly disappear as its habitat was methodically destroyed.

Still here

Against all the odds, the black shama has not yet slipped into extinction. It has clung to survival in bamboo patches and shrubby thickets that survive in places unsuitable for farming. Either the species shows willingness to adapt to changing habitat conditions, or the original assessment of its habitat needs was not accurate. Quite probably, bamboo and shrub habitats are marginally acceptable but not ideal for the black shama.

Many species are not so flexible. Without their principal habitat they cannot survive. If the black shama can survive long enough in the thickets, there may be time for some of Cebu's forests to be restored. Alternatively, the black shama might be a candidate species for moving to available habitat on a nearby island, where it had never occurred naturally.

The status of habitat recovery work on Cebu is not clear, and efforts to relocate the black shama are unknown. The final alternative for the black shama may be that it must permanently adapt to new habitat. It will probably have to in a country such as the Philippines, where political turmoil is frequent and distracting. Social conditions that are unstable will usually prevent any meaningful recovery program from getting off the ground.

Kevin Cook

things that make it possible for an animal to survive. For example, bald eagles (*Haliaeetus leucocephalus*) hunt for fish by perching on exposed tree limbs, from which they can see the water. Exposed tree limbs, then, form part of the cover requirement of bald eagles.

Loss of habitat

A bird's habitat can be lost two ways. It can be destroyed, or it can be degraded. Habitat is degraded if it loses the qualities needed by a species, or if new factors are added to the habitat that subsequently prevent that species from using the habitat. A bird species may still find food and water in its traditional habitat but lose places to nest. A

species may have places to nest and food to eat but lose vital water. An exotic animal may prey on a species' young and prevent successful reproduction. All of these possibilities may harm a species. The quality of habitat makes a difference to every species. Habitat is destroyed if it changes so much that it no longer has its original character. It is habitat destruction that is responsible for pushing the black shama to near extinction.

Forests and woodlands once covered nearly all of Cebu, a medium-sized island in the central part of the Philippines. The black shama inhabited primary forests and the thicker woodlands on Cebu. By 1960 people had cleared most of the trees from the

SHARKS

Class: Elasmobranchii

Sharks belong to the chondrichthyan group of fishes, which means they have cartilaginous skeletons rather than the bony skeletons of the teleost fishes. Sharks were swimming in the oceans of the world 400 million years ago, and many shark groups today have evolved from ancestors dating back 100 million years. Sharks are found in tropical, temperate and cold waters, occupying a range of habitats from freshwater rivers to the deep ocean. Marine sharks are found in all the world's oceans as far north as the Arctic Ocean and to the edge of the Antarctic in the South Atlantic.

There are more than 350 species of shark, from less than 20 inches (50 centimeters) to 40-foot (13-meter) giants. The largest sharks in the world eat plankton, but the majority of sharks are predatory and occupy the top of the marine food chain. Little is known about the biology and ecology of many species. They are known to be long-lived, to produce few young, and to reproduce only every other year or longer. Shark reproductive biology is understood for only a few species. In all sharks the eggs are fertilized internally, but development of the young follows one of several different strategies according to the species. The embryos may be attached by a placenta in the uterus, where they continue their development into fully-formed sharks. This strategy is termed placental viviparity. In other species the embryos develop unattached to the uterus. These embryos are either nourished by large yolks (ovoviviparity) or by feeding on infertile eggs (oophagy).

In some species, larger embryos feed on the smaller ones, and this cannibalistic strategy is termed embryophagy. For some shark species the embryos develop within large leathery egg cases that are laid on the sea bed, where they develop and hatch (oviparity).

Large shark species have a reputation as man-eaters and are generally feared. This is due more to sensational media coverage and Hollywood films than fact. The International Shark Attack Profile (ISAP) indicates that there are probably less than 50 shark attacks each year worldwide. Of these, only a small percentage are fatal, but as many as a hundred million sharks are thought to be killed each year in commercial fisheries, as by-catch from other fisheries, in anti-shark beach netting, and by recreational fishing. This has severely reduced the populations of many species, and several countries including the United States have developed fisheries management plans to reverse these declines.

There is growing global concern over the unsustainable exploitation of fisheries. This is reflected in the 1999 initiative of The Food and Agriculture Organization of the United Nations (FAO), to adopt a new voluntary International Plan for the Conservation and Management of Sharks. Public perception about sharks may also be changing.

There has been a growth in recreational diving, and more tourists pay to see sharks in their natural environment. Sharks are killed for their meat, skin, liver, and fins. The fins are one of the most valuable parts of the shark, and the trade is worth hundreds of millions of dollars. They are the ingredient for shark-fin soup, for which there is a huge demand in Asia. The fins may be removed while the shark is still alive, then it is thrown back into the water to slowly die. "Live-finning" is banned in U.S. waters, but is still carried out elsewhere.

Basking Shark
(Cetorhinus maximus)

IUCN: Vulnerable

Class: Elasmobranchii
Order: Lamniformes
Family: Cetorhinidae
Length: Approximately 22-30 ft. (7-10 m)
Reproduction: Thought to be ovoviviparous
Habitat: Coastal areas and oceans
Range: Atlantic, Indian, and Pacific Oceans; the Mediterranean Sea

THE BASKING SHARK is the second largest fish in the world and can grow to about 30 feet (10 meters). However, few sharks have been accurately measured and there are unconfirmed reports of larger individuals. The most distinguishing features of the basking shark are its cylindrical shape with a pronounced pointed snout and the five large, prominent gill slits that almost encircle the head.

Basking sharks have a wide distribution and are found in both the Atlantic and Pacific Oceans. They are migratory and move from the open ocean to coastal areas at certain times of the year. Basking sharks are observed off the Atlantic coast of the United States from North Carolina to New York in the spring. They move northward to New England and Canada in the summer, and then disappear to unknown locations in the autumn and winter. Basking sharks are seen off the Pacific coast of California in the autumn and winter, moving northward in the spring and summer. Despite its huge size and presence in coastal waters, very little is known about the biology and ecology of this species. Where the sharks go when they disappear from inshore areas is not known.

This shark gets its name from being observed at or near the surface and "basking" with its dorsal fin out of the water. This behavior is not well understood but is thought to be related to mating or feeding. The basking shark is only one of three species of shark that feeds entirely by filtering plankton from the water. The other species are the whale shark (*Rhiniodon typus*), which is also the largest fish in the world, and the megamouth shark (*Megachasma pelagios*).

When feeding, the basking shark cruises along at a speed of about 2 knots (3 kilometers per hour), keeping its mouth wide open. Huge volumes of seawater containing microscopic plankton are forced through the gills, where hair-like structures called gill rakers trap the plankton, which is then swallowed. The basking shark appears to shed its

gill rakers each year, and could be without functional gill rakers for several months. However, if and how it feeds and what it feeds on during this long period is still a mystery.

The disappearance of basking sharks from coastal waters is thought to be linked to this shedding of the gill rakers and to the seasonal variability in the supply of plankton. There are several theories about the basking shark's migration and feeding habits when they leave the coast. It has been surmised that the sharks move into deeper, colder water, where they feed on other organisms. Some researchers have suggested that they hibernate in deeper water. The shark's massive oil-rich liver could act as a source of energy during a period of reduced activity.

Reproduction is another mystery. The gestation period is unknown, with estimates ranging from one to three-and-a-half years. The basking shark is assumed to be slow growing and it has been estimated that it can live for 50 years. The number of years it takes for a male shark to reach maturity has been esti-

mated by some scientists to be five or six years, though other researchers think that it could be twelve or more years.

The basking shark has been fished for hundreds of years by harpooning from small boats. Coastal fisheries have operated off Norway (the largest commercial fishery of basking sharks in Western Europe), Ireland, Scotland, Iceland, the United States (California), Peru, Ecuador, China, and Japan. The shark is exploited for its liver, which was used as a lighting oil and tanning agent in the 19th century, and more recently for its chemical properties. The liver is rich in squalene oil, used in pharmaceuticals, cosmetics, and high-technology industry.

Shark-fin soup
The basking shark is also fished for food and skin. In more recent years, it has been exploited for its large fins, which are used in the making of shark-fin soup. Bask-

The basking shark (*Cetorhinus maximus*) is found in waters worldwide, but due to fishing exploitation, this animal is now classified as vulnerable.

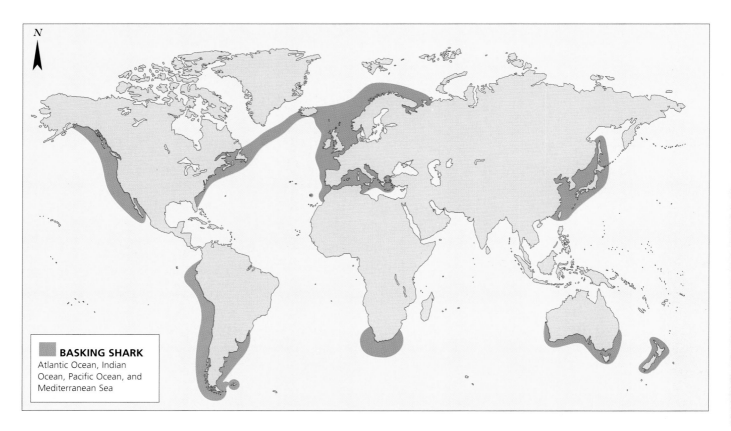

BASKING SHARK
Atlantic Ocean, Indian Ocean, Pacific Ocean, and Mediterranean Sea

ing sharks can become entangled in nets intended for other species, severely damaging the nets. This impact on nets was considered such a problem off the Pacific Coast of Canada in the 1950s that basking sharks were caught and killed.

This action appears to have removed most of this population, and the basking shark is now rarely sighted in these waters.

The basking shark has disappeared from several areas where they were once known to occur, resulting in the localized collapse of the basking shark fishery.

However, without much more detailed knowledge of the distribution and ecology of this species, it is difficult to prove the precise cause of these disappearances. There is concern that local disappearances of basking sharks indicate that the species is being exploited beyond recovery. Overexploitation is believed to be a

serious threat off the coasts of the United States, the United Kingdom, and New Zealand, which has led to basking shark fishing bans in these waters.

Other measures to protect these species are being considered, such as the inclusion of this species under CITES. Scientific research on the biology and ecology of these species is being carried out by the Pelagic Shark Research Foundation in California through the tagging of individual sharks. A shoreline network has also been established to record sightings within the Monterey Bay National Marine Sanctuary. In Europe, the Basking Shark Society is studying sharks in the waters off the United Kingdom. It is hoped this research will reveal where the sharks go when they leave coastal waters and provide information about the biology and ecology of these huge, elusive sharks.

Dusky Shark
(Carcharhinus obscurus)

IUCN: Lower risk

Class: Elasmobranchii
Order: Carcariniformes
Family: Carcharhinidae
Length: 11 ft. (3.6 m)
Reproduction: Viviparous
Habitat: Coasts and oceans
Range: Atlantic, Pacific, and Indian Oceans; sometimes the Mediterranean Sea

THE dusky shark is a large shark that can reach a length of about 12 feet (four meters). It is blue-gray on the upperparts, fading to white on the undersides. The tips of the fins have a darker, dusky coloration. The dusky shark is found in sub-tropical and temperate waters. This species is found around the coasts of Aus-

tralia, Asia, Africa, and North and South America. In the United States, the dusky shark can be observed along the Pacific coast from southern California to the Gulf of California, and along the Atlantic coast from southern Massachusetts to Florida.

The dusky shark is considered more common than many other shark species, although there are no population estimates.

Dusky sharks are found close inshore and in the open ocean. They can be seen swimming close to the surface, and are often seen following ships. They have also been recorded at depths of 1,200 feet (400 meters).

This shark is migratory, and in the eastern North Pacific and western North Atlantic, dusky sharks move northward in the summer months, then return southward to warmer climes when these waters cool in the winter.

Viviparous

Dusky sharks mature at 19 to 21 years and an approximate length of 8 feet (2.7 meters), and are thought to live for 40 to 50 years. Like many other sharks, dusky sharks are viviparous. The embryos develop in a yolk sac, and this sac forms into a placenta that attaches to the uterus. The gestation period is thought to be at least 12 months, and between three and fourteen pups are born, measuring about 36 inches (90 centimeters) long. Reproduction may only occur once every two or three years. The coast of South Carolina is one of the dusky shark's known birthing and nursery areas. There are also nursery areas off the coast of western Australia and Natal in South Africa.

Dusky sharks prey on a wide range of fishes such as tuna, mackerel, eels, and flatfishes. Smaller prey such as shrimps and

The dusky shark (*Carcharhinus obscurus*) prefers temperate and subtropical temperatures. It inhabitats the coastal regions of three oceans, including the Indian Ocean.

barnacles are also eaten. Dusky sharks are known to prey on smaller sharks, and may attack dolphins. While the dusky shark is a large predator, there have been very few reported attacks on people by this species. Dusky sharks may in turn be eaten by larger sharks such as the sandtiger shark (*Carcharias taurus*) and the great white shark (*Carcharodon carcharias*).

The biggest threat to the dusky shark is from humans. Dusky sharks are fished commercially in Australian and United States waters, and are also caught as by-catch in swordfish and tuna fisheries. This shark is exploited for its meat, skin, liver and fins and is also popular for sport fish-

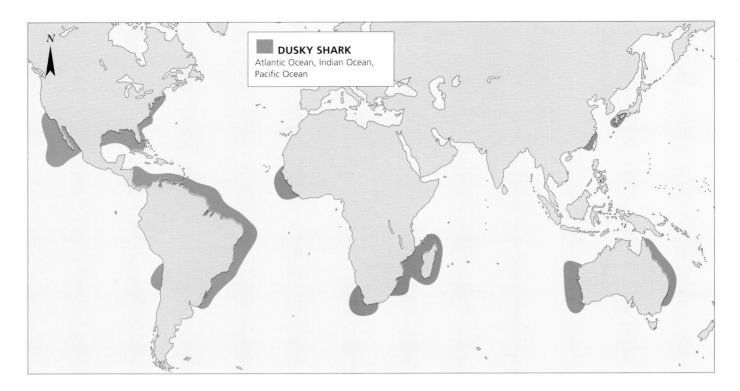

DUSKY SHARK
Atlantic Ocean, Indian Ocean, Pacific Ocean

ing. In the Atlantic shark fishery of the United States, about 80 tonnes (81 metric tons) of dusky sharks have been caught and killed each year since recording began in 1992.

There has been a decline in the number of dusky sharks off the East Coast of the United States, and in these waters the shark is considered vulnerable according to the IUCN Red List criteria. The National Marine Fisheries Service (NMFS) estimates that the population in the northwestern Atlantic and the Gulf of Mexico may have declined by as much as 80 percent since the mid-1970s. Since 1993, the dusky shark has been one of the species managed under the NMFS Fishery Management Plan for Atlantic sharks, though this plan has been criticised for not implementing stricter regulations.

In Western Australia, the dusky shark fishery has taken about 450 tonnes (457 metric tons) of sharks each year since the 1980s. The fishery exploits the young sharks from the nursery areas, but the fishery is believed to be at a sustainable level. A Marine Protected Area (MPA) has been established in these waters to protect the shark breeding population.

The dusky shark, like many sharks, is a long-lived species with a slow reproductive rate. Although the biology and ecology of this species are more fully understood than for many shark species, its population dynamics are still not clear. Management plans are being implemented for heavily exploited shark species such as the dusky shark, often in response to declining catches.

However, it can take many years before the effects of management strategies become evident. If these plans are initiated too late or are flawed because of lack of knowledge, shark populations may never recover to their former levels.

Ganges River Shark

(Glyphis gangeticus)

IUCN: Critically endangered

Class: Elasmobranchii
Order: Carchariniformes
Family: Carcharhinidae
Length: 9 ft. (3 m)
Reproduction: Unknown
Habitat: Large rivers and estuaries
Range: India and possibly Pakistan

THE GANGES RIVER shark is one of several species of shark which live in freshwater. Like other river sharks, there is almost nothing known about this species. There are at least four or five other species of river shark in the world, mostly known from museum specimens collected in the last century. Very few live specimens of river shark have ever been observed.

The Ganges river shark is thought to grow to several feet (meters) in length and to prey on fish. This species has small eyes, and is adapted to living in muddy river water. The Ganges river shark was known to scientists from only three museum specimens until 1996, when a 10-foot (3-meter) adult female was caught. It is also thought that the Indus River in Pakistan may contain Ganges river sharks.

Mysterious species

Another species of the genus *Glyphis* is the Borneo river shark. This mysterious species is only known from a single hundred-year-old museum specimen collected from an unspecified

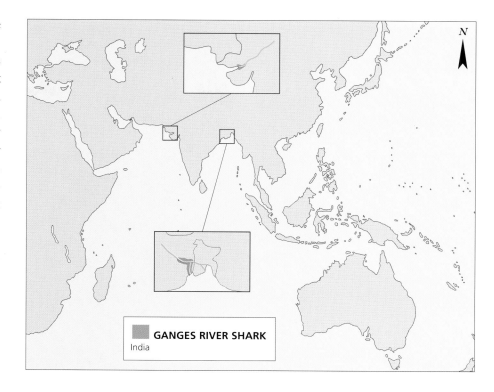

GANGES RIVER SHARK
India

The Ganges River at sunset gives no hint of its muddy waters. The Ganges River shark (*Glyphis gangeticus*) is a species of freshwater shark that has adapted well to living in murky water.

river in Sabah, Malaysia, on the island of Borneo. In 1997, an expedition to the Kinabatangan River in northern Borneo saw juvenile river sharks that had been caught by local fishermen in nets intended for other species. It is not yet certain whether this is the same species as the preserved specimen or if it is another species of river shark. It is hoped that further research will find more evidence of these very rare and little-known sharks.

Great White Shark

(Carcharodon carcharias)

IUCN: Vulnerable

Class: Elasmobranchii
Order: Lamniformes
Family: Lamnidae
Length: 15–21 ft. (5–7 m)
Reproduction: Ovoviviparous
Habitat: Coasts and open ocean
Range: Pacific, Atlantic, and Indian Oceans; and the Mediterranean Sea

THE GREAT WHITE shark is one of the largest predatory fishes in the world and is known to grow to a length of 21 feet (7 meters). There are reports of larger individuals, but none of these have been confirmed or the specimens precisely measured. The shark is darkly colored on the top half of its body, fading to white below the pectoral fins. Great white sharks have a blunt, cone-shaped snout and powerful jaws containing several rows of large teeth. The species is distributed throughout the world's oceans and is found mainly in coastal and offshore areas and around oceanic islands. They generally inhabit cold to temperate waters and rarely occur in tropical seas. In North America, great white sharks have been observed along the eastern coast from Newfoundland to Florida and along the western coast from Alaska to California.

Powerful predator

The huge size of this shark, combined with its very powerful jaws, strong razor-sharp teeth, and high-speed maneuverability make this shark a top predator. Great white sharks are able to cruise slowly through the water for long distances. They can also deliver a fast attack on their prey, ramming it to stun it and then taking a large bite out of the victim. Like most sharks, the great white has several rows of teeth. Shark teeth are continually discarded and replaced. The front rows contain functional teeth, while the back rows hold replacements for lost teeth. The great white shark's upper teeth are triangular and serrated and used for slicing into the prey, while the lower teeth are more pointed, not serrated and are designed for holding. The prey can be marine mammals such as seals and dolphins, though this shark has a broad diet that includes fish, birds, turtles, carrion, and other sharks. Sharks are sometimes injured by their prey. For example, elephant seals can inflict serious damage with their long sharp teeth and claws.

There are no population estimates of great white sharks, but the species is considered rare with scattered, low-density populations. Great whites occur

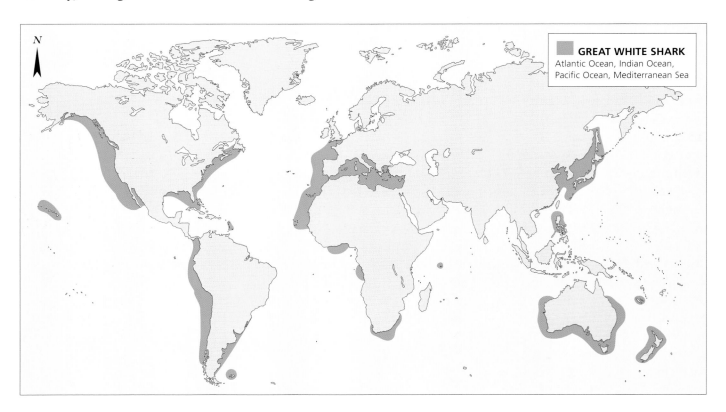

N

GREAT WHITE SHARK
Atlantic Ocean, Indian Ocean,
Pacific Ocean, Mediterranean Sea

Although a formidable predator due to its huge size, the great white shark's reputation for attacking people has been greatly exaggerated.

singly, in pairs, or sometimes in groups at a feeding area. Like most sharks, great whites are slow growing. The males reach maturity at nine to ten years, when they are at a length of 9 to 12 feet (3 to 4 meters). The females mature at 12 to 15 years, when they are at a length of 12 to 15 feet (4 to 5 meters). It is estimated that great white sharks can live for approximately 36 years.

Great white sharks are thought to be ovoviviparous, which means that the embryos do not become attached to the uterus and are nourished instead by large egg yolks. The developing embryos get further nourishment from eating the unfertilized eggs that the female continues to produce (a process known as oophagy). Pregnant females are rarely seen, and the

locations where both adults and new-born sharks occur are presumed to be birthing areas. These include waters off the northeastern coast of the United States, and off Southern California.

It is thought that between two and ten sharks are born, each with an approximate length of 4 feet (1.5 meters). The gestation period is likely to be longer than one year. The great white shark is thought to reproduce only once every two to three years.

Shark-fin soup

The great white shark is not targeted commercially, but many are caught in nets intended for other species, or caught incidentally in other shark fisheries. The large fins are used in shark-fin soup. The great white shark is also a popular sport fish in waters off Australia and the northeastern United States.

The great white shark has a reputation as a fierce predator that will attack people. While

attacks on humans have occurred, they are extremely rare. California has one of the highest known attack rates from great white sharks, with 41 reported attacks between 1950 and 1982, of which only four were fatal. Why sharks attack humans is not fully known, though it is thought that, seen from below, the outline of a diver or a surf boarder may be mistaken for a seal or other prey species. Due to its fearful reputation, attacks by other predators may also be mistakenly attributed to the great white shark. Great white sharks are rare in tropical waters, and attacks attributed to this species in warm waters are more likely to be from one of several other common species in these waters, such as tiger sharks (*Galeocerdo cuvier*).

The ecology and behavior of great white sharks is little known and, despite a wide distribution, they are rarely encountered. Research is being undertaken to gain more understanding about this enigmatic predator. The low numbers of great white sharks has raised concern over the exploitation of this species. Since the early 1990s, the great white shark has been protected in coastal waters off South Africa, Australia, and the United States. Great white sharks continue to be caught accidentally in fishing nets and for their fins. Many also become entangled in protective mesh barriers erected offshore to keep sharks out of bathing areas. Man is also having an ever-increasing impact on the ocean through pollution and over-fishing, both of which may affect the shark's prey species. Ultimately, great white sharks have more to fear from man than we have from them. The dynamics between species in the marine environment is still poorly understood, but it is known that the great white shark is an integral part of the marine ecosystem and removing large numbers will have an impact.

Sandbar Shark

(Carcharhinus plumbeus)

IUCN: Lower risk

Class: Elasmobranchii
Order: Carchariniformes
Family: Carcharhinidae
Length: 6 ft. (2 m)
Reproduction: Viviparous
Habitat: Coast and ocean
Range: Atlantic, Pacific, and Indian Oceans; the Mediterranean Sea

THE SANDBAR SHARK has a stocky outline with a short, rounded nose. The body is gray-brown in color, fading to white on the undersides. A distinctive feature of this shark is the very tall and triangular front dorsal fin. The sandbar shark can reach a length of approximately 8 feet (2.5 meters), although most of this species are between 3 and 6 feet (1 to 2 meters) in length.

The sandbar shark is widely distributed in temperate and tropical seas and is common in sandy bays, harbors, and estuaries. This shark generally keeps to the bottom of bays and deeper water. It can descend to depths of more than 800 feet (250 meters), though it can also be seen at the surface and in very shallow water. In the United States the sandbar shark is found along the East Coast from Florida to Massachusetts, and in the Gulf of Mexico.

There appear to be separate subpopulations of sandbar sharks, and tagging and genetic studies indicate the Atlantic seaboard and Gulf of Mexico sharks are different from the smaller population found in waters further south from Trinidad to the Brazilian coast.

The sandbar shark is usually migratory. It moves seasonally along the Atlantic coast of the United States, and this appears to be linked with changes in

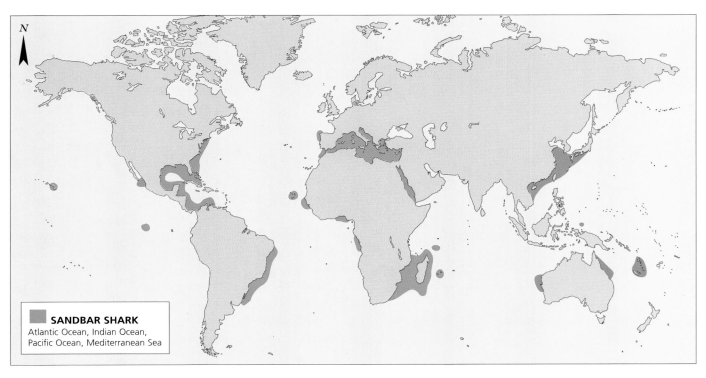

SANDBAR SHARK
Atlantic Ocean, Indian Ocean,
Pacific Ocean, Mediterranean Sea

The sandbar shark (*Carcharhinus plumbeus*) is found in waters all over the world. It has suffered from habitat degradation and overfishing. Time is needed for the population to recover.

water temperature. In the summer months, when the water temperature is about 66 degrees Fahrenheit (19 degrees Centigrade), the female sharks migrate north and give birth to their pups in sheltered bays along the Chesapeake and Delaware Bays.

In winter the sharks migrate to the warmer waters of the Gulf Stream off the Carolina coast, and some even migrate as far south as the Gulf of Mexico and the Caribbean. Not all sandbar sharks migrate; the Hawaiian Islands sharks appear to be residents all year.

It is thought that this species reaches maturity between 13 and 19 years and can live as long as 35 years. The gestation period is between nine months and one year, with sandbar sharks reproducing every two to three years. The number of sharks born is dependent on the size of the female. In the Western Atlantic, where mature females reach about 5 feet (1.8 meters), the average number of pups born is eight to nine. In Hawaiian waters mature females are smaller and have an average of five pups.

The newborn sharks are approximately 24 inches (60 centimeters) in length.

Varied diet

The diet of the sandbar shark consists of a wide range of fish species, and mollusks and crustaceans are also eaten. Adult sandbar sharks may themselves become prey for great white sharks, and other species such as tiger and bull sharks are known to prey on young sandbar sharks.

Commercial fishing

The sandbar shark is fished commercially. The meat is used for human consumption, the skin for exotic leather products, the fins for making shark-fin soup, and the liver for vitamins. It is also caught in recreational fishing.

In the Western Atlantic, the sandbar shark may account for as much as 60 percent of all the sharks caught for commercial use. In the 1970s and 1980s the industry was unregulated and the number of sharks caught increased. This species was overexploited and it has been estimated that its populations in the Western Atlantic were reduced by 90 percent.

The sandbar shark may also be at risk from coastal habitat degradation. For example, the Chesapeake Bay is an important nursery ground for the sandbar shark. Silt and effluents released from on-shore development have increased water turbidity and the frequency of algal blooms. These changes in water quality have altered natural habitats in the bay, impacting on the native aquatic vegetation upon which the shark's prey species depend.

Catch quotas

In 1993 the sandbar shark was one of the species listed under the National Marine Fisheries Service (NMFS) Fisheries Management Plan. This plan imposed quotas on the number of sandbar sharks caught and aimed to reduce catches to allow the population to recover from decades of exploitation. There was concern that the quotas were too high and that the time needed for the population to recover its former level was underestimated.

In 1997 the allowable shark catch was reduced by 50 percent, and further restrictions have since been imposed. Despite these measures, adult females are still rarely seen and it is thought that it may take several more decades for the population to recover to its former level.

Although much is known about the ecology of this shark, its population structure and dynamics are not fully understood. Without this information it is difficult to make management and recovery plans.

Sand Tiger Shark

(Carcharias taurus)

IUCN: Vulnerable

Class: Elasmobranchii
Order: Lamniformes
Family: Odontaspididae
Length: 8 ft. (2.2–3 m)
Reproduction: Ovoviviparous
Habitat: Coastal areas
Range: Atlantic, Pacific, and Indian Oceans; the Mediterranean Sea

KNOWN IN SOUTH AFRICA as the spotted ragged-tooth shark and in Australia as the gray nurse shark, the sand tiger shark is a large, heavily built species. The body is gray-brown on the upperparts and gray-white underneath, with a scattering of reddish brown dots that may fade as the shark matures. The dorsal and anal fins are large and distinctive in that they are both of equal size. The sand tiger shark can grow to be approximately 13 feet (3.1 meters) in length. This shark has three rows of large sharp teeth that can be observed when the mouth is closed, earning its ragged-tooth name.

The slow-swimming sand tiger shark is a coastal species found in temperate and tropical waters. The sand tiger shark inhabits the surf zone to depths of 570 feet (190 meters), though it favors lower depths. Sharks lack the inflatable swim bladders of bony fishes, and to maintain their position sharks usually must keep swimming. However, the sand tiger shark can hang motionless in the water. This is achieved by swallowing air at the surface. This gives it buoyancy, and allows it maintain its position in the water.

The sand tiger shark feeds on a range of fishes and will also prey on small sharks and rays, crustaceans, and large mollusks. Cooperative feeding has been observed in this species, where sand tiger sharks have encircled schools of fish to make them easier to feed upon.

This shark is thought to live for 20 to 30 years and to reach maturity in six to 12 years. In some parts of the range, sand tiger sharks form large schools

The sand tiger shark is characterized by its ragged teeth, which are clearly visible even when its mouth is closed. It has declined severely and now survives only because it breeds well in captivity.

for feeding and for reproduction. This has been observed off Cape Hatteras on the Atlantic Coast. Sand tiger sharks are ovoviviparous in their reproduction, producing eggs that develop in egg cases inside the uterus of the female. The female sand tiger shark has two uteruses, and 16 to 23 eggs develop in each one. The young hatch when they are about 20 inches (55 centimeters) long

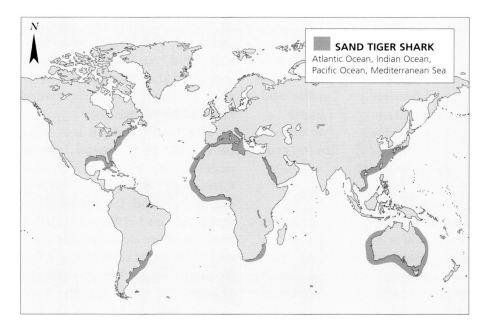

N

SAND TIGER SHARK
Atlantic Ocean, Indian Ocean,
Pacific Ocean, Mediterranean Sea

and feed on the undeveloped eggs. The sand tiger shark is different from other ovoviviparous sharks in that the young sharks will also feed on the other developing young in a process called uterine cannibalism. The result is that only two sharks will complete their development, one in each uterus. The gestation period is between nine months and one year and the young are born when they are approximately 3 feet (1 meter) long.

Severe decline

The sand tiger shark is fished commercially. The meat is used for human consumption and is considered a delicacy in Japan. The fins are used to make shark-fin soup and the liver is used for its oil. The sand tiger shark is easy to find and catch as they form large schools at the same time and place each year when they come together to mate.

Off the Atlantic Coast of the United States the sand tiger population severely declined in the early 1990s due to over-fishing. In 1993, The National Marine Fisheries Service (NMFS) Atlantic Shark Fisheries Management Plan was implemented to reduce the fishery impact on Atlantic sharks and to help populations recover. In 1997 the NMFS plan was updated, and all commercial and recreational fishing was prohibited for the sand tiger shark. The northwestern Atlantic population of sharks is classified as endangered. In Australia, this large and slow moving shark once used to be a target for sport divers.

In 1984 the sand tiger shark became the first fully protected shark species in the world when the New South Wales Government conferred protection to the species. The sand tiger shark is protected in all Australian Commonwealth waters, where these populations are endangered.

The sand tiger shark survives well in captivity and these powerful and yet vulnerable fish can be observed in aquariums, which is the closest many people will ever get to a live shark.

Megan Cartin

SHEARWATERS

Class: Aves

Order: Anseriformes

Family: Procellariidae

Shearwaters glide over the sea with beautiful grace, working the waves for the squids, crabs, shrimps, and small fishes that constitute their meals. The air immediately above the water is kept moving by the push and pull of the waves, and this allows shearwaters to navigate just inches above the surface. When not in flight, shearwaters sit on the water very much like gulls.

Shearwaters are well equipped for life at sea. Their long, narrow wings bear more flight feathers than those of other birds and allow them to maneuver on the shifting air currents above the sea. Short legs and feet end in small, webbed toes. At sea, the birds have no access to fresh water; they get salt water from the food they eat and when they preen their feathers, so regulating body salt is crucial.

Unlike aquatic birds that nest around freshwater lakes and marshes, seabirds do not build floating nests. They return to land only for this part of their annual cycle. The ability to fly great distances in search of food, however, means long periods away from their nests. Long absences for days at a time could almost certainly spell doom for nestlings, as many predators would relish them as a meal. Seabirds found a way to avoid predators—they nest in places where predators cannot reach them, like trees, rock crevices, steep cliffs, and islands.

Shearwaters excavate burrows in loose soil. They choose islands and usually ridgetops, crests, or mountain summits. The slopes allow nestlings to waddle short distances on their inadequate legs to launch themselves. Falling down the slope, they quickly gain momentum to fly.

Shearwaters devote their breeding efforts to a single egg. Parents spend the first several days with their newly hatched chicks. Within a week the parents spend all of their time at sea. They return at night to feed the chicks. This secrecy protects them from larger, diurnal predatory birds such as skuas (*Catharacta* sp.) and frigatebirds (*Fregata* sp.). Despite their extended solitude, shearwater chicks once enjoyed a high survival rate. The breeding strategy succeeded in ranking the shearwaters among the most abundant birds in the world.

When people settled the islands where some shearwaters nested, everything changed. At least two shearwater species are now imperiled because of human activities. Predation by exotic species, destruction of habitat, human settlement, and farming have all threatened shearwaters.

Pink-footed Shearwater

(Puffinus creatopus)

IUCN: Vulnerable

Length: 19–20 in. (48.3–50.8 cm)
Weight: 1–2 lb. (0.45–1 kg)
Clutch size: 1 egg
Incubation: Unknown
Diet: Small squids and fishes
Habitat: Pelagic, nests on islands
Range: Eastern Pacific Ocean from southern South America to Alaska

THE PINK-FOOTED shearwater cannot compete with the legend of its homeland. The bird nests on just three islands, and one of them is named for a controversial character of literature.

"Robinson Crusoe Island" sounds like an amusement park attraction, but it is an island that lies 417 miles (667 kilometers) off the coast of Chile in the archipelago known as the Juan Fernandez Islands. Farther west lies its companion, Alexander Selkirk Island. Once known as Más a Tierra and Más Afuera, the islands were renamed Crusoe and Selkirk, respectively, by the Chilean government to honor the fictional tale about a real man.

A sailor from Scotland, Alexander Selkirk found himself stranded on an uninhabited island in the South Pacific Ocean. Four years and four months later, Selkirk was picked up by another ship.

Fact and fiction

When he returned home, he published his book The Life and Adventures of Alexander Selkirk in 1712. English writer Daniel Defoe followed in 1719 with his famous tale Robinson Crusoe.

More than 250 years later, the Chilean government designated the Juan Fernandez Islands a national park and agreed to include them in the United Nations' International Biosphere Reserve program.

These necessary steps were taken because of events that

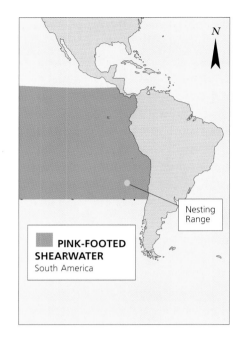

PINK-FOOTED
SHEARWATER
South America

Nesting Range

severely deteriorated the island's plant and animal life.

During the 1500s sailors released goats (*Capra hircus*) on the islands. Repeated landings on these islands during the early centuries of maritime exploration exposed the islands to many invasions of rats. Black rats (*Rattus rattus*) and Norway rats (*Rattus norvegicus*) both became established on the islands. In 1935 European rabbits (*Oryctolagus cuniculus*) were deliberately released on the islands. Coatimundis (*Nasua nasua*) were also released sometime between 1935 and 1940. Besides the animals, many plants were introduced to the islands. Most notable among them were eucalyptus trees (*Eucalyptus* sp.) and bramble (*Rubus ulmifolius*).

Human settlement

Of course, people eventually settled on the islands, too. They brought farming, house cats (Felis sylvestris), and dogs (Canis familiaris) to the islands. The collective result of various human

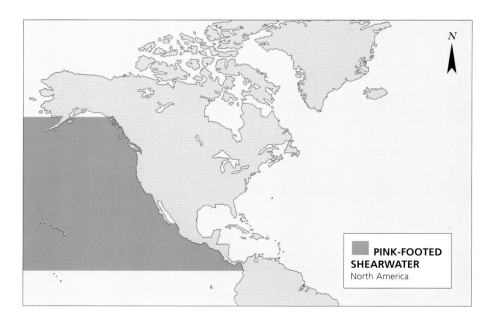

PINK-FOOTED
SHEARWATER
North America

activites has been the destruction of habitat and the decline of native animals. The pink-footed shearwater is one of the losers.

Appearance and sound

One of the larger shearwaters, the pink-footed variety sports the typical two-tone plumage of its family. The upperparts are uniformly sooty brown, although the bird appears to be colored deep charcoal to nearly black from a distance. The dark color covers the entire face and extends down the sides of the neck. The underparts are white from chin to tail, but the line between upperparts and underparts has a strongly mottled pattern. The flight feathers of the wing appear dark gray to charcoal underneath, and the small feathers are silvery white and variously mottled. The beak, foot, and toe are a dull, fleshy pink color. Shearwaters produce wails, screams and choking sounds. They are used to allow individuals to recognize each other, especially at night. There may also be a territorial aspect.

The pink-footed shearwater's bill is longer and thinner than that of other groups of seabirds. Shearwaters eat mainly fish and squid, which they catch by crashing onto the prey, or they capture it underwater.

Pink-footed shearwaters can escape the winters south of the equator by moving north. They are one of the few bird species that breed and also nest south of the equator, then move north of the equator.

During the North American summer, pink-footed shearwaters commonly range as far north as the Gulf of Alaska. Being shearwaters and pelagic in habit, they do not routinely wander close to shore but are more likely to stay at sea and be seen by people aboard ships farther off the coast. The numbers of pink-footed shearwaters has dwindled due to worsening conditions on their nesting islands.

Nesting

Pink-footed shearwaters nest in burrows only on the Juan Fernandez Islands and on Mocha Island, which lies a few degrees of latitude further south and is a coastal island. Feral goats and rabbits have severely overgrazed

Shearwaters, like the Newell's shearwater shown here, are among the birds known as tubenoses, a group that includes albatrosses (Diomedeidae) and storm-petrels (Hydrobatidae).

the Juan Fernandez Islands, eating plants that help anchor the soil on the steep slopes preferred by the shearwaters. Plants also help hide the openings from seabirds that chase the shearwaters. Coatimundis, cats, and rats prey on eggs and nestlings. Cats also catch adults at night as they return to their burrows to feed their chicks, and they catch fledglings as they emerge from their burrows for their flight to sea.

Egg collecting

Mocha Island has been drastically changed by the presence of humans. For example, egg collecting in decades past totally eliminated a cormorant colony on Mocha. Even though the world population of pink-footed shearwaters has been historically quite high, conditions now threaten the species. Its population is estimated at between 10,000 to 20,000 individuals.

National Park

Recommendations have been proposed for controlling or eradicating exotic mammals on the Juan Fernandez Islands. Mocha Island has been proposed as a national park. The response to these recommendations has been either slow or absent. Perhaps the real-life troubles of a seabird hardly match the romance of the world's best-known castaway. However, if the situation is ignored or corrective action delayed, the pink-footed shearwater population could begin to decline very rapidly. An entire species might become as imperiled on Robinson Crusoe Island as Alexander Selkirk was almost three centuries ago.

Townsend's Shearwater

(Puffinus auricularis)

IUCN: Vulnerable

Length: 12–14 in. (30.5–35.5 cm)
Weight: Unknown
Clutch size: Probably 1 egg as in related species
Incubation: Unknown
Diet: Squids, crustaceans, small fish, garbage
Habitat: Pelagic; the central Pacific population nests on the Hawaiian Islands; the eastern Pacific population nests on the Revillagigedos Islands of Mexico
Range: East-central Pacific Ocean from Hawaii to Oaxaca, north to Baja, Mexico

PIGS THREATEN THE survival of a rare seabird. This bizarre situation is due to humanity meddling with the world's wildlife. The bird

in question has its own identity, but ornithologists cannot agree what it is. The bird is all-black above and all-white below. The black extends from the beak across the middle of the cheek and down the side of the neck. The white of the lower belly extends upwards slightly onto the rump. The feathers of the underwing are white, but the flight feathers are black.

A confusing name

For many years ornithologists considered this bird a subspecies of the Manx shearwater (*Puffinus puffinus*), named for the island where the species once nested prolifically. A man named Mathias Newell collected a peculiar "Manx" shearwater on Maui in 1894. It was described as a subspecies in 1900 and named "Newell's Manx shearwater" (*Puffinus puffinus newelli*). At the time, ornithologists treated the Manx shearwater as a species of global oceanic distribution. In the 1980s they split the Manx into several species. The original

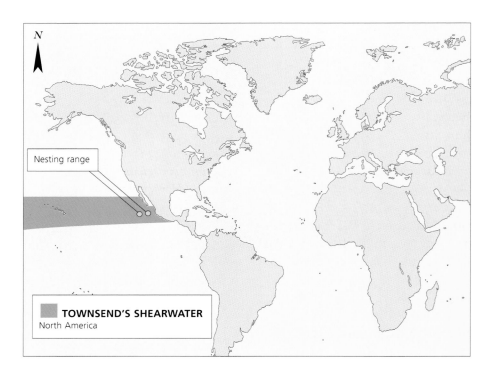

Nesting range

TOWNSEND'S SHEARWATER
North America

While the classification of shearwaters is somewhat confusing, ornithologists agree that the Newell's and the Townsend's shearwater species are distinct—and severely threatened.

Manx shearwater remained a recognized species of the Atlantic Ocean. Pacific Ocean birds were split into black-vented shearwaters (*Puffinus opisthomelas*) and the Townsend's shearwater (*Puffinus auricularis*). The Hawaiian birds were then reclassified as a subspecies of the Townsend's shearwater and became known by the clumsy name of Newell's Townsend's shearwater (*Puffinus auricularis newelli*).

Reclassification

More recently, some ornithologists have granted the Hawaiian birds status as a discrete species called Newell's shearwater (*Puffinus newelli*), which is listed by the ESA as threatened. The classification of shearwaters remains an open debate, and more revisions will eventually be recommended. Both Townsend's and Newell's shearwater face severe threats.

The first threat

When Polynesians settled on the Hawaiian Islands around C.E. 800, they brought many exotic species with them. Europeans who came later did the same. The Polynesians brought pigs (*Sus scrofa*) and Polynesian rats (*Rattus exulans*), while the European and American settlers followed with dogs (*Canis familiaris*), house cats (*Felis sylvestris*), black rats (*Rattus rattus*), Norway rats (*Rattus norvegicus*), Indian mongooses (*Herpestes auropunctatus*), and common mynas (*Acridotheres tristis*), among others. These exotic species helped to devastate many plant communities, and also reduced numbers of the bird species that lived amid them. Similarly, on the Revillagigedo Islands off the west coast of Mexico, visitors brought their own form of exotic species in the form of livestock. A permanent settlement was estab- lished on Socorro Island in 1958.

In 1979 the Mexican government installed a weather station on Clarion Island and assigned 11 men of the Mexican Navy to attend it. Settlers brought pigs, chickens (*Gallus* sp.), and goats (*Capra hircus*). The livestock was intended to supply the human residents with fresh meat. House cats accompanied the people as their pets, but disaster followed.

The pigs helped devastate the Townsend's shearwaters. Pigs root around in the soil, and their keen sense of smell detects potential food. With their powerful snouts they dig out delicacies such as mushrooms, grubs, worms, and rodents. While snuffling about, they discovered shearwater burrows and willingly took the contents, whether egg or nestling. Pigs cannot swim, so a shearwater at sea has nothing to fear from a pig, but the bird's technique for raising its offspring leaves their young defenseless. Pigs symbolize the enormous threat that exotic species present to shearwaters.

Feral house cats are another hazard. They lurk in the dense vegetation around shearwater burrows. They easily catch and kill adult shearwaters returning to their burrows. Cats also catch the fledgling shearwaters as they prepare to leave their burrows for their first flight.

Mongooses and rats directly invade shearwater burrows to feast on eggs and nestlings. The common myna also eats shearwater eggs. Yet all these exotics account for only part of the shearwater's troubles.

Artificial stimulus

During their first venture from their burrows, shearwater fledglings often become disoriented by artificial lights. Instinctively, the young shearwaters wait until after dark to leave their burrows. The bright lights of athletic fields, parking lots, resorts, and other human habitations attract the newly airborne shearwaters. Lacking any flight experience, the shearwaters fly into power lines, buildings, towers, and other structures. Stunned and injured birds fall to the ground, where they become easy prey for cats or are hit by cars. Those that survive may become vulnerable to mongooses.

Once at sea, the shearwaters experience new difficulties. They avoid natural enemies such as sharks and seals but face additional human-made hazards. Nets used by commercial fishers catch hundreds of thousands of shearwaters each year. The collective effect on Townsend's and Newell's shearwaters has been population decline.

The Hawaiian range

The Newell's shearwater suffered more thoroughly and sooner than the Townsend's shearwater. The Newell's formerly nested on all the Hawaiian Islands. Before the first decade of the 20th century ended, the Newell's shearwater had vanished from every island except Kauai. By the 1930s it was thought to be extinct.

A single Newell's shearwater struck a window on Oahu in 1954. Later, the species was found nesting on Kauai. Their attraction to lights on Kauai became apparent in the 1960s, and the problem grew steadily worse through the 1970s.

A plan

An innovative campaign to enlist people to help shearwaters began in 1978. Twelve stations were set up around Kauai, each with wire cages in which people could put the shearwaters they found. State and federal biologists collected them each day, then the birds that were healthy were released. The cages were taken to a remote cliff, and their doors opened. The shearwaters that stayed behind were examined and treated, when possible, for internal injuries.

In the first year, 1,023 Newell's shearwaters were recovered and 861 were released. The total reached 1,836 in 1985, with 1,653 birds released. The birds appear to learn from the experience as only a small percentage returns to the lights after the first night.

A 1988 survey counted only 57 active shearwater burrows. Even if the Newell's shearwater laid three eggs per burrow, that would only account for roughly 300 birds. Shearwaters usually lay only one egg. Thousands of birds circling Kauai lights just years before suggest one of two possibilities. Either the population crashed dramatically in three years, or—more likely—the burrows are extremely difficult to find. The Newell's shearwater usually selects forested or wooded slopes that are well grown with ferns, and there they dig their burrows.

The shearwater has been found on Hawaii and Molokai as well as Kauai, and evidence suggests they may occur on Oahu as well. These islands still have exotic animal problems, and the Newell's shearwater probably will not fully recover on any of these islands. To reduce shearwater colli-

sions, lights on Kauai have been fitted with shields so they are less visible from above.

Further recovery work has included placing the eggs of the Newell's shearwater in the nest burrows of wedge-tailed shearwaters (*Puffinus pacificus*). Ornithologists remove the wedge-tailed shearwater's egg so that the parent birds raise a Newell's chick instead. Called "cross-fostering," this technique has succeeded in getting young Newell's shearwaters raised in other locations. It is hoped that they may expand their nesting areas when they are mature enough to breed.

Common mynas have been conditioned to avoid shearwater eggs. Ornithologists injected chicken eggs with ammonia, tabasco sauce, or mensurol (a foul-tasting bird repellant). The holes in the eggs were sealed with wax and the eggs placed in burrows. When the mynas broke open the eggs, the awful flavor deterred them from further raids. The extent to which the technique has actually been used to deter mynas is unknown.

No help in sight

No specific action has been taken for the Townsend's shearwater on the Revillagigedo Islands. Pigs must be controlled or the shearwater may perish.

The Newell's shearwater, or Newell's Townsend's shearwater, appears secure; but accidental introductions of predators is always a threat. If people are vigilant and continue helping it, the bird should make a good recovery in Hawaii.

Kevin Cook

See also Albatrosses, Christmas frigatebird, Cahow, Petrels.

GLOSSARY

actinopterygii: the scientific name for bony fish

amphibia: the Latin scientific name for amphibians

apically: relating to, or situated at the apex

arboreal: living in or adapted for living in trees; arboreal animals seldom, if ever, descend to the ground (see terrestrial)

aves: the Latin scientific name for birds

barbels: a slender growth on the mouths or nostrils of certain fishes, used as a sensory organ for touch

bilabiate: flowers with upper lip projecting over lower lip

bipedal: any organism that walks on two feet

bract: a leaf at the base of a flower stalk in plants

buff: in bird species, a yellow-white color used to describe the plumage

calyx: the green outer whorl of a flower made up of sepals

captive breeding: any method of bringing several animals of the same species into a zoo or other closed environment for the purpose of mating; if successful, these methods can increase the population of that species

carnivore: any flesh-eating animal

carnivorous: flesh eating

carrion: the decaying flesh of a dead organism

cauline: growing on the upper part of a stem

clear cutting: a method of harvesting lumber that eliminates all the trees in a specific area rather than just selected trees

clutch, clutch size: the number of eggs laid during one nesting cycle

corolla: the separate petals, or the fused petals of a flower

cotyledon: the first leaf developed by the embryo of a seed plant

cryptic plumage: coloration designed to camouflage or conceal

deciduous: dropping off, falling off during a certain season or at a regular stage of growth; deciduous trees shed their leaves annually

decurved: curving downward; a bird's beak is decurved if it points toward the ground

defoliate: to strip trees and bushes of their leaves

deforestation: the process of removing trees from a particular area

diurnal: active during the day; some animals are diurnal, while others are active at night (see nocturnal)

dominance: the ability to overpower the behavior of other individuals; an animal is dominant if it affects

others of its own species in a way that benefits itself; also, the trait of abundance that determines the character of a plant community: grasses dominate a prairie, and trees dominate a forest

dorsal: pertaining to or situated on the back of an organism; a dorsal fin is on the back of a fish

ecology: the study of the interrelationship between a living organism and its environment

ecosystem: a community of animals, plants, and bacteria and its interrelated physical and chemical environment

endemic: native to a particular geographic region

estrous: the time period when female mammals can become pregnant

exotic species: a plant or animal species that is not native to its habitat

fasicle: small, slender bundle (describes the arrangement of leaves)

feral: a wild animal that is descended from tame or domesticated species

fishery, fisheries: any system, body of water, or portion of a body of water that supports finfish or shellfish; can also be used as an adjective describing a person or thing (for example, a fisheries biologist)

forest: a plant community in which trees grow closely enough together that their crowns interlock to form a

continuous overhead canopy

fry: young fish

gene pool: the total hereditary traits available within a group; when isolated from other members of their species, individual organisms may produce healthy offspring if there is enough variety in the genes available through mating

gestation: the period of active embryonic growth inside a mammal's body between the time the embryo attaches to the uterus and the time of birth; some mammals carry dormant embryos for several weeks or months before the embryo attaches to the uterus and begins to develop actively, and this dormancy period is not part of the gestation period; gestation period is the time length of a pregnancy

glabrous: smooth, and hairless

granivore: any seed-feeding animal

granivorous: seed feeding

guano: manure, especially of sea birds and bats

habitat: the environment where a species is normally found; habitat degradation is the decline in quality of a species' home until it can no longer survive there

herbivore: any plant-eating animal

herbivorous: plant eating

hibernate: to spend the winter season in a dormant or inactive state; some species hibernate to save energy during months when food is scarce

hierarchy: the relationships among individuals of the same species or among species that determine in what order animals may have access to food, water, mates, nesting or denning sites, and other vital resources

home range: the area normally traveled by an individual species during its lifespan

hybrid: the offspring of two different species who mate; see interbreed

hybridization: the gradual decline of a species through continued breeding with another species; see interbreed

immature(s): a young bird that has not yet reached breeding maturity; it usually has plumage differing from an adult bird of the same species

in captivity: a species that exists in zoos, captive breeding programs, or in private collections, perhaps because the species can no longer be found in the wild

incubation: the period when an egg is kept warm until the embryo develops and hatches

indigenous species: any species native to its habitat

inflorescence: a group of flowers that grow from one point

insecta: the Latin scientific name for insects

insular species: a species isolated on an island or islands

interbreed: when two separate species mate and produce offspring; see hybrid

invertebrate(s): any organism without a backbone (spinal column)

juvenal: a bird with an intermediate set of feathers after its young downy plumage molts and before growing hard, adult feathers

juvenile(s): a young bird or other animal not yet mature

litter: the animals born to a species that normally produces several young at birth

lore(s): the irregularly shaped facial area of a bird between the eye and the base of the beak

migrate, migratory: to move from one range to another, particularly with the change of seasons; many species are migratory

montane forest: a forest found in mountainous regions

neotony: immature characteristics in adulthood

nocturnal: active at night; some animals are nocturnal, while others are active by day (see diurnal)

nomadic species: a species with no permanent range or territory; nomadic species wander for food and water

old growth forest: forest that has not experienced extensive deforestation

omnivore: any species that eats both plants and animals

ornithologist(s): a scientist who studies birds

parietal: relating to the walls of a cavity

pelage: the hairy covering of a mammal

pelagic: related to the oceans or open sea; pelagic birds rarely roost on land

perennial: persisting for several years

petiole: slender stem that supports a foliage leaf

plumage: the feathers that cover a bird

predation: the act of one species hunting another

predator: a species that preys upon other species

primary forest: a forest of native trees that results from natural processes, often called virgin forest

primate(s): a biological ranking of species in the same order, including gorillas, chimpanzees, monkeys, and human beings (*Homo sapiens*)

quadrangular: four-sided (stems of plants)

range: the geographic area where a species roams

recovery plan(s): any document that outlines a public or private program for assisting an endangered or threatened species

relict: an isolated habitat or population that was once widespread

reptilia: the Latin scientific name for reptiles

riffle(s): a shallow rapid stretch of water caused by a rocky outcropping or obstruction in a stream

riparian: relating to plants and animals close to and influenced by rivers

roe: fish eggs

rufous: in bird species, plumage that is orange-brown and pink

secondary forest: a forest that has grown back after cutting, forest fire, or other deforestation; secondary forests may or may not contain exotic tree species, but they almost always differ in character from primary forests

sedentary species: one that does not migrate

stellate: star-shaped (flower)

tectonics: geological structural features

teleost: bony (fish)

terrestrial: living in or adapted for living principally on the ground; some birds are terrestrial and seldom, if ever, ascend into trees (see arboreal)

territory: the area occupied more or less exclusively by an organism or group, usually defended by aggressive displays and physical combat

threatened species: any species that is at risk of

becoming endangered

tribe: a more specific classification within the biological rankings of family or subfamily

tubercle: a prominent bump on a fish's body connected to a spine

veld: a grassland region

with some scattered bushes and virtually no trees; other terms are *steppe, pampas,* and *prairie*

ventral: on or near the belly; the ventral fin is located on the underside of a fish and corresponds with the hind limbs of other vertebrates

vertebrates: any organism that has a backbone (spinal column)

woodland: a plant community in which trees grow abundantly but far enough apart that their crowns do not intermingle, so no overhead canopy is formed

---

INDEX

The scientific name of a plant or animal is entered in *italics*; its common name is in roman type. Page numbers in *italics* refer to picture captions.